REALITY SHIFTS
When Consciousness Changes the Physical World

"Ever wondered where that missing sock went when you last searched the clothes dryer? Thought about why those keys you so carefully tucked into your jacket pocket suddenly disappeared only to be found underneath the cushion of your favorite television sofa? If so then you have experienced what Cynthia Larson calls a *Reality Shift*. In her book of that title subtitled *When Consciousness Changes the Physical World*, she explains in clear and unambiguous language just what these reality shifts are, why they occur, and how they can be used to influence and change your life for the better. Larson even goes into how the latest ideas from quantum physics can help us understand these shifts and most importantly believe in them as part of our reality, not just our imagination. No, Martha, you are not going crazy, just witnessing the reality shift around you. I recommend this book for its clarity and for its message of hope. Readers will be encouraged to enjoy reality shifts both literally and in actuality—when they occur—and will be taught how to make them happen more often."
– *Fred Alan Wolf, Ph.D., National Book Award-winning author of Taking the Quantum Leap and many other books, including Dr. Quantum's Little Book of Big Ideas, and The Yoga of Time Travel*

"In REALITY SHIFTS, Cynthia Larson helps restore a sense of majesty and wonder to our everyday world. If you think science has explained away the magic of existence, you need seriously to read this book."
– *Larry Dossey, M.D. author of Power of Premonitions, Reinventing Medicine and many more*

"Modern science has now addressed the problem of consciousness. We each experience consciousness every day, in some of the myriad and fascinating ways described in REALITY SHIFTS. But no one yet quite understands why this is so. Speculations, theories and experiments from quantum science have now been entered into the debate which suggest that our world is far more mystical, complex, interactive and even humorous than the sterile, mechanistic dogma of classical scientific thought. Read, enjoy, be amazed, ponder REALITY SHIFTS."

– *Edgar Mitchell, Sc.D., author Psychic Exploration, The Way of the Explorer, Institute of Noetic Sciences Founder, Apollo 14 Astronaut*

REALITY SHIFTS

When Consciousness Changes the Physical World

Cynthia Sue Larson

REALITY SHIFTS
When Consciousness Changes the Physical World

PRINTING HISTORY:
First edition 1999
Café Press edition 2006
First trade paper edition 2012

RealityShifters® is Registered Trademark
All Rights Reserved @ 1999 by Cynthia Sue Larson. Printed in the United States of America. No part of this book may be used or reproduced in any manner whatsoever without written permission, except in the case of brief quotations embodied in critical articles and reviews.

Published by RealityShifters
P.O. Box 7393
Berkeley, CA 94707-7393
www.realityshifters.com

Copyright © 2012 by Cynthia Sue Larson
Cover art by Tessala Larson
About the Author photo by Matt Larson
Back cover author photo by Richard Hiersch

ISBN-13: 9781461075219
ISBN-10: 1461075211

CONTENTS

	Acknowledgements	1
	Permissions	2
	Preface	3
1	Introduction to Reality	5
2	Why Reality Shifts	33
3	Reality Shift Experiences	75
4	Shifting Reality	111
5	Allowing Reality Shifts	143
6	Feeling Inspired Powers Reality Shifts	169
7	Lucid Dreaming	203
8	Living Lucidly in a Shifting Reality	231
9	Shifting Reality for Healing	257
10	Everyday Life with Reality Shifts	289
	Affirmations	297
	Bibliography	299
	About the Author	304

Acknowledgements

I am deeply grateful for and offer heartfelt thanks to all my friends, family, colleagues and neighbors who helped make this book a reality.

Permissions

I am honored to have received permission to quote some of my favorite authors:

Excerpt from *Hands of Light* copyright 1988 by Barbara Ann Brennan. Reprinted by permission of Barbara Brennan.

Excerpt from *The Future of Love: The Power of the Soul in Intimate Relationships* copyright 1998 by Daphne Rose Kingma. Reprinted by permission of Doubleday, a division of Random House, Inc.

Excerpt from the book *Creating Miracles* copyright 1995 by Carolyn Miller, Ph.D. Reprinted by permission of H J Kramer, P.O. Box 1082, Tiburon, CA 94920. All rights reserved.

Excerpts from *Openness Mind* copyright 1978 by Tarthang Tulku. Reprinted by permission of Dharma Publishing.

Excerpts from *Knowledge of Time and Space* copyright 1990 by Tarthang Tulku. Reprinted by permission of Dharma Publishing.

Excerpt from *A Dictionary of Mind and Spirit* copyright 1991 by Donald Watson. Reprinted by permission of Andre Deutsch Ltd.

Excerpt from *The Spiritual Universe* copyright 1998 by Fred Alan Wolf. Reprinted by permission of Moment Point Press, Inc.

Preface

Reality is shifting all around us in this everyday, ordinary life. We most commonly notice reality shifts when we set something down and it vanishes or reappears somewhere very different from where we know we left it. Reality shifts are physically observable changes that occur without any direct physical intervention. We may note that the more attention we pay to the idea that reality shifts, the more we see our reality shift.

We live in an incredibly dynamic universe that gives us what we wish for, like a waking dream. Reality is fluid, occasionally discontinuous, and fully responsive to our thoughts and feelings. Scientific studies have shown that our wishes and thoughts do not come only from our brains, but from every cell in our bodies. We attract to us that on which we most focus our attention. The better our wishes are aligned, the better we can notice how the universe responds to our every question and thought.

Our thoughts and feelings seem to shift reality to create the coincidences that make our lives exciting and rewarding, with our wishes and prayers coming true. Even our own bodies are capable of miraculous transformation, as I've found by participating in healing for myself and others. We really do have the power to change reality with our thoughts and feelings, and to see our dreams come true. We can heal ourselves and others and even the things we love. In each moment of life, we can choose to enjoy our lives by opening our minds and hearts to feel the incredible energy of pure love, letting go of feelings of anger about the past and worry about the future. There is a great abundance of love, joy, inspiration and prosperity in this universe, and it is freely available to us all.

I have witnessed some amazing reality shifts: I've seen magazines transport themselves; I've watched bruises vanish from my hand; I've observed a previously dead cat walking around in my backyard, very much alive. These experiences are exhilarating and awe-inspiring for me.

I love to share reality shift experiences with my friends and family, such as the time two friends and I noticed a large sundial sculpture appear out of nowhere at the Berkeley Marina one day, looking as if it had been there for many years. On a different occasion, my daughter showed me that an illustration in a book we read every day was completely different. I once took my husband's coat out of the laundry, and was surprised to see that its fabric was different. I've watched car keys materialize out of thin air under a friend's hands, as we wondered how to get into his locked car when we couldn't locate the keys.

I've talked to total strangers about reality shifts while waiting in movie or grocery lines, and found that many I've talked to have witnessed reality shift, and want to know what's going on. Most people I've talked to experienced situations where objects inexplicably vanished or relocated, and are eager to hear stories of shifting reality and an explanation for why reality shifts. The tremendous interest in this subject has given me the impetus and support to summarize my own experiences with reality shifts, and to investigate this phenomenon.

I hope the stories in this book spark a sense of recognition for you, so you may increase your awareness of reality shifts, validate your own reality shift experiences, and be reassured that reality shifts are a natural part of life. This book may be considered a how-to guide for those eager to explore the changing nature of reality, while others may prefer to read and contemplate the significance of reality shift stories. I wrote this book to embody a unique synthesis of physical phenomena, spirituality, and personal development, because I believe that ultimately the greatest practical application for shifting reality is in changing oneself.

Chapter I

Introduction to Reality

*"I would rather live in a world where my life is
surrounded by mystery than live in a world
so small that my mind could comprehend it."
– Harry Emerson Fosdick*

What is Reality?

"Whatever works" – Carol Stieger

Reality is the fundamental essence of existence. In order to know what is real from what is not, we rely upon our senses, our reasoning, and our intuition. Our senses provide us with the physical input our mind requires to comprehend the world, and our mind gives us a framework in which to place our experiences. Our intuition helps us feel what really matters to us, and whether something feels out of place or just fine. Intuition is the inner teaching that lets us know what is right for us, and what we truly need.

Many dictionaries say **reality** is:
"the state of things as they are or as they appear to be, rather than as one might wish them to be,"

and define **real** as:
"existing or occurring in the physical world; not imaginary, fictitious, dream-like or theoretical."

What we wish for, dream and imagine is the very framework and foundation of everything we create. In other words, the essence of all that is real springs forth from all that is not yet real. Every great invention starts out as a mere idea; everything we build begins as something previously only imagined. When we contemplate the difference between fantasy and reality, we look into the very essence of how creation works; we get a sense of the innermost workings of the universe itself and how something comes from nothing.

The difference between fantasy and reality seems clear to most people. Dreams are something we wake up from, whereas reality is what we awaken into. Dreams are fanciful and unpredictable, whereas reality feels more familiar and stable. We can tell the difference between fantasy and reality because fantasy is purely our own creation—something we either dreamt, or wished for, or imagined somehow—while reality is what already exists that we do not believe to be totally our own creation.

Sometimes it is difficult to be conscious of dreaming as we are dreaming, and the fantasy *does* feel real to us during the time we are dreaming. We may even believe we are already awake because we awoke from a dream within a dream, and it's easy to feel quite startled to wake up out of what we already thought was wakefulness. The jolt of awareness that a more conscious state is possible informs us, "*Now* you are truly awake!" In other words, we most clearly notice the difference between different states of mind by experiencing the boundary between these experiences.

Reality, like a dream, is in a continual state of change and transition. Nothing stays the same for very long. The weather changes, the continents change shape and drift across the oceans, and even we ourselves change tremendously with time. Any attempt to hold onto something is essentially futile, because constant change is the rule in life, as it is in dreams. We may feel a need for our world to be somewhat solid and stable, because we want something dependable under our feet that we can rely on to be there and build upon. We think we want things to stay somewhat fixed and solid, even though we actually need fluidity and change in order to grow and develop. A lack of change feels like stagnation, where the flow of fresh air and water has stopped; it's an unpleasant experience for most people. Feeling and hearing a breeze, breathing fresh air, and drinking fresh running water feels immensely more pleasurable and healthy than breathing stale air and drinking stagnant water.

If you're thinking to yourself, "Not everybody has to change," then consider the idea that every job that exists on earth deals in change, including yours. Farmers work with earth to grow food from the sun's energy, truckers transport food from farms to grocery stores, grocery store employees keep the new food on the shelves, and customers buy and eat the food. Bankers collect the money from individuals and businesses, and update financial records after each transaction. Sanitation engineers take the garbage from our businesses and homes and transport it to solid waste management areas for recycling, reuse, burial, or incineration. Secretaries answer telephone calls, take messages, type memorandums, and file papers for managers who design and manage projects that produce goods and services. Every human job is focused on changing something, no matter how small a thing it may seem to be.

If you feel like you want to change the world, where do you start? The biggest change we can make in life and the most exhilarating is to change ourselves. Changing ourselves changes our behavior, and when we change the way we act in the world, we're changing both the quantity and quality of our interactions. If we wish to change our behaviors, we need to change a couple of things we have full control of in our lives—our attitudes and beliefs. Our attitudes and beliefs form the basis for our every action in life, and this is truly the way we "make something out of nothing," and create new realities from what were previously unconscious desires.

Sometimes, we know we need to change because we feel a need for something different in our lives, and we recognize that if we continue on the way we've been going, we'll end up precisely where we're headed! This realization can give us the necessary jolt to snap out of our habitual lives and consider that there might be a better way to live than what we've been doing so far. Sometimes we have to crash into a wall several times before we notice that this hurts, especially if we are rather hardheaded. If we feel like we keep running into walls, we might ask ourselves if we've fenced our belief system in too thoroughly for our own good. Other times we feel an urge to change because we find ourselves in a *completely* different situation than we've ever previously encountered, and we know we need to be able to adapt ourselves, because all the old notions of what works and what doesn't work don't apply outside of the old boundaries of our beliefs. Only when we question these new and unusual experiences can we begin to increase our knowledge of what lies beyond the boundaries of what we comprehend.

Sand Crabs

When I was a child, I saw an extraordinary thing one day at the beach. My family and I were vacationing at a remote island in the Pacific Ocean, and we spent a leisurely day on a quiet, uninhabited beach. I sat by myself on a part of the beach populated by a whole colony of sand crabs. These little crabs lived in holes in the sand that each crab dug for itself, and at any sign of movement, the crabs would scurry quickly down into their holes for safety.

I observed one of the crabs moving sand with a claw with absent-minded proficiency, and I was mesmerized to see the effortless way it obtained a scoop of sand and lifted it into the air. This activity looked like so much fun to me that I made a similar ball of sand and playfully tossed it toward some crabs. The sand ball hit an unsuspecting crab, which immediately scooped up a ball of sand and held it aloft while standing up as high on its back legs as possible. The crab looked as tense and concerned as a crab can look, with moist grains of sand from the sand ball I'd just tossed still clinging to its shell.

The crab continued standing high on its back legs, surveying the area and assessing all the crabs in the vicinity to determine who might have tossed a sand ball. After several long moments of careful consideration, the crab steadied itself as it fixed its gaze on one particular crab. It suddenly flung its ball of sand at this unsuspecting crab, which it hit with incredible precision! The targeted crab immediately scooped up a ball of sand and returned fire.

In a matter of minutes, a dozen little crabs were all flinging sand balls at one another with reckless abandon. None of the crabs suspected the perpetrator of the whole sand ball fracas was not a crab at all, but a human.

My experience with these sand crabs shows me that crabs interpret what happens to them in terms they can understand, which may not be the truest sense of what is actually happening. We humans are not so different from crabs, in the sense that we are also only capable of interpreting experience based on what we *know* of reality. Some forces are simply outside our realm of comprehension. The sand crabs had no prior knowledge of humans, so they did not imagine I might have been the one who threw the first sand ball, though my interaction with them had the effect of moving almost every single crab on the beach into action.

We live within a conceptualization of a universe of which we have limited understanding, just like the crabs on the beach with no knowledge of anything besides other crabs throwing sand balls. We have much in common with those crabs, since we usually only consider other humans like ourselves to be capable of affecting our lives. When Captain Cook's sailing ship first approached the island of Tahiti in the South Pacific it was not noticed by the inhabitants, even when Captain Cook and his crew pointed it out to them, since no Tahitians ever saw such a vessel before. Just as Captain Cook's ship was invisible to Tahitians, I was invisible to sand crabs on the beach. This shows that we can't contemplate what we have no comprehension of, even when it is right in front of us. The range of our knowledge of reality is limited by our pre-existing beliefs, assumptions and expectations.

How We Construct Reality

We like to comprehend our environment, so we name things and ideas in order to think and talk about them. It is the unique way our brains and sensory systems work together that often convinces us that we are directly experiencing something, when in fact our brain filters all our senses. Our brains influence both how we conceptualize ourselves and elements of our environments; how we select and store information. Some minds work in visual images, seeing pictures, while others structure experience in words, ideas, or according to how something feels. Every person has a unique way of paying attention and storing and retrieving their impressions of what they pay attention to. Whether we interpret our experience in feelings, visual images, or words, the *way* we order the universe therefore limits our observational concepts.

It's a well-known fact that our visual perception is "full of holes." We have no photoreceptors in the middle of our retinas, and we only see our visual range of the spectrum of light. The visual range is a relatively narrow bandwidth from red to violet; we do not see infrared or ultraviolet frequencies without technological tools to help us. We compensate for these perceptual limitations by filling in the holes with what we believe is there, and what we fill in can be more than half of what we believe we are seeing. Our brains do this so seamlessly that we are seldom conscious of visual gaps. This may be why we can see more information by moving around and getting a new perspective, and why we often notice, "something seems different" in visual puzzles in the Sunday newspapers, but don't know exactly what changed unless we compare each minute detail between nearly identical pictures.

Dr. Karl Pribram, a neuroscientist at Stanford University, proposes that our brains perform computations to construct physical reality. This holographic model of the brain suggests that we are viewing only a very limited version of reality that we are capable of understanding. We already know we do not perceive everything there is, but Dr. Pribram also suggests that if we saw reality without the mathematical computations our brains perform, we would observe a very different universe in the frequency domain without any sense of time or space—just events. The holographic model of the brain helps explain how our brains can store so much information in so little space, and also how we can best recall a memory when we illuminate it with the same kind of feeling we had when we stored the memory. Our brains also allow us to easily transfer learned skills, so we find it easy to trace the shape of a valentine heart in the air with our nose, even if we've never before done such a thing. Pribram's holographic brain model explains that if our brains are converting all our memories into interfering waveforms, they are able to flexibly roll every idea around to be played with and experienced from many different perspectives.

The very process of labeling and archiving information greatly affects what we allow ourselves to experience. By constraining the way we identify and sort the significance of an experience, our memory structures give our minds order and cohesiveness. These memory structures can also block our ability to fully comprehend any given experience. We can empathize with the crabs on the beach who notice that a ball of sand has appeared nearby, yet have trouble noticing that it was thrown by a human being, since they have no way to comprehend such a thing as a human. Even though something very *large* is right in front of us like a gigantic human being near a group of crabs, or an enormous sailing ship sitting just offshore a Tahitian beach, we may not notice it if we've never seen any such thing before. We tend to perceive what we are ready and willing to perceive, and not much more ... unless we open ourselves to directly experiencing reality. Fortunately, we can increase our awareness of something simply by paying attention to it.

Have you ever noticed that when you are thinking seriously about something, like buying a new car, you suddenly see lots of new cars all around? If you are thinking of getting a dog, it seems like dogs are everywhere. If you are thinking of having a baby, everyone seems to be having babies. What we attend to brings that idea or thought more into our awareness, and we are likely to feel its presence has increased in our lives. I've found it to be true that when I appreciate how reality shifts around me I begin to notice many more such changes going on.

When I notice more reality shifts, I also see how much I create for myself by how I choose to feel in response to my environment. I interpret the behavior of people and things around me according to my own beliefs and attitudes, coloring each experience with how I choose to feel about it. I can choose to live in a world of anger about past injustices, or in a world of worry about the uncertain future, or in a world of acceptance of the love that is here right now. We can live in any world we choose, although much of what we are choosing we are only unconsciously aware of. We often don't pay conscious attention to the background sounds, smells, sights, and other sensations around us, yet they have very profound effects upon us. Likewise, we rarely pay much attention to the unconscious currents in our minds. Whether we admit it or not, we all start with our own unique perceptions of the world upon which we base our personal conception of reality.

Our concept of reality is a subset of the totality of all that reality encompasses—much in the same way as our house, car, office, and shopping areas are not the entire universe, even if we do spend much of our time in those enclosed places. As we change how we think about things, we can open our minds and our senses to new possibilities with fewer constraints on what we will and won't believe in, and then we can begin to experience miracles as we become more involved in being fully present.

Belief Structures

"There will be some fundamental assumptions which adherents of all variant systems within the epoch unconsciously presuppose. Such assumptions appear so obvious that people do not know what they are assuming because no other way of putting things has ever occurred to them."
– Alfred North Whitehead

Cultural attitudes are perhaps the strongest influences upon how individuals form belief structures to view reality. Children start out with beginner's minds and hearts; they are able to learn whatever language and social norms they are exposed to. Eskimo children learn how to hear and interpret the different sounds of ice and snow under their feet, while Australian bushman children learn how to make special sounds that have no equivalent in other human languages, and how to find the locations of underground roots and unseen animals. Native American children learn how to smell the rain coming, and how to recognize the changing of the seasons by what the plants and animals are doing. Children born with physical handicaps learn to interpret and explore their world by making fuller use of their entire complement of mental, intuitive, and sensuous skills and abilities. Children of all cultures learn over time what experiences to be wary of, and how to make sense of the information they perceive through their senses.

Just as every culture teaches its children what is considered most important to survival and success in that perceived environment, each family and subgroup within each of these cultures has its own mini-belief system. As children, we learn what is real and what isn't real from our parents and the other people around us, so we learn to view the world in ways we can communicate to others. We learn to value and sort our experiences based on our beliefs of who we are as individuals and in groups. Experiences that are not part of our beliefs are not easily stored or accessed in our minds, so they often go undetected in our consciousness.

It's amazing how people can live such different lives, mostly because we each have such unique internal belief systems that form the basis for all subsequent knowledge we are conscious of. We can be remarkably ambivalent about the parts of life that we don't value or believe in, effectively shutting out much of what other people may consider to be the essence and core of their lives. While our individual experiences are so remarkably unique and varied, collectively we experience All That Is.

The psychologist Jean Piaget recognized a period of *reality adjustment* in the pre-adolescent child during which *magical thinking* fades away. What Piaget did not consider is that this "magical thinking" is a primary and very valuable process of directly experiencing the universe. Children are born with the ability to conform to any belief structure, and they start out wide open to all possibility, free of assumptions such as "effect must always follow cause in time," and "wishes have no effect." As we grow up, each of us replaces our totally open way of directly experiencing the universe with a belief structure uniquely customized by immersion in culture and family whose language and ways of living support and sustain the concept of the consensus reality. We pay little attention to this process of changing the very way we experience the world, because we unconsciously reframe ourselves and reframe our life experiences in accordance with our newer belief structures.

Barbara Ann Brennan remembers her own childhood on a farm in Wisconsin in her book, *Hands of Light*, where she writes about how she would sit perfectly still alone in the woods, waiting for small animals to approach her, and blending into her surroundings.

> *"In those quiet moments in the woods I entered into an expanded state of consciousness in which I was able to perceive things beyond the normal human ranges of experience. I remember knowing where each small animal was without looking. I could sense its state. When I practiced walking blindfolded in the woods, I would feel the trees long before I could touch them with my hands. I realized that the trees were larger than they appeared to the visible eye. Trees have life energy fields around them, and I was sensing those fields. Later I learned to see the energy fields of trees and the small animals. I discovered that everything has an energy field around it that looks somewhat like the light from a candle. I also began to notice that everything is connected by these energy fields, that no space existed without an energy field. Everything, including me, was living in a sea of energy."*

Barbara continues to explain that she did not consider these early childhood experiences to be extraordinary; she simply accepted them as being natural and probably well-known by everyone. As Barbara grew up into a young woman, she forgot all about them. I believe all children are open to this kind of direct experience, and each of us experiences our own unique interpretation of it.

What we believe can be so powerful it can produce physiological changes in our bodies. "Hysterical pregnancies," where women mistakenly believe themselves to be pregnant result in women gaining weight, retaining water, and ceasing their menstrual flow for many months. People given placebos typically experience both the benefits and the side effects identical to ones they would have if they were taking the drugs being distributed for the studies. People who believe they have received the "evil eye" often die of unknown causes within days of being cursed.

Our cultures, like our egos, serve to provide us with a sense of identity. They do this by giving us boundaries we can recognize, and by helping us sort our experiences into those that are internal and those that are external. Our beliefs give us these boundary lines of demarcation. Our beliefs tell us things like "you can't read someone else's mind," "you must work hard and be competitive in order to succeed in life," and "happiness comes from financial security and social status."

In general, our Western culture believes in cause and effect, where what happens has been brought about by forces that acted earlier in time. While many religions and spiritual people believe in miracles and the power of prayer and wishes, the more prevalent point of view in academic circles is that "You don't get something from nothing." Some scientists believe nothingness may actually be the very source of all that is, but most people in academia would not agree with that.

Experiences that jeopardize our beliefs in the boundaries we've chosen and adopted as our own are generally met with some resistance or resentment, unless we are open to expanding our sense of boundaries and limitations. Love allows us to open ourselves to new beliefs and experiences, and helps us heal the wounds we feel from holding onto anger and fear. As our boundaries expand in love, so does our conscious awareness.

When we think and believe according to how we've been conditioned, we tend to behave in the same ways we've learned to interact with our environment. We keep doing what we've done and believing what we've believed. Our habitual behavior rewards us until such time as resources are depleted or we lose interest in the sheer monotony of our repetitive patterns. When we maintain our belief structures, we keep creating for ourselves an experience of stability and some degree of predictability that works well as a framework for us to live by.

The biggest problem with static belief structures is that they do not allow for ecstasy, ec-static being essentially the experience of feeling oneself free of stasis—or literally to stand outside, go beyond, be beside oneself. When we wish our lives would continue as they've always been, we doom ourselves to a depressing state of boredom for the simple reason that we are no longer challenging ourselves to our full ability to grow and change. Going beyond our ordinary concept of self is what always brings us the greatest sense of joy in life. Going beyond our own boundaries brings us an ecstatic awareness of how we are truly created in connection with all that is.

Even after making a breakthrough and catching a glimpse of the universe beyond the ways we normally sense it, we usually return again to seeing the universe as solid and physical almost immediately. When we manage to see outside the normal boundaries of experience, we often interpret our experience in terms of our own predispositions to see the images from our framework of understanding. For example, Christian saints and mystics see images of the Christian faith like Jesus or Mary, while Aboriginal karadji would see Mimi Spirits, a Lightning Figure, or a Sun Woman.

We also may find ourselves having trouble changing our attitudes and beliefs as we become more and more habituated to them; new experiences and ways of looking at the world are best adopted when they are reinforced. My younger six-year-old daughter's mind was still flexible enough for her to say to me, "Mom ... I just saw one of those things ... what do you call it?" When I replied, "A reality shift?," she nodded excitedly, and said, "Well I just saw one! I was playing with my horse and it's tail moved when I wasn't even touching it! I watched it and it moved from that side to the other" as she pointed to indicate it had swished from right to left. Her mind is more open to seeing a toy move by itself, simply because she hasn't yet constrained her mind to a certainty that a toy horse's hair tail cannot move by itself.

The more experienced we are, the easier it is for us to say, "I know that" upon encountering something familiar. We feel delighted to recognize a familiar concept, and are quite happy to find confirmation of our beliefs. The problem with stopping at this point and categorizing new experiences in terms of something familiar is that we risk completely missing out on the unexpected ... the unanticipated ... the surprising ... the amazingly, astonishingly new. If we look and listen a little more carefully, we can release ourselves from the constraints of predetermined judgment, and open ourselves up to expanded awareness of multiple coexisting harmonious meanings. As soon as we stop our questioning process, we essentially imprison ourselves in whatever set of beliefs we happen to be holding onto at that moment.

When we understand that our belief structures are creations of our minds, we can start noticing how varied individual belief structures can be from person to person. What one person considers realistic and matter-of-fact can seem outlandish to another person. Even the idea that other people actually *see* images in their minds may seem outlandish to some people, let alone *what* those people see. When enough people shift their belief structures and look at the world in a whole new way, cultural paradigms shift.

Social Resistance to Expanded Consciousness

> *"It is demonstrable that many of the obstacles for change which have been attributed to human nature are in fact due to the inertia of institutions and to the voluntary desire of powerful classes to maintain the existing status."*
> *– John Dewey*

Cultures gradually expand boundaries to be slightly more inclusive. This expansion of awareness is apparent in the gradually improved cultural attitudes of accepting individuals for who they are regardless of race, religion, gender, sexual orientation or economic class. Obviously, there is still a long way to go before we can accept and love ourselves and each other as fully as possible, but many of us have come a *very* long ways towards feeling genuine unconditional love, even when others don't behave or look like we do.

Listening to different viewpoints is not a prelude to being converted to a particular point of view, but it is an excellent way to gain deeper understanding of oneself and one's own belief structure. As we hear what others experience, we gain an opportunity to view the universe from a new perspective. We can accept others as being true to themselves, and perhaps even learn a little about who they really are. When we are afraid to listen to different perspectives because we do not wish to risk losing or modifying our beliefs in the process, we are choosing to remain in stasis.

Few people enjoy being told what to believe, and most of us prefer the freedom to see the world as we believe it really is. It can feel so delightful to be able to say, "I'm RIGHT, and here's *more* proof that I'm right," but such proclamations seldom hold the same amount of fascination and exhilaration for those listening to us. We can examine why it is that we feel so strongly that we want to prove we are right, and take a closer look at what it is that we are hoping others will see and adopt into their own belief systems.

There's generally little advantage in trying to control or manipulate people to behave according to our perception of their highest potential, since any remaining desires to try out all other possibilities will just come out *more* strongly when they are suppressed, and not always in ways that feel healthy or pleasant. Suppression usually leads to more extreme and more deeply manifested problems, since it's a forced way of holding onto unexpressed feelings until they explode out in uncontrolled ways.

Most of us prefer to fit in with what we consider to be normal behavior for the social groups we belong to, even when this requires that we suppress our truly unique individual feelings in the process. Humans are social animals, and we strongly prefer acceptance to rejection. Individuals are often socially ostracized for failing to conform to the norm, so most of us carefully consider how what we say and do affects how other people think of us.

Fortunately for all of us, there are some individuals who take the risk of being mavericks, and blaze new trails for the rest of us to consider. Some of history's most revered artists and scientists experienced some fairly severe social resistance to expanding consciousness as they stretched the boundaries of what the rest of us have come to take for granted. Copernicus risked being denounced heretical to show us that the Earth revolves around the sun, and Darwin faced ongoing criticism about his theories of evolutionary biology. Society may eventually come to appreciate these new beliefs and ways of looking at the universe, but typically there's a great deal of resistance and discomfort when new ideas are first presented.

New ideas are not comfortable to hear, precisely because they *do* demand a re-ordering of the way we comprehend the universe. Many of my friends are artists, poets, and musicians who are especially conscious of social resistance to new ideas as they make their own paths in life.

There is no line, but you've just crossed it

I have an artist friend who was taking pictures of himself in a photo booth at the Transbay Terminal in San Francisco one day to experiment with that art medium as an idea for the students in his art class to try. He was using confetti and other props to make the self-portrait strips of photos much more artistic, when he was stopped by a police officer who queried him about what he was doing. Even though there was nobody else waiting for the photo booth and my friend was cleaning up the confetti mess, the police officer felt some kind of infraction had occurred, and asked him to stop what he was doing and clean up right then, or risk being cited.

Since my friend was not undressed or doing anything hurtful or suggestive, he was mystified and upset that he had been threatened with receiving a citation. When he consulted legal counselors who specialize in assisting artists, he was informed by a lawyer that the only law that he could think of that could apply was something similar to the law that regulates public bathrooms. It's private, but you can't do everything you want. The lawyer explained, "There is no line, but you've just crossed it." In other words, unspoken and unconsciously supported beliefs exist that serve to maintain the belief boundaries we live within.

The beautiful thing about creative people like artists, actors, writers, musicians and inventors is how they show us our world in new ways. They invite us to see ourselves and how we perceive in ways that challenge our beliefs; they encourage us to transcend limitations we're often unconsciously living within. There are so many different ways to create our realities, and when we see some of these different possibilities, the world becomes a sparkling place of infinite creativity and delight.

I have a friend who shares her unique kind of creativity conducting "mystery tours" that give people opportunities to explore beyond their ordinary boundaries. She often only gives people the barest and most mysterious clues as to where they're going on a mystery tour, such as informing them they need to wear "white gloves and a hat," or "tights." When people show up for her mystery tour, they discover they'll be learning to fence, play bocci ball, perform circus acrobatics, or perhaps tour a Twinkie factory. These mystery tours achieve legendary status because of the memorably creative way they provide such exciting and unpredictable ways of stretching peoples' concepts of what one can experience.

All of us are artists, if only in the sense we are creating ourselves as the lead character in the story of our life. We often are not aware of the variety of choices available to us in every moment, since it's so easy to get trapped in the habit of maintaining perspectives we've "always had" rather than being open to something new. To the degree we are willing to open our minds, we free ourselves from the prison of our habits and belief structures. We can end any painful cycle in life by simply opening a circle of belief that constrains us too tightly. Every new experience is an opportunity to learn, grow, laugh and love, if we allow this to be true.

What Are Reality Shifts?

Reality shifts are physically observed changes that occur without any direct physical intervention; they are mysterious appearances, disappearances, transformations, and transportations that occur in and around us. Some reality shifts seem to result from the intention of prayers and wishes, and some involve healings related to prayers, while the reason for others is not at all obvious. Reality shifts may occur due to choices made by unconscious thoughts and feelings, creative consciousness, or the conscious and unconscious collective. Reality shifts feel miraculous to those who witness them, giving one a sense of awe and wonder at the mystery of how something that seemed so solid and fixed could be affected as if by magical forces beyond one's comprehension.

I started thinking and talking about reality shifts in 1997 when I noticed some startling changes in which real physical objects and people changed, and I felt a burning need to discuss this with my friends and understand what was going on. These experiences were shocking and a little bit frightening to me at first, until I realized reality shifts have been happening around me for much of my life, and that no harm comes to me from experiencing them. In fact, observing reality shifts sharpens my awareness to what's happening around me and around my perceptual acuity. I also feel like I'm gaining a back-stage view of how the universe operates, getting a chance to see how even apparently solid objects can behave rather fluidly and how consciousness creates reality.

The reality shifts I experience involve things undergoing rather marked changes that I don't anticipate, like seeing artwork in a children's book changing to a completely different illustration, a large sundial sculpture sometimes being there and sometimes not, and keys falling out of the air. Other shifts involve a dead cat being alive again, a person's name vanishing off of a conference agenda on all pages in the room, bruises vanishing right before my eyes, and rain starting and stopping as I look up at the sky.

These reality shifts are incredibly mysterious transformations that happen right in front of me, many of which I experience with others. It's so much more meaningful to share these things it's easier to know that something magical really *did* occur when more than one person shares the experience, since corroboration helps reassure me that I am not imagining things. Shared experiences of reality shifts also help because they encourage me to talk about what happened, describe it in words, and place it in memory.

You have probably already experienced many reality shifts. I believe most of us have. Possibly you noticed a sock or two missing after you washed it, somewhere between the washing machine and the drying machine, most inexplicably leaving you one or more lone socks with no mates. This experience is so commonplace that it's routinely joked about, yet I haven't heard anyone other than stand-up comics ask the question, "*Where* do all the missing socks *go*?" Often socks are so small that they can and do hide inside other laundry items, and can even get mistakenly folded up inside towels and sheets, or hung up on hangers with shirts or dresses. What's most curious is when the socks simply seem to vanish altogether, and all other possibilities have been investigated. When you have thoroughly checked everywhere possible and *still* can't find the sock, you begin to wonder what could possibly have happened to it. Since it's just a sock and not something or someone more important to you, the incident may not capture much of your attention, even when the sock reappears mysteriously in a place you'd already checked and you're certain it hadn't been before.

    Perhaps you've had an experience where you are *absolutely* sure that you set down your wallet or keys in a certain place, only to return and *not* be able to find them there. You then search around the place a bit more unsuccessfully, and return again to that same place where you first looked ... and *there they are*. You probably figured at that point that you must have been distracted or inobservant—certainly they must have been there all along, and somehow you just didn't notice them the first time you checked there. There is something strange and surprising about this, but since you've found what you were looking for and have no reason to continue contemplating the matter, you give it no further thought.

    You might think that by paying *more* attention, you could stop these events from occurring ... yet I've found the opposite to be true. I've had many experiences with reality shifts such as the hypothetical one described above, and surprisingly, the more attention I pay to reality shifts, the more I observe them happening around me, and the more likely it is that I find reality shifting in accordance with how I would prefer my reality to be.

    I've noticed reality shifts all my life, but hadn't noted or talked about them because these experiences fell outside the realm of what our culture considers possible. I doubted that I saw something that wasn't really there, because it vanished again. It was easier to believe I was just daydreaming and imagining things than to admit I just saw something so magical and mysterious. Many people can notice how reality shifts around them, so it's time for us to share stories of reality shifts, and open a discussion about this magical universe.

Skepticism, Mindfulness and Reality Shifts

> *"If you would be a real seeker after truth, it is necessary that at least once in your life you doubt, as far as possible, all things."*
> – Rene Descartes

So if reality shifts around us all the time, why don't more people acknowledge this phenomenon? Once people hear about reality shifts, why don't they all enthusiastically embrace this idea? Why would *anyone* feel a need to doubt something they can experience relatively easily for themselves?

At the heart of skepticism is a desire for objective examination of new ideas, rather than subjective airbrushing or "wishful thinking." Skeptics remind us of the importance of minimizing our subjective personal judgments so we may more fully experience what is *really* here. There is a significant difference between mindfulness and skepticism. Whereas mindfulness is the nonjudgmental awareness encouraging us to accept what we perceive, skepticism encourages us towards ever-vigilant doubtfulness.

Many people believe that maintaining an attitude of skepticism is healthy, because it protects us against being taken in by false claims. Doubt is considered to be the starting place for science, since new discoveries are not to be believed based on some researcher's word alone—they must be proven to be valid and true. Scientific experiments must be repeatable in order to verify the logical process from assumptions to experimental procedure to results, or else the results are highly suspect. We do not trust what we do not respect, and so the basis of good science is the reporting of observed phenomena stripped clean of the personally subjective components of perception.

My Random House College Dictionary defines skeptic as:

> **Skeptic** - *a person who questions the validity or authenticity of something purporting to be factual; a person who maintains a doubting attitude, as toward values, plans, statements, or the character of others; a person who doubts the truth of a religion; a member of a philosophical school of ancient Greece, who maintained that real knowledge of things is impossible; any thinker who doubts the possibility of real knowledge of any kind.*

The underlying premise of skepticism is that certain widely held beliefs are all that can be commonly proved to be true, so only that which is readily apparent to our senses and can be demonstrated to us upon demand may be considered valid, and all else must be continually questioned. When skepticism encourages that we remain in a state of disbelief regardless what is being sensed, it's clear that disbelief will greatly affect our perceptions ... just as any belief system affects perception. Rigid adherence to a state of disbelief is just as limiting as rigid adherence to any other kind of belief system.

In fact, we are all limited by our assumptions. It's challenging if not impossible to thoroughly doubt and question our own closely held beliefs ... such as the one that maintaining a constant state of doubt is advantageous to us. Doubting such doubt leaves us with nothing at all as the basis for all that is. While a person with a mindful attitude of acceptance would lovingly accept this discovery, a skeptic quite possibly would doubt this finding as well. At some point, even the most passionate skeptics among us accept ideas and beliefs as their basis for comprehending this universe. If this acceptance is a rigid one of holding some beliefs more tightly than others, we risk becoming closed-minded, and ignoring many innovative new ways of seeing the world.

There are numerous examples throughout history of how skepticism and doubt often appear in retrospect to be attempts to cling to long-held conservative beliefs. Christopher Columbus faced such skepticism when he attempted to get financing for his voyage to the new world, and found that most of the people who could afford to pay for his trip felt it was a waste of money, since they were skeptical that he would find anything of value on his voyage before he fell off the edge of the earth.

Many things we take for granted now such as cars, computers, microwave ovens and satellite communications for television and phone calls were not considered possible when they were first publicly discussed. People greeted these tremendous new technological inventions with considerable doubt and distrust. The Wright brothers were faced with immense skepticism that they could make a real flying airship, since everyone who had ever tried to get a mechanical device airborne with people aboard had failed spectacularly.

Skepticism is not merely a historical aberration, but continues to appear even in more recent times. In 1985, scientists laughed at and ridiculed a proposal by fellow scientists to view a single molecule with a new type of scanning tunneling microscope. A decade later, when scanning probe microscopes, or SPMs, became the standard equipment in research labs around the world and a Nobel prize in physics was awarded for the development of the scanning tunneling microscope, the skepticism of physicists and microscopists finally wore off.

Experiential proof overcomes conservative skepticism, since many people can accept new beliefs when they directly perceive them. I therefore strongly encourage people who wish to explore the nature of reality shifts to try the exercises at the end of each chapter of this book. Reality shifts do not readily lend themselves to experimental validation, since they do not occur upon demand, nor do they force themselves on us so those who wish to ignore them are incapable of doing so ... but they definitely *do* occur when they are allowed to happen. Dramatically recognizable reality shift experiences seem to most frequently occur when they are *needed*.

To those who doubt that reality can move as I describe, I suggest they retain mental equilibrium by equally doubting that reality does *not* shift. Skeptical people are capable of having the most intense kinds of experiences when they remove their mental barriers and perceive the vast difference between what they had believed possible and what they find themselves experiencing. In other words, to see is to believe.

My Background & Beliefs

My awareness of reality shifts came to me in spite of the fact that I was raised in a very pragmatic family, and I didn't attend church or receive spiritual training. My parents emphasized the importance of logical, rational thinking for best understanding the universe. My father is a civil engineer who believes that math and science provide us with the best way to comprehend the universe, and who shared many hours with my sister and me studying mathematics, science, and literature when we were growing up. My mother was a grade school teacher who provided my sister and I with a loving, relaxed and supportive learning environment in our childhood. My family traveled every summer to different parts of the world, so as I grew up I saw people living in very different cultures… ranging from the friendly laid-back attitudes of the Pacific islanders to the rush-rush excitement of people living in big cities like Hong Kong, Stockholm, Tokyo, and Paris. There are many different ways for people to live and relate to one another, and I'm grateful to have witnessed this firsthand while growing up.

Both my parents believed in the value of continuing education, so my sister majored in Molecular Biology and I majored in Physics when we were encouraged to go away to college as teenagers. I continued my university studies to get a master's degree in business administration after receiving a bachelor's degree in Physics, and then worked as a data center project manager for a bank for several years. My educational schooling in physics, psychology and business reinforced the values of practicality and rationality I learned in childhood from my family.

Aside from a short time in the Girl Scouts when I was young, I have not belonged to religious or spiritual affiliations, so my spiritual experiences have been relatively unbiased by religious training. My grandmother lovingly shared with me her belief in Christianity, but I did not attend church or bible study classes. It is wonderful to observe these experiences relatively free of religious bias or expectation. I am not seeking to add any additional belief structures to overlay on myself, because I have found a deeper appreciation for direct experience. I love to be able to continue questioning without ever assuming that, "*Now* I understand what's going on here." I prefer to ask questions indefinitely without stopping at concepts of agreed-upon reality and assuming that since two or more of us agree upon something, then that's all there is to it.

I also feel it is important to let you know that I do not take drugs; my experiences are not augmented by any kind of controlled or uncontrolled hallucinogenic substances. While I have experienced various extra-sensory phenomena throughout my life, I consider myself to be a very practical, organized person, not someone who is carried away by flights of fancy. I excel at planning and managing projects with many people, and have a reputation for being straightforward and honest.

I'm excited to share with you some examples of reality shifts I've encountered and heard about, as well as ways to experience reality shifting so you can feel the joy and wonder of witnessing miracles first-hand. I wrote this book based on my own experiences and some of the experiences of those close to me. It's my sincere desire to share reality shifts stories in order to open up a dialog about the way reality shifts, so we may all become more conscious of the effect our thoughts and feelings have on the universe. I've included sections on reality shifts I've experienced that seemed to have occurred for no apparent reason, reality shifts I noticed corresponding to wishes or prayers, reality shifts that resulted in healings of people and things, ways to allow reality shifts and feel inspired, lucid dreaming, lucid living, thoughtful contemplation about the why and how reality shifts, and a sense of what it's like to live everyday life knowing that reality shifts.

When you experience the shifting nature of reality, you may find, as I have, that life feels like a dream.

Life is But a Dream

When I see remarkable and surprising things happen, it gives me a jolt similar to how I feel when awakening from a dream. I feel startled out of complacency each time I experience a reality shift, as the experience of witnessing something I considered stable undergoing a surprising transformation feels shocking to me. It must be very easy to fall back asleep again and react mostly unconsciously to the world, because I have been continually reminded of the shifting nature of reality again and again when things instantaneously and without any apparent physical cause appear, disappear, transform, or transport. The meaning of these reality shifts has grown for me over time. I am now aware that reality shifts carry a message for us that we are all able to transform our lives through our thoughts and feelings. Each time these reality shifts occur, I feel a reminder from spirit that space and time are *much* greater than I am normally able to comprehend or appreciate, and I sense an implicit grandeur to the universe.

At the time I first became consciously aware of reality shifts, I had no mental framework for placing such experiences. Now that I've witnessed hundreds of reality shifts, I've become more accepting of shifts occurring around me as I see reality is not constrained by limitations I've previously believed in. I've had experiences that have shown me that people who are separated across time and space remain interconnected on a deep level. I've noticed patterns in my experiences, such that some reality shifts feel like wishes being granted, others feel like spontaneous healing is occurring (which is a special kind of prayer), and still others seem like incredible synchronicities. Wishing and praying for people to heal seems to shift reality. Wishing and praying for changes in our lives also shifts reality. Our minds are very influential in constructing our sense and our experience of reality, and reality behaves very much like a dream. Reality is responsive to our thoughts and where we place our attention.

Buddhist meditation practitioners are familiar with these reality shift gaps and discontinuities, and typically advise against either identifying oneself too strongly with the reality shifting (such as thinking, "I'm *amazing!* I can warp the very fabric of reality!"), to the other extreme of feeling reality shifts should be guarded against because they threaten our normal view of reality. As with all things in life, reality shifts are best enjoyed when balance is found in learning to appreciate the mysteries and wonder inherent in everyday life. Reality shifts are gifts that give us a glimpse of the underlying interconnectedness between all levels of space and time.

Some religions and spiritual faiths explain that what we consider to be reality is actually a dream. Life feels like a dream when we are startled out of complacency and routine by inexplicable synchronicity, epiphany, déjà vu, rapport, and miracles. Many of us have felt like what's happening has happened before, or that we have some kind of memory of it already. Many of us feel instant rapport for a person, place, or thing, without any real reason for feeling so close. If a wish fulfilled is a miracle, then I believe millions of miracles happen here on Earth every day, because so many people experience their wishes being granted. I believe we are creating our lives from our thoughts and feelings every day, and when we focus our attention more closely on what is possible, we can better appreciate our power to completely transform our lives.

The people who inspire me most are those who live their lives lucidly, with full appreciation for what really matters. People who have had near death experiences inspire me because they often decide to radically open their beliefs in accordance with their spiritual path and knowledge of the ways that they are directly creating reality. People who've been declared dead and then come back to life frequently resume their lives with much greater interest and vigor than before, and with much greater appreciation and enjoyment of life. They stop worrying about things they no longer consider of importance, they don't get angry about things "going wrong," and they change their values ... knowing that the only things we take with us when we die are the love, knowledge and joy of living each day to its fullest. These people remember the interconnectedness of all things and the preciousness of life, while losing their fear of death.

Learning to flow with life and develop a more expanded sense of experience gives me feelings of joy, stability and freedom. When I sense the way reality changes, I feel more aware of who I am and how I fit in the universe, and less constrained to live according to expectations. When viewing experience from the perspective of participating in a waking dream, I am in a much higher frame of reference that allows me to perceive these reality shifts as the physical embodiment of choices I am making. Our true spiritual nature is love, joy, and freedom—and nobody deprives us of these things. We can be our own jailers, trapped in static limitations of our beliefs and attitudes, or we can choose to free ourselves to fully experience this present moment.

I long to live in a world that responds to my thoughts and feelings, yet still surprises and delights me in new and ever-changing ways. Such are the qualities of my most enjoyable dreams, and such my life becomes when I wake up to what's really possible. I notice my belief boundaries expanding every time reality shifts, as well as in every 'ordinary' moment of each day.

Introduction to Reality Exercises

Arm Folding

Quickly fold your arms in front of you, without looking to see which arm is on top of the other. Now quickly unfold and refold your arms the opposite way. How do you feel crossing your arms this way? If you feel uncomfortable or awkward, do you know why that is?

This exercise shows how we can get so accustomed to doing things a certain way that habitual patterns can become impediments to changing our ways. We rarely notice our most typical ways of thinking and behaving, because things we do often tend to become habitual and unconscious. Now *visualize* crossing your arms the new way, just the opposite of how you usually cross your arms. Don't actually cross your arms the new way—just imagine how it looks and feels to cross your arms differently. After picturing this clearly and then quickly crossing your arms the new way, do you notice any difference? Why do you think this is?

Imaginary Rubber Band

We often overlook how much influence our minds have over every aspect of our lives. We tend to be so immersed in our thoughts we don't examine how thoughts affect our experience.

Clasp your hands together with your two forefingers both pointing upwards parallel to one another at a distance of about one to two inches apart. Study your forefingers, and imagine that there is a tight rubber band around them. Now say aloud to yourself slowly in a deliberate tone of voice, "I can feel the rubber band bringing my fingers closer ... and closer ... and closer ..." If you notice your fingers moved closer together, why do you think this was? If you notice your fingers didn't move together, why do you think they stayed apart?

Heaven's Boughs

I climb my tree with book in hand,
and feel the rough bark scratch me.
Barefoot toe-holds lift me up into the leafy bower ...
heaven's gateway of poking twigs
and twisting branch of roughened bark
and fragrant bough.
Ants walk here towards the sky
as I twist and turn
finding a nest of branches to embrace me,
my barefoot toes wiggling in ecstatic delight.
Sunlight dances through cathedral leaf patterns
above me ... birds sing nearby.
I can feel myself steady and embraced in love
yet swaying gently ...
slowly ...
in these scratchy arms.
I feel so much Love here,
I rest my head and fall asleep ...
wakening much later to gaze
into a blue jay's intense eyes.
We are brothers, he and I.

Chapter 2

Why Reality Shifts

*"Nature is full of infinite causes
that have never occurred in experience"*
– Leonardo da Vinci

When I talk to people about reality shifts, I am often asked, "So *why* do these things happen? I can't find my wallet anywhere ... is this a practical joke?" The first reason for experiencing things appearing, disappearing, transporting and transforming is simply to awaken us to the fact that *it can*—reality *does* shift. Perhaps there need be no other reason. Some of us require a whole lot of reality shift experiences before we are finally willing to admit something mysterious is going on that defies immediate comprehension. Once we acknowledge that reality may be an ever-changing creation of our collective minds, we open ourselves to a dialogue between ourselves and the universe. The significance of some reality shifts seems much like dream symbolism, where people, objects, and events have meaning far greater than surface appearance suggests. Observing reality shifts thus deepens my appreciation for the mystery of life, and the miracle of being part of such a creative universe.

My scientifically minded sister once asked me "What is the *mechanism* for these things to happen!?," after she experienced her first psychic communication with me when we were continents apart. As far as I know, there are no mechanisms existing within material reality that allow people to send and receive communications with one another across time and space, heal others, make and receive wishes, and see people and things transform, appear, and disappear. All these things seem magical, mysterious, and miraculous because they defy some of our most basically held assumptions—yet they have all happened to me and people I know.

Many scientists believe if we look in the right place, we'll find mechanisms to explain every experience. This mechanistic view is based on assumptions of material realism, which Amit Goswani outlines in his book, *The Self-Aware Universe*, as being: strong objectivity, causal determinism, locality, physical or material monism, and epiphenomenalism. Scientists adopt such assumptions as a philosophy of scientific realism, without remembering their assumptions arose from postulates about the nature of reality—not experimental results. These assumptions began when Rene Descartes divided the world into matter and mind, and with scientists subsequently challenging the mind, or spirit, component. Results from modern quantum physics experiments indicate that mind is an essential component in the universe, and that mind and matter are unified by consciousness.

Quantum physics is the study of atomic and subatomic particles and waves, the smallest known and most elementary components of the universe. Scientists studying those most elementary particles, or quanta, hope to find ways to better observe and predict quantum behavior. Intriguingly, quanta seem to only manifest as material particles when we look at them, and otherwise tend to behave as waves. We can actually *see* this dual wave/particle behavior in photons, which are the most basic quantum particles in light. Photons demonstrate wavelike behavior when we shine light through a narrow slit and see a diffraction pattern of light and dark bands, and particle behavior when light particles physically strike film in our cameras that we can develop into pictures.

Scientists wishing to prove their assumptions of material realism at the subatomic level have been surprised to find just the opposite, because quanta do not behave mechanically. Waves of light sometimes behave like particles, but we can only predict quantum particle behavior with probabilities. We are also unable to observe all the information about a given quantum particle at a given time. These findings require a reassessment of some fundamental assumptions, since our ability to explore and understand the universe depends upon our flexibility at improving our core beliefs.

Start with Good Assumptions

Before we can seriously contemplate why reality shifts, we need to start with good working assumptions for our scientific exploration of the universe that agree with what we observe. All science is based on assumptions. We need to honestly assess our starting assumptions before attempting to build an explanation for what's going on. We'll examine how the assumptions of material realism hold up to scientific findings, and revise these assumptions to match what experimental results appear to show us. It's good scientific practice to revise assumptions when they just don't match reality; for example, we now assume the world is spheroidal, not flat, and that the Earth revolves around the sun. We'll stick with these beliefs until reality shows us a more accurate perspective.

Material realism's first assumption of *strong objectivity* asserts there is an objective material universe "out there" that is independent of us. For example, we hope to understand chemistry by studying the interaction of chemicals, and physics by studying how physical bodies interact ... yet we do not consider ourselves to be in any way entangled in what we are observing. We often imagine that we can be perfect voyeurs, having no appreciable impact whatsoever on the subjects of our study. The validity of this assumption becomes questionable when we see how inextricably connected the observer is to quantum physics experiments; the observer plays the decisive role in determining what is observed.

The second assumption of *causal determinism* is the familiar idea that once we understand the forces causing change in a given system, we can accurately predict the effect those causes will have. We would expect to be able to predict what would happen when we roll a marble towards a bunch of other marbles, if we knew where all the marbles were and the position and speed of the striking marble. As we will see in this chapter, quantum physics challenges our ability to understand all that we need in order to make such predictions, since the uncertainty principle does not allow us to know both an object's velocity and position. We cannot accurately make predictions in the realm of quantum physics, other than having a sense of statistical probability for certain outcomes. Werner Heisenberg proposed in his uncertainty principle that quanta must be described as waves while they travel and particles when they are viewed, and Niels Bohr added that it's impossible to specify the observed atom's wave function separately from it's observing electron. Chaos theory is another challenge to causal determinism, as the universe appears to behave unpredictably at its very core.

The third assumption of *locality* in material realism is the concept that objects exist independently and separately from one another. We study each experimental subject with the assumption that it is separate from other objects so we can conduct different experiments in different conditions and believe that we are studying an isolated, independent subject. At odds with this assumption is the observation of some twin quantum particles that have shown separated objects can and *do* remain in synchronization with each other across time and space ... continuing to correlate their angles of spin with each other. This was first considered in the "Einstein-Podolsky-Rosen paradox," later verified in the laboratory, and mathematically demonstrated by Bell's theorem.

Assumptions of *material or physical monism* and *epiphenomenalism* assert that subjective mental phenomena are simply epiphenomena of matter. In other words, the material world is the primary mover and shaker, and things we think we observe through our minds are irrelevant, "immaterial" inconsequential side effects. Quantum physics shows us the weakness of these assumptions when we consider how observers who take quantum measurements collapse quantum waves at the moment they make that observation.

If the assumptions forming the basis for material realism are so shaken by findings of quantum physics experiments, what assumptions can we start with that accommodate these results? We can start by refining and revising the above assumptions of material realism into assumptions that *include* mind along with matter, and that better agree with the findings of quantum physics:

> **Subjective Interconnectedness**
> Each part of the universe has its own unique subjective perspective and is interconnected to all that is
>
> **Change is a Handshake between Sender & Receiver**
> Change occurs when a sending wave and receiving wave meet and agree that a choice is

being made for change, like two hands shaking between the past and future

Consciousness is Nonlocal
At the subquantum level, all points in time and space are equal to all other points in time and space, and a change contemplated in one place and time can have long distance and temporal effects

Mind and Matter are One, Unified by Consciousness
When consciousness changes, it affects the material world, because mind and matter are inseparable

We will keep these revised assumptions in mind as we take a look at some scientific theories that can help us understand how and why reality shifts occur, and review experimental findings these assumptions support.

Learning from Scientific Theories

Scientists by their very nature offer ever-evolving hypotheses and theories as they find things out. Science helps us gain a better grasp of what's going on, as long as we remember that scientific theories are all ideas that start with words like "maybe," "perhaps," and "what if." In other words, today's scientific wisdom might well be tomorrow's discarded theories, but in the meantime these theories can give us something wonderful to contemplate.

Another important consideration to keep in mind is that scientifically proven theories can only be proven within the domain being studied. Theories can be tested, yet different levels of science are not all-encompassing. The behavior of subatomic particles can be predicted with reasonable accuracy based upon physical models and theories, but it would be a mistake to assume that the behavior of people can also be predicted by the same theories. Physics is helpful for providing us with a better idea of what's going on in the physical universe, because it works with the simplest, most basic levels of reality. Physics does *not* help us understand our inner psychology, social dynamics, or even how living organisms on Earth interrelate with one another and their ecosystems—although all those disciplines depend on physics.

When we consider theories in physics as they relate to all that is, it helps to remember that we are using physical "what if" models as analogies for larger, more complex things, like ourselves. Once we keep in mind the fact that scientific theories are precisely that, and that caution is advised when extrapolating from quantum particles to human consciousness, we can start having fun contemplating what may be possible based on scientific theory.

Physicists note that the fact that we are consciously aware observers changes what we are observing. Noticing a reality shift means we are consciously aware of a different past than the one that we are currently a part of, and the very process of observing has a huge impact on reality itself. It's quite possible that we create what we believe we are observing, so what we pay attention to becomes more real as we invest more of our attention in it. Realizing this is much like realizing that we are all dreaming, whether we are sleeping or not, and that each one of us is creating our life of experienced realities as a work of art. When we give more attention to reality shifts, we see more of them.

Do you remember the movie, *Groundhog Day,* starring Andie MacDowell and Bill Murray? That movie tells the story of a character who has no idea what's going on, but begins to notice that he is reliving the same day over and over again. This story presents the notion that at some level, we really are aware of all the possible choices we might make in life ... that at some level, *we know* there are an infinite number of universes of reality for us to exist within. For most people in life and in that story, the full infinite variety of choices is not consciously perceived; but for the main character, the choices themselves become the focal point of all attention. When a person understands that many socially held values feel empty and meaningless when one's spirit is not satisfied, one discovers what is really worth living for.

Quantum physics gives us some exciting new ideas for contemplating our universe in conjunction with the notion that consciousness may be the underlying foundation of reality. What if some of the theories from quantum physics appeared in our everyday lives? What if we could experience being particles of matter some times, and waves of energy other times, apparently materializing and dematerializing? What if we could make discontinuous quantum jumps from one place to another, transporting ourselves instantaneously? What if we could jump to another state of being, like jumping to a parallel universe?

Our thoughts and wishes behave as energetic wave forms that continue to exist even after we've thought and released them, and we cancel out many things we think we are wishing for when our thoughts conflict. All things are indeed possible, yet we often get in our own way. We can get a better idea of this feeling of how we know all possibilities are there and how some wishes act to cancel each other out by considering the famous "double slit" experiment in quantum physics.

Particle/Wave Duality

> *"As far as the laws of mathematics refer to reality, they are not certain; and as far as they are certain, they do not refer to reality."*
> *– Albert Einstein*

The "double-slit" experiment in quantum physics is an important starting point for observing what's going on behind the scenes in reality. The double-slit experiment consists of a stream of subatomic quantum particles (such as electrons, atoms, or light) being directed toward a screen, with a barrier in front of the screen. The particles must pass through two parallel slits in the barrier before they hit the screen, and each slit can be opened or closed independently. The tiny quantum particles are directed towards the screen in a trickle, so only one particle passes through the slits at a time. The screen is very sensitive, and shows a tiny spot every time a particle hits.

The surprising thing about the double-slit experiment is that if one or the other slit is closed down, *more* particles reach certain parts of the screen than when both slits are open. This is *very* surprising since the barrier is less open with one slit closed and only one slit open, so one might reasonably expect fewer particles would hit the screen. In fact, with only one slit open, particles hit parts of the screen they would *never* hit with both slits open!

This behavior of quantum particles can be explained if one imagines the particles are traveling like waves when they pass through the slits and travel towards the screen, where waves are capable of interfering with one another and canceling each other out. This does explain the interference, but it doesn't explain why the quantum particles hit the screen as point like spots ... much more like particles than waves.

This experiment is the basis for showing how quantum particles have the disconcerting quality of being both particles and waves, yet we only observe them as being one or the other at any given time. This experiment suggests the possibility that when we have conflicting thoughts and intentions, they cancel each other out. It seems our intentions travel like waves to create what we consider to be the materially real, or particle-like parts of our reality.

Reality behaves fluidly when it shifts from one possibility to another ... yet the transition phase is something I rarely witness in reality shifts. Most of the reality shifts I've seen occurred in such a way that they seemed to jump from one state to another with no in-between transitional phase. It seems as if when reality is in the process of shifting it is like a wave, and when it settles again to another physical arrangement it is behaving like a particle.

A deep connection exists between observers and the observed in quantum physics. This connection appears to be *so* strong that it doesn't seem possible to separate the observer from what's being observed. I feel this particle/wave duality and observer effect is also manifested at more organized levels, so we notice synchronicities based on where we focus attention. When we are aware of something, we are in some sense "creating" it—because until someone comes along to encounter a given experience, that material possibility can occupy an infinite number of possible wavelike positions simultaneously. This is true of subatomic particles, and I have personally witnessed this observer effect in my own life every time I encounter a surprising synchronicity such as this one:

Songs from Beyond

In February 1998, on the day after my friend died, I went to a florist's shop to send a bouquet to his widow. After arranging the delivery, my daughter and I browsed through a nearby shop that sells beads.

I noticed the music in the store sounded like it was my dead friend talking to me. The lyrics to the songs were uncannily like something he would want to tell me, and it started really hitting me hard. After two or three songs like this, I thought, "Well, at least they're not playing Lean on Me," since that song *really* reminds me of him. Well, guess what song played next?! I was astounded to hear the beginning notes of "Lean on Me," and I rushed over to the sales clerk asking, "WHAT ARE YOU PLAYING?!" She must have thought I looked a little crazed, but she politely responded, "Time-Life Blues hits from 1972 ... it's a compilation."

Every time this sort of synchronicity occurs, I consider how consciousness seems to help select the most memorable experience. So if we somehow *know* all the possibilities are available to us in every moment, how can we access them? Where are all those possibilities hiding, and how can we experience and choose between them? The concept of parallel universes presents us with a way to visualize how so many things can be possible, and how our consciousness can select what we experience.

Parallel Universes

> *"Space is big. You just won't believe how vastly, hugely, mind-bogglingly big it is. I mean, you may think it's a long way down the road to the drug store, but that's just peanuts to space."*
> *– Douglas Adams*

In Fred Alan Wolf's book, *Parallel Universes,* Wolf describes how physicists first attempted to explain otherwise inexplicable paradoxes with the concept of parallel universes in the 1950's. The notion of parallel universes began around 1935, when Albert Einstein and Nathan Rosen recognized a bridge between our universe and another possible universe in black holes. The idea for parallel universes coming together in black holes began when the black holes were mapped by Martin Kruskal to show how the flow of time goes different directions at the boundary of the black hole.

These parallel universes consist of space and time, just as this universe we are in, and they exist alongside our universe. There are an infinite number of parallel you's and me's out there existing in the same space and time we live in, but normally not perceived. In these universes, an infinite number of different choices are being made at each moment, and each universe contains different outcomes from these different choices.

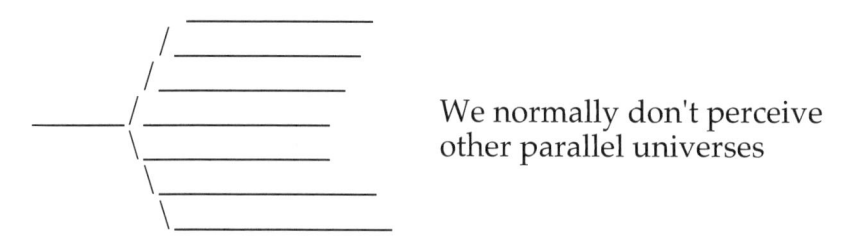

```
              /‾‾‾‾‾‾‾‾‾‾
             /‾‾‾‾‾‾‾‾‾‾
            /‾‾‾‾‾‾‾‾‾‾
    _____ /‾‾‾‾‾‾‾‾‾‾          We normally don't perceive
          \_‾‾‾‾‾‾‾‾‾‾          other parallel universes
           \_‾‾‾‾‾‾‾‾‾‾
            \_‾‾‾‾‾‾‾‾‾‾
             \_‾‾‾‾‾‾‾‾‾‾
```

Parallel universes provide a fascinating concept for the imagination, for they encourage us to consider living completely different lives simultaneously—just not being conscious of them all (unless one is schizophrenic)! In another universe, I am a man instead of a woman, and I got married as soon as I finished high school. In another universe, you and I know each other and are friends. In yet another universe, one or both of us may already have died. Any and all of these possibilities exist, along with universes that are almost exactly identical to this one, with only the tiniest differences—like a slightly different illustration in a children's picture book, a woman vanishing as she walks down the street, or a statue appearing that had not been seen before! Some universes are *greatly* different from this one, perhaps because events diverged tremendously from earlier observation points. Every observation and choice has an effect on the universe, where different possibilities spring forth like branches on a tree. Each branch in turn has more branching points, until the end point of two different branches on a tree are in completely different places.

When reality is considered to consist of parallel universes, an explanation for why observers affect the physical systems that they observe begins to present itself. Parallel universes help us comprehend how people make decisions in their lives, by unconsciously "feeling out" how the choices they make will affect everything else. If all possibilities are occurring somewhere, perhaps consciousness is the connection that allows us to get some sense of how things would feel if we felt or acted in different ways. At some level, we *know* about all possible futures, yet we are not conscious of all these possibilities for the simple reason that such information would overwhelm our capacity to comprehend it all. We might then have unconscious feelings that would give us an intuitive sense that one reality path is preferable to another. Parallel universes help explain reality shifts, which appear as a leap in consciousness from one universe to another, so we actually see two (or more) different universes, all looking and feeling equally real in every way. It's possible consciousness is constantly moving from parallel universe to parallel universe, and we only notice this is happening when we are fortunate enough to witness a discontinuity in the transition from one to another, much as one might be startled to discover the gaps between still images on a roll of movie film.

Bent Coin

In September 1998 I observed a reality shift when a friend was feeling very stressed at helping me straighten up my house before another friend arrived. He carefully picked up a penny from the floor and placed it down flat on top of the clothes drier, in such a way that it made a *"Thwap!"* noise, as it's flat surface contacted the flat surface of the drier.

A few minutes later, I found a very warped penny sitting on top of the drier! I'd never before seen a penny bent like this one into a curve, like it was transformed into a rocking chair, and I asked, "Have you *ever* seen anything like *this* before? What on Earth can bend a penny to look like this?" That's when my friend told me the penny had been flat only moments earlier! He told me he'd had a tough time picking it up, until it became soft and a corner bent upward so he could hold onto it. He said something similar had recently happened to him while holding a friend's pewter ankh pendant in his hand that became warm in his hand, softened, and bent. When he handed it back, she exclaimed, "You bent my ankh!" so he took it back unconsciously smoothing it between his fingers, and it straightened back.

Mysteriously warped penny next to normal penny

This particular kind of reality shift is referred to as psychokinesis, which was defined by Thalbourne as *"the direct influence of mind on a physical system without the mediation of any known physical energy."*

John Taylor studied metal-bending, and observed what he called a "shyness effect," where the spoons or keys that were bent were never actually observed to be bending. Taylor's shyness effect matches my own observations that I've rarely seen reality shifts in the in-between phase; instead, reality shifts seem more like quantum leaps where reality shifts from one universal possibility to another. In the case of the bent coin, reality seemed to shift from a universe where there was a normal flat penny sitting on top of the drier to a different universe in which the coin sitting atop the drier was bent. Almost all of the reality shifts I've seen have been like this, where I noticed a point in time when something appeared, disappeared, or transformed instantaneously. There was no "morphing" or fade-out, but instead an immediate transition.

Perhaps it's simply because we are somewhat trapped by habitually observing our lives—tending to see what we expect to see rather than what is actually here—that we hardly ever notice the jumps from one reality to another. We need to be able to observe the fluid wave-like nature of reality in order to witness the in-between infinite place between universes of possibility. We are constantly constrained by what we believe, or knowledge, as well as space and time. Tarthang Tulku writes about the effect of noticing these constraints in his book, *Knowledge of Time and Space*:

> *"It is as though we had been trapped in the narrow angle of a triangle, squeezed on one side by linear time and on the other by empty space. At the base of the triangle, determining its structure, is the knowledge that space and time make available—not only limited, but separated from us by a distance we have no hope of crossing. Though linear time moves freely, it presents us with one 'measured-out' triangle after another, each as confining as the last. Though empty space allows an infinite number of positions, each one traps us in the same way.*
>
> *If we could somehow open space or time, knowledge would become available in a new way. We could move out of the narrow angle in which we have been wedged to explore the space that the triangle encloses. We could question the dynamic that creates the triangle and propels us from one triangle to the next. We could reach out to know knowledge directly, perhaps finding as we did so that the triangle itself shifted shape or dissolved entirely. No longer confined like an animal in its pen, we could start to live a richer way of being."*

This opening of the boundaries of the physical world occurs when we expand our peripheral vision—our "triangles" of awareness. When we learn to attend to all that is, and become more open to full direct experience, we live a much more innately rewarding and exciting life.

So if all these parallel universes exist, *how* does everything hold together? There seems to be a strange quality about existence that keeps everything simultaneously interconnected to while at the same time everything functions independently. One of the most popular physical models for understanding how everything is interconnected is the holographic universe model proposed by physicist David Bohm and Stanford neurophysiologist Karl Pribram.

Holographic Universe

The holographic model of the universe is especially appealing because it provides a theoretical foundation that accommodates new assumptions of non-local consciousness, subjective interconnectedness, and mind and matter being unified in consciousness. Our best-known physical examples of holograms are visual three-dimensional representations of scenes, in which every small piece of the image contains the entire image as seen from one particular perspective. If you break a holographic image into hundreds of pieces, you'll find you now have hundreds of tiny holographic images of the same scene, with each image *slightly* different as if photographed from slightly different locations. Because the universe moves, it cannot be considered a hologram (which doesn't move); our universe is dynamic, like a holomovement.

David Bohm's holographic concept of our universe asserts that the tangible reality of our everyday lives is really an illusion, like a holomovement. Every piece of the universe is whole in itself, and each of these whole pieces are in turn part of a larger whole. Underlying the tangible "explicate" level of reality is what David Bohm refers to as the "implicate" (which means "enfolded") order. Bohm uses this terminology because he considers the manifestation of all form in the universe as the result of countless enfoldings and unfoldings between these two orders. An electron, for example, is not one thing, but instead is a totality or ensemble enfolded throughout the whole of space. All particles are not lost even when they appear to be destroyed ... they are simply enfolded back into the deeper order from which they sprang.

Bohm believes that because everything in the universe

consists of the seamless holographic fabric of the implicate order, it is as meaningless to view the universe as composed of "parts" as it is to view the different geysers in a fountain as separate from the water out of which they flow. Electrons are not really "elementary particles"; that is just a name given to a certain aspect of the holomovement. The arbitrary way people decide to divide our experience of reality up into parts and then name those parts is more a product of convention and a reflection of our existing belief boundaries than it is a true representation of what is going on.

Bohm points out that our almost universal tendency to fragment the world, ignoring the dynamic interconnectedness of all things, may be responsible for most of our problems in science, in our lives, and in society. People who believe that we can clear-cut forests or strip-mine for minerals without impacting the environment find that we may also then experience massive erosion, soil loss, damaged streams and rivers, and destroyed habitats. People who believe we can prescribe drugs or have surgery that affects only one part of our body can instead experience that other parts of our bodies are surprisingly affected as well. Bohm passionately believes that not only does our current fragmentation of our world into parts not work, but it could lead to our extinction.

Fritjof Capra notes that within the holographic paradigm, time doesn't follow linear flow, and can exist multidimensionally through several dimensions simultaneously. In other words, every moment can be said to exist everywhere, always. I've experienced such multidimensional moments myself:

Time Stands Still

> I was just about to read a Rudyard Kipling picture book, *The Beginning of the Armadillos*, to my younger daughter as we settled into chairs in a waiting room for my older daughter's appointment, when the office door swung open and a woman brought me a picture book. This book was *The Woman Who Fell From the Sky*. As I held the beautifully illustrated picture book, I felt immediately compelled to read it, but my younger daughter insisted we read her selected story first. The

story she chose looked like a long one, and I was concerned we only had twenty-two minutes before my older daughter's appointment was over, and it would be time to leave.

I sighed as I looked up at the digital clock in the waiting room, noting it was 4:08 PM. I wished I could read without rushing, so I decided to not worry about having enough time. I later timed myself reading this book, and clocked it at eleven minutes.

When I finished the armadillo story, I looked up at the clock and saw it was 4:08 p.m. ... the clock had not moved during the entire story! My daughter came out at 4:30 p.m., right on time, and the clock in my car also agreed it was 4:30. Somehow, I'd read a story for eleven minutes, yet no time passed at all.

All experiences we think of as being real are actually composed of neurophysiological processes occurring in our brains. We experience some things as happening inside ourselves, and others as happening outside, because that's how the brain localizes inputs it receives when creating the internal hologram map we believe to be reality. Sometimes our brains can't distinguish between what's felt inside and what's outside, so we feel phantom touch sensations that feel real even when we're not physically being touched.

When we contemplate the concept of a holographic universe, we glimpse the deepest interconnections between everything, which seems paradoxical when we consider how our own humble lives can seem so isolated and alone. It is the distance between ourselves and others that captures our attention: the distance from this solar system to another star system light years away, or simply the distance between this universe of possibility and another. Everything can seem separated by such vast quantities of space, that it's hard to imagine how it could all be interconnected. One way to get to better understand the interconnectedness of everything is to look in the "empty" spaces to see what is there.

Zero Point/Implicate Order

> *"Zero is the ideal of each existent — the nonexistent totality of what would wish to be; the wholeness or fullness toward which all existence tends."*
> Tarthang Tulku

Space presents humans with a vastness that boggles our attempts to know it. We wish to comprehend the source of all things, and are struck by the paradox that places that seem full of nothing more than pure vacuum of empty space can be so full of energy.

Physicist David Bohm proposes there is an infinite ocean of energy, and tells us a little bit about the vast and hidden nature of what he refers to as the implicate order. When physicists calculate the minimum amount of energy an energy wave can hold, they find that every cubic centimeter of empty space contains more energy than the total energy of all the matter in the known universe! Bohm points out that matter does not exist independently from the so-called empty space. Space is not empty nothingness, it is *full*, and is the grounds for the existence of everything. As Bohm explains,

> *"This excitation pattern is relatively autonomous and gives rise to approximately recurrent, stable and separate projections into a three-dimensional explicate order of manifestation."*

Bohm asserts the implicate order is the foundation that gives birth to everything in our universe. It contains every configuration of matter, energy, life, and consciousness possible.

Another name for the emerging paradigm of getting something from nothing is Zero Point energy, so called because some physicists are now considering that space appears to have a vast quantity of intrinsic energetic potential. If what we imagine to be "empty" space is actually full of energy being held in balance while nearly infinite amounts of energy converge so that they cancel each other out, then each point of space with any kind of asymmetry would appear as matter. This suggests that all forms of matter may be considered to be various asymmetries of the zero point field.

But what good are all these theories if we can't experience them? What value do such lofty and intellectual concepts have to us in our everyday lives? Humans learn best from direct physical experience, and even the most intelligent scientists rely on their ability to sense and perceive reality in order to understand it. If we wish to directly experience how reality is selected, we can attempt to sense our experience on the quantum scale.

Sensing on the Quantum Scale

Our perception of reality shifts implies that we are, indeed, capable of sensing on the quantum scale where discontinuities in this universe have been scientifically shown to exist. Noticing that a reality shift has occurred is essentially an act of observing a quantum state selection—observing the point in time and space where potential reality becomes actual reality. Our ability to perceive reality shifts is thus a form of high sensory perception we can develop if we choose.

Our unconscious, habitual patterns are malleable when we learn new things, so anyone is capable of developing an awareness of reality shifts. In a multiverse of parallel universes, we are the ones who choose what we consciously experience, beginning with the experience of noticing our minds are making such choices. Each of us can change our life from within. We make choices every minute of our lives that have tremendous impact and influence.

Fred Alan Wolf describes these choices as "qwiffs," which is a cute nickname for quantum wave functions. When we consider the particle/wave duality of quantum particles, we imagine how the qwiffs can either *flow* like waves or *pop* like waves vanishing to be replaced by some physical form, like a bubble. When qwiff waves are flowing, they are not being observed. They "pop" at the moment an observer pays attention and sees a bubble where once only a wave had been. Essentially, we *"pop a qwiff"* every time we choose to do anything, selecting one reality from an infinite range of possible realities we might wish to experience.

When a possibility is selected, it typically remains in the particle form we expect ... like a green bubble ... yet, it is also possible for the particle form to pop again to another state, like a purple bubble, if we allow for such an observation to be made. In other words, by allowing ourselves to *observe the observation* of reality choices being made, we can witness more than one pop from a qwiff. When we notice that reality has shifted, we recognize we are in a different universe of possibility than the one we occupied before, because we allow ourselves to *pay attention to the way we pay attention.*

The Observer's State of Mind

The standard explanation from quantum physicists is that the observer's role is vital in how reality is selected. Typically, once an observer "chooses" a possible reality, that's *it*; the quantum wave function or "qwiff" has popped, and the universe has provided us with an expected physical environment. Once we think we know what we're experiencing, we don't typically examine the experience in detail, since we seldom believe it can be possible for the universe to change its mind. Each change of mind arises from a choice (wish, desire, or prayer) someone makes.

Observing the universe "change its mind" is what reality shifts are all about. As long as we've moved our concepts of reality by an amount we are comfortable experiencing, we are invited to witness how reality *becomes* reality! Our ability to witness such behind-the-scenes activity is determined by our frame of mind. People can be skeptical about reality shifts—even *highly* skeptical, conservative, cautious and practical—and as long as they are *open* to the possibility of seeing reality shifts, they can see reality shift before their eyes.

Jane Katra writes in *Miracles of Mind* of seeing a US government agent in the Philippines observing psychic surgeons at work. A healer asked him if he would allow her to heal a very old skin abnormality of his, and he rather reluctantly agreed. He was amazed and transformed by witnessing his old, familiar, ridged purplish bump on his forearm heal right before his eyes.

Our state of mind matters in order for us to see and work reality shifts in our lives. It seems necessary for an observer to be *open-minded*, *conscious*, and *attentive* to the area about to change, in order for that person to observe reality shift. If we aren't willing to allow for the possibility of reality shifts, we won't experience them. If we don't consciously focus our attention where shifts occur, we won't see things transform, transport, appear and disappear, or witness changes in time. It would be a real shame if the universe's magic tricks were performed for nobody's benefit; it's wonderful to know we are becoming more aware of consciousness itself, in order to more fully appreciate the miracle of existence.

We Are Energy

The most important thing to realize when contemplating how we influence reality shifts is that *we exist as pure energy*. Not just people, but every single physical object, animal, and thing in existence consists of energy. Native American people, with their appreciation for direct experience, have an understanding that spirit (energy) permeates everything. Spirit is not just something that inspires people and animals, but also trees, grasses, rocks, streams, and mountains.

Just as Barbara Brennan discovered she could see auras around everything when she was a child, many people have noticed and described these energy fields for thousands of years. People who see auras regularly describe them as colorful, egg-shaped patterns of energy, and some people experience them as movements and waves of energy, rather than seeing energy fields. This energy has been known as prana (Hindu), ka (Egyptian), mana (kahunas), ch'i (Chinese), dunamis, pneuma (Greek), baraka (Sufi), Jesod (Jewish Cabbalists), fluid of life (alchemists), and wakan or wakouda (Sioux). If you have not seen or felt energy fields, it can be hard to accept that they exist, even if people have been observing them for thousands of years.

Throughout history and across many cultures, spiritually centered individuals such as monks, priests, saints, shamans, magi, mystics and sorcerers have seen the essential reality as energy and consciousness ... something like webs or filaments of light, and not the three-dimensional material world most of us think of as 'real'. Ancient seers believed that we do exist, but not only in the way we interpret ourselves to be, since our interpretation is something we created, something we expect to experience brought to us to sense in the ways we expect to sense it. In other words, ancient mystics talk about reality similar to David Bohm's idea of an implicate order. Psychics and seers describe individual human energy fields appearing like egg-shaped forms of light, with filaments or threads of light issuing from a central core. There is a smaller but more intensely glowing point of awareness at the periphery of the individual's aura, and most mystical and shamanic traditions believe the position of this point of attentive awareness is directly responsible for what the individual experiences. When this point of attentive awareness moves, the individual experiences a different realm.

The more skeptical among us may be interested to know that the existence of the human energy field has been experimentally confirmed by Valerie Hunt, a physical therapist and professor of kinesiology at UCLA. In her experiment, aura readers were also participating in experiments simultaneously with Hunt to record their observations. Hunt discovered that an electromyograph device, ordinarily used to measure the electrical activity in muscles can pick up another field of energy radiating from the body, much subtler and smaller in amplitude than the traditionally recognized biological function fields, which range in frequency from 100 to 1600 cycles per second, and occasionally higher. Most brain electrical activity ranges from 0 to 100 cycles per second, muscle electrical fields go up to about 225 cycles per second, and electrical energy measured in the heart goes up to about 250 cycles per second; higher than any other biological function yet measured electrically. The astonishing thing about Hunt's discovery is that the high frequency fields she measured were not emanating from the brain, heart, or muscles, but from the *chakras*. Hunt also found that the electromyograph showed patterns that matched the frequencies the aura readers saw. Hunt watched the electromyograph patterns on an oscilloscope screen, and observed that the patterns she saw would invariably correspond to the colors the aura readers were seeing.

Hunt discovered there is correlation between people's frequencies and the primary focus of their consciousness. People concentrating on the material world vibrate in the lower range, not too far from 250 cycles per second. People who utilize psychic senses and healing have frequencies between 400 to 800 cycles per second, and people who do trance channeling are in the range of 800 to 900 cycles per second. People with frequencies above 900 cycles per second are what Hunt calls 'mystical personalities', and are aware of cosmic interrelatedness of all things. Using a very special piece of equipment, Hunt measured frequencies on some of these people as high as 200,000 cycles per second!

When I meditate and raise my level of vibration, I can viscerally feel the sensation of higher frequencies in and around me. At times, I've awakened in the night to feel the bed I was sleeping on vibrating audibly, and so strongly it seemed something was shaking the bed. The shaking appeared to be an oscillation from the energy vibrations I felt. When these higher frequencies vibrate within me, I feel great love, and the most incredible things happen. This high-energy vibration is strongly associated with reality shifts. The more of this high energy I feel, the more likely I am to notice reality is shifting around me!

Hunt also made the astonishing discovery that the human energy field responds to stimuli *before* the brain and body respond. Hunt conducted experiments to measure both EMG and EEG readings of the brain simultaneously when she made a loud noise or flashed a bright light, and she found the EMG of the human energy field was first to respond. This finding indicates our energy fields respond to stimuli before we consciously react, and it also suggests the possibility that each part of our body has its own form of intelligence. Our language reflects cellular body knowingness with phrases like "my *gut feeling* tells me," or "I've got *cold feet* about this."

Despite the fact that Hunt successfully measured the human energy field, she doesn't believe it is purely electromagnetic; Hunt suspects there is probably more to it than that. Since we don't really know what *any* field is, it's not too surprising that we don't know all there is to know about the nature of human energy fields. Scientists give these fields names such as electrical fields, gravitational fields, or magnetic fields, and describe their properties. Once things are named and described, we often feel more familiar with them.

In the late 1950's, neurophysiologist Benjamin Libet found that we create time and space in our brains, working with brain surgeon Bertram Feinstein at Mount Zion Hospital in San Francisco. Libet's experiments placed electrodes on patients' brains and skin, and detected both a temporal referral (time displacement) and a spatial referral (spatial displacement). Spatial referrals had been known about for some time; that is, direct stimulation of a person's brain gives the person a sense that sensations are occurring elsewhere in the body. Libet discovered a temporal referral—about a half-second delay between when something stimulates our brain, and when we are consciously aware of it. This means our decisions and responses in the world are mostly made unconsciously. Libet found by questioning people about when they first became aware of stimulation that then we refer our first moment of conscious awareness *back in time* to the moment of sensation, and *out in space* to the location of the stimulus. The astonishing implication about Libet's findings is that his experimental subjects felt there was no delay in awareness at all. Libet's experiments are extraordinary for clearly showing that conscious awareness requires first a fast neural signal (unconscious detection), and later the arrival of other neuronic signals.

Brain waves appear to be related to the human energy field and human behaviors. Researchers who study psychokinesis believe they've found medical correlations with peoples' ability to cause mechanical or electrical failure in appliances, and there may also be an association between psychokinesis and theta brain waves. Psychokinesis is the ability of people's minds to influence physical systems without physically interacting with those systems. People who have Parkinson's disease have watches that go haywire much more often than average, and epileptics have similar experiences with electrical appliances breaking down around them. Epileptics have very different brain rhythms than most people.

> **Beta** is the state characterized by excitement, full sensory awareness and alertness;

Alpha is the state of more passive awareness and deep relaxation as bodily sensation diminishes;
Theta is the state of drowsiness and beginning unconsciousness; and
Delta is the deep sleep state.

We can change our mental rhythms in ways that enhances our ability to sense and interact with our world, by learning to relax. Stefan Ossowiecki was a gifted psychometrist who correctly described individuals and scenes associated with them by physical contact with objects belonging to those individuals. Ossowiecki's psychometric abilities were tested during the Second World War with objects from the Warsaw Museum, and he correctly identified the age and use of objects he held, and provided detailed descriptions of what life was like for people who'd used those things. Ossowiecki described how he feels before doing psychometric work as:

> "I begin by stopping all reasoning, and I throw all my inner power into perception of physical sensation. I affirm that this condition is brought about by my unshakable faith in the spiritual unity of all humanity. I then find myself in a new and special state in which I see and hear outside time and space ... I seem to lose some energy, my temperature becomes febrile and the heartbeats unequal ... As soon as I cease from reasoning, something like electricity flows through my extremities for a few seconds ... then lucidity takes possession of me, pictures arise, usually of the past."

The feeling of electric energy Ossowiecki describes is very similar to the way I feel highly energized when reality shifts around me. I notice an increased awareness of expanded consciousness during times I feel alert and simultaneously highly relaxed, with a sense I am more consciously connected to everything in the universe as I let go of a rational, reasonable "Beta" state awareness of the world.

Our Dimensional Identity

Some scientists believe our universe consists of much more than the three spatial dimensions plus time we are consciously aware of. This provides us with a clue to realizing we're not seeing all there is—much is hidden, the same way most of the underwater portion of an iceberg is hidden from view from above. Some scientists working in the field of membrane theory in physics suggest there may be eleven dimensions operating in our universe—with hidden dimensions coiled tightly around the three dimensions we experience, so we see no obvious sign of them—yet they are absolutely necessary for our universe to exist as it is. All we can actually *perceive* to exist are the dimensions of length, depth, height and time.

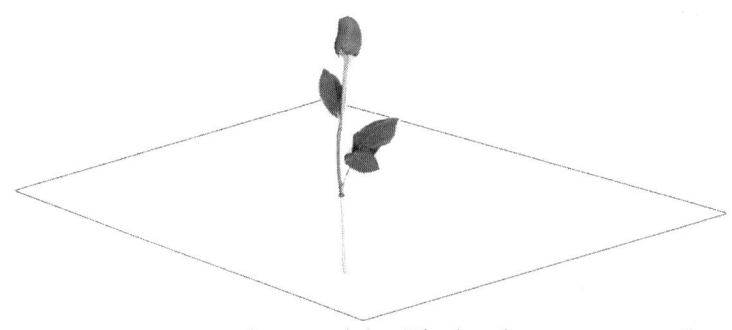

A rose visits Flatland

There are higher levels of dimensional consciousness than this one of height, width, depth, and time ... and these higher levels provide a mechanism for miraculous and amazing things to happen here in our world. It's easier to picture this as we contemplate an imaginary "Flatland," a universe existing only in two dimensions moving through time. When we examine the Flatland world, we see Flatlanders moving about in a flat plane of existence. They do not perceive anything that doesn't bisect their two dimensional plane. Visualize a piece of paper with Flatlanders living right on the top of the page, and imagine how they might react when we raise or lower some other object (such as a rose) right through their universe. Any such movement could easily seem mysterious and magical, and quite inexplicable.

Just as we incorporate two-dimensional awareness into our everyday reality, we can also access higher levels of consciousness where we see how seemingly unrelated parts of the universe are interconnected. Ken Wilber lists ten basic structures of consciousness that describe the hierarchical developmental path of human consciousness:

> **Undifferentiated Mind** is the primary matrix, primary narcissism, oceanic, protoplasmic, adualistic
>
> **Sensoriphysical Mind** is the physiological beginning of a sense of self and differentiation, the "hatching" or birth of the physical self
>
> **Phantasmic-Emotional Mind** structures and builds emotional boundaries, with an egocentric and narcissistic point of view that the world is an extension of oneself
>
> **Representational Mind** uncovers techniques to conceptualize the world in images, symbols and concepts; preoperational cognition
>
> **Rule/Role Mind** involves script analysis, and an ability to take the role of another, to put oneself in another's shoes; paradigm shifts occur and experiences from the past are reinterpreted according to how one fits with one's group
>
> **Formal Reflexive Mind** is worldcentric and introspective with a global perspective; thinking about thinking and questioning the questions
>
> **Centauric** is existential vision-logic or network-logic; synthesizing and integrating awareness between the mind and body in a relatively autonomous self

Psychic is nature mysticism and the feeling that "you are the mountain," while still knowing your body and mind's boundaries

Subtle includes waking consciousness, heightened sensory perception, extremely subtle bliss currents and cognitions, expansive states of love and compassion and a feeling of oneness with deity

Causal is a kind of formless mysticism; a state much like dreamless sleep with a sensation of utter fullness beyond containment or objectification and therefore the essence of pure nothingness and nonduality

Each one of these levels of consciousness, or states of dimensional awareness has an energetic vibration to it, and they are all equally important. We can be aware of many levels of consciousness simultaneously, or contemplate one level for some time. The higher levels (Psychic, Subtle, Causal) are states of awareness where we know we are at one with all that is. When we experience the Causal, we can *feel* that we are creating reality.

The interesting thing to note with dimensional awareness is that while higher dimensional awareness is important, the lower dimensions need our attention as well. Some days our attention may be focused on the introspective contemplation of the meaning of life and reality shifts in the Formal Reflexive Mind level, while we may spend others wholly focused on our own lives in the Phantasmic-Emotional Mind level. Some stretches of time can feel like our minds are focused on the simplest, purest, feeling of creation—very undifferentiated and one dimensional—like a ray of light.

Our unconscious minds spring up from our very beginning in life, where the self doesn't consciously acknowledge all that it is, and it begins hiding and not being fully honest about all that is being created by itself. When we alienate parts of ourselves, we split thoughts off into repressed thought forms that continue on as unconsciousness, not growing and developing with our conscious awareness, but remaining right where each trauma occurs.

```
                    / Potential
        Trauma    /
                  \
                   \ Actuality
```

We heal these traumatic breaks by returning to face fears we encountered where we repressed some part of our genuine feelings. Returning to the emotional place of trauma and empowering ourselves to be strong there is a powerful way to reintegrate and heal ourselves. Healing is the process of remembering a state of good health and physically embodying it. Our trauma points require extra attention and love.

Valerie Hunt's measurements of the human energy field can be mapped to these levels of consciousness; the higher levels vibrate at a noticeably higher frequency. Perhaps in the not too distant future we will gain a better understanding of what levels of consciousness we are utilizing, and we will learn to stretch our awareness of our energy body frequencies, much as we can learn to stretch awareness of other bodily functions with biofeedback.

Synchronicity in the Space-Time Continuum

Albert Einstein's publication of his special theory of relativity in 1905 marked an incredible turning point in physics. Prior to relativity theory, scientists considered space and time to be linear, absolute, and universal. Relativity theory brought us the concept that space and time are inextricably linked in a four-dimensional space-time continuum. There *is* no universal flow of time, since time itself is relative, so different observers sequence events differently in time if they move at different velocities relative to events they're observing. According to relativity theory, it's even possible for two observers to witness events occur in reverse time; one observer will see two events occur exactly opposite how the other observer saw them. Relativity theory is supported by our new assumption of subjective interconnectedness, which is that strong objectivity is not always (if ever) possible.

In 1964, physicist J. S. Bell published a mathematical theorem ("Bell's theorem") suggesting that subatomic particles are connected in some way that transcends space and time, so two nonlocally connected twin particles would behave similarly. In 1982, physicists Alain Aspect, Jean Dalibard, and Gerard Roger succeeded in conducting an experiment at the University of Paris that showed twin particles actually *did* continue correlating their angles of polarization with each other, even after they'd traveled in opposite directions down pipes and filters ... just as Bell's theorem had predicted they would! This physical proof that two entities remain mysteriously instantaneously interconnected even when physically separated confirms what many of us personally experience, and supports our assumption of non-local consciousness.

It can feel extraordinary to experience synchronicities with others, much as if we are like twin particles remaining mysteriously interconnected, regardless of physical separation. We notice synchronicities of interconnection when we change and someone else experiences the same change at the same time. These changes are instantaneous, can happen across great distances, and don't require any "mechanism" or energy signal in order to occur. All they require is a complementary choice being made by sender and receiver.

Twin Soul Synchronicities

An example of shared synchronicity is the time my hair became naturally curly at the exact same time in October 1996 as my friend's. I was in California at the time, and my friend was in New York. Shortly before my hair curled, I'd looked at a picture of my friend as I wished to know what it was like to have naturally curly hair, and wondered if her hair was naturally curly.

A couple of years later, this same friend and I experienced synchronous simultaneous change in June 1998, when our bruises vanished as we separately and without discussion with each other decided to stop accepting negativity (darkness) into our lives. We were still located on opposite coasts of America, and discovered after the fact that we had both experienced this same transition at the same time!

My personal reality shift experiences demonstrate to me that our choices (wishes and desires) have an extremely powerful effect on reality, and that we can consciously remain aware of both the previous and the new reality. There may be an infinite number of universes, and when each one of us makes a choice, we pull the possibility into this universe when that possibility feels attracted by the love and energy of our wish or prayer. Reality shifts give me the feeling of sensing energy shifts occurring just beneath the surface of things where all universes of possibility are interconnected. If anything is possible, the toughest job might simply be knowing what we want.

Mystics from every religious orientation point out that we are dreaming all the time, whether we are awake or asleep. Mystics also persistently remind us that nothing happens in either the past or the future; only the here-now exists and is real. Recently, studies have helped show that indeed, the present can and *does* change the past.

Changing the Past

> *"You are led through your lifetime by the inner learning creature, the playful spiritual being that is your real self. Don't turn away from possible futures before you're certain you don't have anything to learn from them. You're always free to change your mind and choose a different future, or a different past."*
> *– Richard Bach*

When we consciously make choices like wishes or prayers, our intentions have a definite effect upon past, present, and future. The reality shifts I observe show me that wishes alter the future and the present. Studies by Helmut Schmidt show people can also change the past. Helmut Schmidt conducted experiments in which radioactive material was placed in vials, so emissions of randomly decaying particles were recorded on an electric counter. This recorded decay information for each vial of radioactive material was then stored on floppy disks that nobody saw at that time. The disks were used at a later time to generate a sequence of positive and negative random numbers, which were shown to people who were asked to attempt to change the sequence to favor positive numbers.

Schmidt found that not only did observers succeed in affecting the numbers, but the fact that they *could* do this indicated that their present intention to produce more positive numbers had somehow changed a random event in the past (the radioactive decaying particles' emissions). Schmidt feels that the simplest explanation for these startling results is that this was a *non-random* event, because the sequence of numbers produced were clearly biased. Even though these isotopes had *already* decayed before the study participants wished for the results to go one way or another, the participants could tilt the decay rates in the direction they'd been requested.

In physicist Fred Alan Wolf's book, *Parallel Universes*, Wolf describes a principle of self-consistency that requires whatever sequence of events is occurring to be logically consistent. As long as we don't cancel out the actions involved in noticing how the present changes the past or the future changes the present; *anything* is possible. Physicist John G. Cramer's work considers how time waves collapse when the traveling wave is observed. Waves from the past and from the future may send and receive energy in order to bring about events, and when they encounter one another, the wave collapses to a particular choice. Cramer calls the original time-forward wave the *offer* wave, and the conjugate time-reverse wave the *echo* wave. The implications of Cramer's work are quite profound, because they indicate that every time we observe something, we send out a wave toward the future and a wave toward the past. This is like a handshake between sender and receiver, with a mutual agreement upon a choice being selected. The interesting thing about the present affecting the past is that it seems reasonable to consider that decisions made in the future also affect our present. So long as events don't cancel each other out, consistency is maintained.

An experiment that showed how decisions can be made at the last minute was conducted in 1985 by three physicists at the University of Maryland. Carroll Alley, Oleg Jakubowicz, and William Wickes devised an experimental apparatus consisting of electronically controlled mirrored surfaces that could be inserted after a photon had entered an apparatus with two well-separated channels. When the mirror was inserted just before the observation point, the photon could be made to interfere with itself. When the mirror was left out, the photon didn't undergo any such interference. When the mirror was inserted, the experimental data confirmed that the photon had to pass through both channels simultaneously! This is amazing, because the decision at the very last nanosecond to insert the mirror *did* affect whether the photon traveled through one of the channels or both simultaneously. This experiment suggests that the present can affect the past. Much of what we call coincidence or synchronicity could be caused by this property of our minds to send and receive time waves, selecting a reality we choose to experience.

I've also encountered experiences where it seemed that what physicist John A. Wheeler calls "delayed choice" was occurring ... where the present changes the past.

Cindy's Birthday Song

In June 1995, I was driving through England with my husband, in a rented car with a tape deck, although we had no cassettes with us. I thought how nice it would be to find some good music, so we stopped at a sandwich/magazine shop at the Sunningdale train station just outside London, to look at tape cassettes in a bin by the cash register. I was delighted to find a tape entitled, "The Hits of 1962," since I was born that year. I examined the tape more closely, and was absolutely *stunned* to see it had a song titled, *Cindy's Birthday,* by Shane Fenton and the Fentones!

This experience felt like a possible reality manifested specifically for my appreciation and amusement, because I was paying attention and "looking" right there, right then. Our observations of synchronous events are a way of making choices to observe something that determines what will be from all the infinite possibilities, essentially deciding what the past had to have been in order to bring about this experience now. This raises the concept of how the present, future and past all cooperate to create the experience we call "now."

Creating the Future

> *"Every person, all the events of your life are there because you have drawn them there. What you choose to do with them is up to you."*
> – Richard Bach

I love to imagine our present being created in partnership with our futures and pasts ... with intentions from all across time and space involved in what we experience now. It's possible that what we feel as our highest sense of mind or spirit is actually the sum totality of ourselves, and that inspiration we feel to make a particular choice comes from much more complete knowledge of all possibilities than we consciously comprehend in our ordinary day-to-day state.

Directing My Life Movie

I've had lucid dreams that showed me an infinite array of what appeared to be movie strips. These movie strips dangled down from a great height, descending beyond what I could see. Each frame of these infinitely long movie strips was itself a moving picture, providing me with the revelation that I was looking in movie frame windows where real world action was taking place, with each window of possibility positioned between a window above and one below.

I felt I could choose between any one of the window frames on any of the movie strips ... an infinite range of possibilities within an infinite range of possibilities. Every choice seemed connected to all others. I got the feeling that an infinite number of universes exist, and when we make wishes in our lives, we are choosing a unique, specific experiential path.

My dreams about an infinite number of movie strips of infinite length are very much like the idea that reality consists of parallel universes. As each choice in each universe is made slightly differently, the movie story line changes accordingly. To the degree our consciousness moves between parallel universes, we may get "hunches" or intuition that inform us how different choices feel after we make them. Similarly, we may realize we've had a feeling of déjà vu, because we sense we've been at this same decision point before; experiencing another time is just as possible as experiencing another space.

The feeling I get from these lucid dreams is one of infinite possibilities. The key to making choices lies within each of us, starting with our thoughts and feelings. If anything is possible ... how would you choose to live your life? If all you take out of this life is the love you share and things you learn, what do you most feel inspired to become and do? You can view your life as a story, considering what you most enjoy, and intending to live more true to that feeling and vision.

When my life "movie" is not following a plot line I enjoy, I stop for a while to get a better sense of what I need. I can change the way I "play my role," especially when it seems my life hasn't fit me well the way it was going. Sometimes the best thing to do is rediscover how refreshing life feels when lived from inspiration rather than habitual reactions. It's exhilarating to face fears and start living as the lead character instead of a supporting role. I remind myself that everything I need to face each day is right here with me; I can be creative and handle situations so they feel best to me. I make a conscious choice each day to not worry or be angry, and to be grateful and appreciative for the many blessings in life.

People who have near death experiences (NDEs) are usually greatly transformed—becoming happier, more optimistic, more loving and affectionate, more compassionate, and more spiritually oriented, and much more appreciative of the "simple things" in life. With eyes freshly opened to the sheer joy of being alive, they see how materialistic our values can become. There is no limit to how much love and joy we can feel in our lives, when we value these things first. Telepathy and healing abilities, as well as 'remembering' the future are common in people who have had NDEs. The spiritually aware kahunas of Hawaii are widely esteemed for their psychic and precognitive powers, and consider the future to be fluid, but in the process of 'crystallizing', with significant events crystallizing furthest in advance.

Some researchers have been surprised to discover how hypnosis subjects describe their experiences after death and before birth. Their experiences of death match the NDE descriptions of seeing white light and getting a full life review, and these hypnotic subjects remember even more. Michael Newton's book, *Journey of Souls,* describes experiences of hypnotic subjects recalling periods of time between lives where people reviewed what they learned from past lives, and made plans for their next lives. Newton's hypnotic subjects told how spirits work together in groups, often encountering the same souls again and again in different roles, depending on what issues need to be worked on and understood.

One intriguing possibility is that we all undergo amnesia, so we don't recall details of past lives or future significant events—ensuring self-discovery in the present. We all experience times of change that involve taking risks. Whether or not we act upon opportunities, we have free will to choose what we do. We are masters of our destiny. As Newton says:

> *"If souls choose a life where their death will be premature, they often see it in the place of life selection. I have found that souls essentially volunteer in advance for bodies who will have sudden fatal illnesses, are to be killed by someone, or come to an abrupt end of life with many others from a catastrophic event. Souls who become involved in these tragedies are not caught in the wrong place at the wrong time with a capricious God looking the other way. Every soul has a motive for the events in which it chooses to participate."*

Newton believes our relationships are the most vital parts of our lives, so the importance of coincidentally meeting the people we planned is paramount. One of Newton's subjects describes going to 'recognition class' to learn how to recognize people in life by how they look, move, or talk. These signs register for us so we know, "Oh, good, you are here now," at turning point moments in our lives. The subject goes on to tell

Newton the most important recognition sign to remember from this preparation class, and Newton is told it will be his wife-to-be's laugh, the scent of her perfume when they dance, and her eyes. She will recognize his big ears, stepping on her toes dancing, and how it feels when they first hold each other.

Michael Newton noted many such signs before he felt compelled to find the woman he would marry. One day, he spontaneously recalled an advertisement for a watch with a tag that read, "To Peggy" he'd seen many years ago that had made quite an impression on him. He then received that exact kind of watch as a gift. Then one day, he heard the words, "It's time to meet the woman in white ... Go now," so he thought about where a place might be that people wear white, decided to go to the hospital, and asked for Peggy. He discovered Peggy was just coming off her shift, and they talked for a while as friends who hadn't seen each other for a long time. Peggy told her friends after this initial encounter that she'd just met the man she was going to marry, and they did indeed get married! I once had a similar experience.

Recognizing my Husband-to-be

When I was fourteen, I became completely mesmerized by a boy in the middle of the classroom taking apart a mechanical pen on the first day of school in my Algebra II class. My attention was riveted on him. I felt there was something about the way he was assembling and disassembling the pen that seemed familiar ... even though I knew I hadn't seen him do this before. Then I experienced a vision of him at the ages of 25, 35, 45, 55, 65, 75, ... watching him growing older in a few minutes! I was seeing his life flash before my eyes, as if to point out he would be an important part of my life for decades to come. I did marry him, several years later!

I later learned my boyfriend's family purchased a blue station wagon the very year I'd gotten my favorite toy Matchbox car when I was ten years old ... a blue metal station wagon with little doors that opened and shut. When I got my toy station wagon, I'd had an image of the boy I would marry along with knowing he had a sharp sense of humor, and loved to take things apart.

These stories of recognition sound romantic and seem to imply that fate and destiny play a major role in our lives, yet I believe we are free to choose our life course, and are doing so every moment. There are people we feel drawn to and feel a strong need to interact with. If we ignore that strong attraction, we miss an important opportunity! Open, mindful interaction brings great rewards. The more mindfully we live, the more creative, imaginative, and fulfilling our lives become.

Believing in fate or destiny can be a trap, since it encourages us to limit ourselves to more confining definitions of what we think possible. We may view such limitations as fine if they are judged to be "good" ones, such as when we feel fated to find our mate or a desirable job ... but an unfortunate thing about believing in fate, destiny, or other predictions of our future is that such beliefs can lead to disregarding our ability to transform our thoughts and feelings. The most important thing to consider when contemplating how destiny and fate shape our lives is: we create our own reality by choosing how we respond physically, emotionally, and intellectually to every situation. The more honestly we see how we choose to respond to the world, the more clearly we can see the world around us, and the freer we are from "getting stuck" in some unfortunate fate.

People who feel like helpless victims of circumstance deny their powerful abilities to co-create reality. Any time we consider ourselves to be innocent victims, we revel in a perceived state of moral superiority where we feel justified to aggress against others, because grievances entitle us to compensation. Righteous resentments can be used to gain sympathetic attention and support, while manipulating others with guilt. Adopting an attitude of "poor me" allows us to escape responsibility by avoiding choice making. In actuality, there are no victims. We all have some degree of responsibility for what happens to us; the degree of responsibility we accept is considered by therapists as a useful way to ascertain mental health. Responsibility comes with the awareness that we choose our own thoughts. When we elect to love instead of attacking someone in the belief we are defending ourselves, we allow reality to shift to heal the situation.

Any time our lives feel disappointing is an opportune moment to remember we are the ones who create our lives based on what we imagine and believe is possible and deserved for ourselves. No outcome is inevitable, since we are creating this present moment right now. We're free to change any unrewarding ways of living *right here, right now*. Everything you do comes from what you think, and you can change your thinking and your reality in this very moment.

Choosing the Present

> *"We are confronted with insurmountable opportunities."*
> *– Walt Kelly*

What we consider to be our consciousness is not contained in our biological brains, but is instead independent of our physical bodies ... thus allowing that consciousness to move to another parallel reality and retain memories of a different universe. We are continually contemplating an infinite assortment of possible realities, and reality shifts are a discontinuous way of noticing how these possibilities can be brought to manifest here in this world. Reality shifts occur when we are in a dreamy state of energized awareness in which we are clear about what we prefer. This preference manifests itself in ways that feel like living a waking dream, with an infinite range of possibility present in every moment.

On an unconscious level, we really *do* know all the possibilities facing us in every moment, and we tend to choose ones we resonate with (or perhaps they choose us), in much the same way that one tuning fork when struck creates sympathetic vibrations in another tuning fork of the same frequency. Our gut level physical bodily feelings greatly influence what reality we experience, since we tend to get the experience that we are attuned to receive. When we feel blessed and radiant, we perceive life to be glorious and enlightening rather than oppressive, and view the universe from an appreciative frame of mind and heart.

Some people believe our lives are planned beforehand to some degree, since people who survive brushes with death report hearing, "it's not your time yet," and are told to return to life. These peoples' lives no longer run habitually on autopilot, as they become more aware and honest about who they are and what they are doing. Such mindfulness makes their lives more creative and compassionate.

Possible Causes of Reality Shifts

Now that we've considered many scientific and spiritual explanations for how reality shifts, we can think more deeply about *why* it shifts in ways we can detect. It seems the main reason reality shifts in ways we can observe is simply because such discontinuities catch our attention and help us gain greater understanding of the nature of the material world, our minds, and consciousness itself.

When we consider consciousness as the primary causal force in the universe, several possible explanations for reality shifts arise. Consciousness studies devoted to better understanding reality shifts can expand upon these possible causes, and create ways to test these hypotheses.

Dissolution ("Fadeout")
At the point where one reality path connects to another, the transition is usually so seamless that it goes undetected. Reality shifts are noticeable when the dissolution of one reality into another leaves a noticeable gap, so we notice a startling appearance, disappearance, transformation or transportation. These kinds of reality shifts feel like a movie segue where one scene fades out and another fades in—yet there's a *noticeable* difference between the two scenes. Something has changed.

Tangled Hierarchy ("Escher Effect")
Since the universe's conscious self-awareness is a loop of self-referential circularity as we contemplate our own consciousness, points of discontinuity occur at every place where an

observer oscillates between two possible vantage points. When we view the universe from first one perspective and then another, the oscillation between two points of view creates a discontinuity, or reality shift. When we consider ourselves as being purely material body and ego, and then believe ourselves to be pure eternal consciousness (spirit), and go back and forth between feeling first physical and then consciousness, reality shifts at the point of discontinuous transition. You can see this effect illustrated in some of M.C. Escher's artwork.

Slipstream Consciousness ("Groundhog Day Effect")
Conscious thoughts occasionally create turbulence and low-pressure areas in which overlapping discontinuities occur, much the way clouds of dust and debris become airborne and fly along in the wake of fast-moving race cars. In this way, we may find ourselves experiencing nearly the same experience twice in a row, as time becomes turbulent and swirls around us when we get swept along with fast-moving consciousness. If a whole day repeats, we're experiencing something like what happens in the movie, *Groundhog Day*, and if years repeat, we're experiencing something as described in the book, *Replay,* by Ken Grimwood.

Rejoinder Feedback ("Jimmy Hendrix Effect")
Occasionally, the sending and receiving waves putting our conscious wishes into effect oscillate in a feedback pattern, like what happens when a microphone picks up and amplifies sounds coming out of the speakers it broadcasts through. This kind of feedback gives some musicians a signature sound, like Jimmy Hendrix had, and it can also create reality shifts as the sending and receiving points continue their "handshake" to a point of discontinuity.

Why Reality Shifts Exercises

Most Essential Self

If everything unimportant about your life could be cleared away, what would remain? Who are you at your very core, and how are you unique in the universe? If you can imagine yourself as almost being nothingness, what little bit of something are you ... what do you feel you just have to communicate or explore?

Parallel Worlds

Imagine your life as three different sets of possible realities, each one different than the life you are living right now. To get the fullest sensation of how it feels to select the life you lead, write down as detailed a description as you can visualize for each possible reality. How do you feel about these possible life paths?

Preferred Reality Shifts

Think about how open you are to witnessing reality shift around you. What kinds of shifts would you be comfortable with, and what kind of changes would not feel so comfortable? Do you feel ready to observe reality shift?

Freedom

This morning I arise and realize my love will set me free.
REAL freedom this time ...
the freedom to be me.

I'd thought freedom meant I'm unwanted and alone
But now I find in my heart I know I'm coming home.

Home to where my heart is
Soaring high up above
Home to feeling honesty, integrity, and love.

These things are all within me
and they've been here all along.
It's just taken time for me to be still enough
to hear their quiet song.

In silence I can feel love
In silence all is known
In silence I remember
How on love's wings I have flown.

Chapter 3

Reality Shift Experiences

Where Inspiration meets Intention, Anything is possible

Right now, at this very moment, you are creating reality. We all are. Most of us are unconscious about what we are doing, but every single one of us is choosing each moment's set of experiences. You may suspect there's more to reality than meets the eye if you have witnessed reality shifting around you, although you may not have known what to call this phenomenon, or how to explain what's going on.

People notice reality shifts occurring in their daily lives when objects appear or disappear from their wallet or purse, but they don't necessarily grasp the significance of what they have seen. Mechanics often refer to mischievous "gremlins" in their shops who have a penchant for moving tools around or taking them away to later be replaced exactly in a very obvious spot where they *should* have been all along, such as the top shelf of the tool box. Most everyone I know has put something "right where it's *supposed* to be," and then found it missing for no apparent reason. Experiencing reality shifts by oneself can leave us feeling we must be confused, tired, or forgetful, or that we can't trust our senses or our mind.

Even the rare person who maintains confidence in their memory, observational skills and mental acuity may find it simply too hard to believe that *reality* has shifted. Only after seeing and talking about reality shifts with other people is it easier for us to believe than disbelieve. It helps to consider with a truly open mind the possibility that our minds create reality, learning through personal and shared experiences. I've found my perception of the fluidity of reality has greatly increased as I've become more and more observant of my surroundings, without assuming that reality will meet my expectations and match my beliefs.

Many of us live our lives to experience love in all its shapes and forms, yet we rarely remember who we are and how we create. We typically focus our conscious attention on what annoys, frustrates, or intrigues us without regard to how we've set up each experience. In other words, we tend to get caught up in the drama of life without noticing how our own needs and desires are a constant, steady force shaping the world around us and influencing which reality we are selecting to experience. We can be limited by our expectations to seeing only what we believe can be true, and miss out on great opportunities. Successful businesses understand this, so companies like AT&T don't consider themselves only to be in the American Telephone and Telegraph business. Such limited beliefs would severely limit AT&T's successful outreach into other markets. Similarly, if we insist on believing our minds don't directly create reality, we limit ourselves by choosing to ignore a vast realm of possibility. The most innovative people on Earth begin their creations with an open mind, for this is how to best receive inspiration. Some of us have trouble opening our minds, because we are afraid of welcoming something into our lives we don't understand. We want to know why these reality shifts occur, and what they mean.

When we wonder why reality shifts occur, the answer might best be expressed as, "Be Cause." Reality shifts remind us we are the cause of them; we are powerfully affecting this world and the universe with our thoughts and feelings. We can choose to become conscious of how we make choices every moment, and learn to accept the responsibility such awareness brings. We cause incredible changes in every aspect of reality, and our lives are miraculous at their very core. Many of us are beginning to comprehend that our thoughts and feelings create our life path according to the deepest longings of our souls. We influence all situations we experience, and every person we meet. We choose how we respond—what attitude we greet the universe with in each moment—and the universe responds by shifting reality.

My most intense personal experiences with reality shifts began as hair-raising incidents where I felt astonished to sense something was *completely* different than what it had been before, and there appeared to be no logical explanation for the change. These reality shifts showed me changes in what I had always considered to be solid, fixed parts of the world I would never expect to change, and I kept asking myself if I was indeed observing things correctly as these miraculous appearances, disappearances, transformations and transportations occurred.

After witnessing some amazing reality shifts on my own, I desired with all my heart to share these experiences with others. My wish was granted, and I feel extremely fortunate to have shared reality shift experiences with others, gaining reassurance that I'm *not* losing my mind or imagining things! It's so much more enjoyable to have companions to share perspectives on what might be happening under the surface of what we take to be solid reality.

This chapter includes accounts of some reality shifts involving treasured objects mysteriously vanishing or moving.

Vanishing Necklace

My friend Lisa's mother, Joan, had her picture taken at age three wearing nothing but a lovely bead necklace. The little girl didn't feel comfortable being photographed naked, and she refused to smile at all unless she could wear her favorite beads.

A little while after the photo was taken, Joan was sitting on the floor quietly playing with the necklace when her grandmother thought to herself that as soon as she was done with the task at hand, she should take the necklace away from the little girl for safe keeping. Nobody came or went from the room, but when Joan's grandmother walked over to get the necklace, it was *gone*. Joan was still sitting on the floor and nobody had any idea what happened to the beads. The necklace *never* showed up anywhere in that house again.

When Joan grew up, she told her daughter, Lisa, that her grandmother related the story to her together with the idea that someone who really needed those beads had taken them, maybe someone in heaven. My friend Lisa remembers seeing them in that old family photograph.

Grandfather's Knife

In 1950 when a friend of mine was six years old, his grandfather died. By the time he turned eight, his grandfather's estate was finally probated and a moving van pulled up with all kinds of treasures. There was a book about their family, a Shonninger piano, and a small Irish silver and porcelain pillbox from the 1800's, and the grandfather's folding pocket knife with tortoise shell handles and silver bolsters.

The 8 1/2 inch knife had a shaving-sharp Damascus blade, although it had not been sharpened for years. My friend's mother recalled that her father kept it under his pillow at night "for emergencies," and she cut herself on it playing with it when she found it there as a child. She had often told her son how sharp it was. Knives usually need to be re sharpened after a while, due to the nature of the steel; this knife did *not.* It was one of the sharpest, most carefully done edges my friend had ever encountered before or since. It was truly a classic hand-made knife of the highest order. This was an elegant fish-skinning or wood-whittling or gentleman's dress knife. It was extraordinarily beautiful and lustrous ... it glowed.

With the lack of respect some eight year old boys have for rare and precious things, my friend decided to try mumbeldypeg in the dirt outside the back door under the bedroom window with it, since his boy scout knife handle was too heavy for throwing, even though he sensed such usage would be a sacrilege to this outstanding example of the knife maker's art. He threw the knife a distance of five feet once, and heard it *"Thump!"* as he saw it stick, but fall over in the dirt. He picked it up and blew the dirt off, not really cleaning it ... and thought to himself, "This is too good a knife to be throwing ... it's old ... it could get scraped." But he also thought to himself, "I WANT to throw it!" He threw the knife a second time, thinking, "I really want to stick it *good* in the ground." This time, it *vanished*.

My friend saw the knife land near the sidewalk. It hit with a solid "thunk," and he went to pick it up, thinking he'd seen just the end of the handle, but there was NOTHING there. He thought perhaps the knife might have buried itself. He kept an eye on the spot where it vanished, and called his older brother to come help with the search. The two next-door neighbors also came over out of curiosity; they had seen the knife at a distance and wanted to look at it close up. They were pretty put out when my friend couldn't produce it, thinking he was being snotty and hiding it from them.

Since the place where the knife vanished was going to be planted with grapes, my friend got a rake and hoe and he and his brother tore up and turned over all the ground in the area, digging up every inch. Even if the knife had somehow impossibly bounced on the other side of the driveway, they would have found it, but they found nothing there. My friend was *very* disappointed and looked for the knife for many years later, offering a standing reward for it's recovery ... but it never reappeared.

My friend felt perhaps his grandfather was looking out for his safety, or perhaps the knife was not meant to be thrown, and was being saved from being damaged or ruined by an inexperienced young boy.

Meeting My Future Self—Who Took Letters from Desk

When I started dating my first boyfriend in January 1978, I was madly, passionately in love with him. The first letters he wrote to me in 1977 were so special to me that I treasured them as my most precious possessions, and placed them lovingly in a secret hidden space under a drawer in my desk. I used to read these handwritten letters again and again, savoring the love I felt in them; they brought me great comfort and joy.

About one year to the day after I first got these special love letters from my boyfriend, they mysteriously vanished from their secret location. Right before they vanished, I began to feel increasing stress and anxiety about leaving my boyfriend behind while traveling with my family in Europe for eight weeks that summer.

The author in 1978

On the night the letters vanished, June 24, 1978, I had an incredibly vivid dream that my future self came into my bedroom to take the letters away. In my dream, I watched in amazement as I saw myself as a grown-up glowing with light and floating from the closet doors over to my desk, where she got the letters and told me with her graceful, soothing presence that she was taking them to my future for some reason; she then floated back to disappear into my closet doors again.

When I awoke, I recalled my dream and felt I really wanted to read the letters from my boyfriend, so I opened the drawer in my desk, and found ... *no letters there at all.* They were completely gone without a trace. This astonished me, and I did not believe that my dream vision of my future self could have actually carried them away. I went immediately to my sister to demand that she return those letters if she was the one who took them. She strongly and convincingly denied any involvement in moving the letters. I felt heartbroken that they had been taken away from me without a trace or explanation.

At that time, I didn't consider the possibility that somehow my spirit really did carry the letters off to some other time and place ... it just seemed too far-fetched that the letters could be spirited away like that. I wrote in my journal several other explanations for how the letters could possibly have vanished, but none of them satisfied me. My sister did not take them, I didn't give them back to my boyfriend, I didn't put them somewhere else, and I didn't throw them away by accident. It seemed highly improbable that the dream I'd had was in any way connected with the letters disappearing from my desk ... yet no other explanation seemed possible. Perhaps one day, those letters will return to me at a time when I need them most.

Missing Person

My husband and I attended a workshop one summer when I was 32 in the royal borough of Windsor, just West of London at the Monkey Island Hotel on an island on the river Thames. My husband was the guest of honor, since he wrote the software program that was the subject of this workshop. I noticed with great anticipation that there would be a speaker named Steve attending from the international architectural firm of Ove Arup, and I was interested in hearing how people were using my husband's software at the biggest architectural firm in the world. I took note of what time of day Steve would be making his presentation on the conference program, and was happy to see that I'd get to hear him talk in mid-afternoon, a while after lunch. This would be *great!* I was really excited to hear him talk about how his large trend-setting company was using my husband's software for computer visualization.

At the break in the workshop, I left the room to have some refreshments with the other attendees, and when I returned and looked again at the workshop agenda, I noticed with great surprise that Steve was *no longer listed!* I turned to my husband and he asked me before I even got a chance to open my mouth, "Hey, wasn't a speaker from Ove Arup scheduled to talk this afternoon?" I agreed I'd noticed a man from Ove Arup scheduled to speak, but "Steve" was no longer on the program. My husband also recalled Steve's name, though neither of us remembered his last name, and we wondered how his name could so suddenly be absent. Perhaps he'd canceled out, and someone re-typed all the agenda sheets and switched them at the break with sheets we'd been given in the morning.

I quickly walked around the room to look at the agendas on each person's desk, certain there must be some explanation why my husband and I would have seen Steve's name on our programs that morning but were unable to see it anywhere on the agenda now. It seemed strange that agendas would be switched for every person so secretly and thoroughly without an announcement that a change was being made, but I investigated anyway, wondering what happened to Steve. I determined the papers had probably not been switched, because they were all tucked away in the individual odd places that each person had put them; it seemed highly unlikely that new agenda sheets would be secretly substituted for the originals. It slowly dawned on me that something incredible had happened, and we were now in a reality where Steve from Ove Arup was *not even attending the workshop!*

The Lady Vanishes

I was walking and talking with my husband in 1996 in my parents' neighborhood one sunny morning when I noticed a casually dressed, middle-aged woman walking alone towards us on the sidewalk on the other side of the street, about 40 feet away. She seemed preoccupied with her thoughts, looking down at her feet as she moved along at a moderate pace. She was walking on a sidewalk between the paved asphalt street and large expanses of green lawn and small shrubs and flowers.

I continued talking with my husband, not looking directly at the woman, but generally looking around when I noticed she was suddenly *not there at all*. She had vanished *POOF!* into thin air. There was no place she could have hidden so quickly, such as inside a car or behind a bush, tree, or house. She was simply gone.

I felt mildly disoriented by her disappearance at first, but also relaxed, as if this was a normal thing to observe. And then, after contemplating what had just transpired, I realized that a woman disappearing as she walks down the street is NOT normal. The more I thought about it, the stranger it seemed, and my initial reaction that a woman disappearing might possibly be normal struck me as increasingly odd as well. I wondered how often this sort of thing happens without being noticed at all! I asked my husband if he'd seen the woman, and he told me he'd been preoccupied talking with me and hadn't noticed her at all.

Sundial Sculpture Appearance

I met with two friends, Jan and Cliff, for brunch at a restaurant in the Berkeley Marina one seemingly normal day. We continued our conversation with a leisurely stroll around the marina, as we often enjoyed doing when we got together. I told my friends about some reality shifts I'd seen, and how much I wished they could see one, too ... when one occurred right on the spot! We were walking together towards the pier, when my friend, Cliff, asked us, "Do either of you recall ever seeing that statue here before?" as he pointed at a giant sculpture of a sundial. Jan replied, "No ... I don't." I felt tremendously excited, because I'd seen that sculpture there, but *never* when I was there with these two friends! The sundial seemed to rise up proudly towards the sun to greet us as we walked in awed silence to get a better look.

We walked around the ten foot tall concrete sculpture as children sat and climbed around on it. This installation is in a central location people notice, right in the middle of a square at the foot of the Berkeley pier. Amazingly, the sundial sculpture's absence had previously allowed us to clearly see another giant sculpture situated up on a hill above the sundial when we were on the pier and walking back towards the shore ... but now that the sundial *was* there, we noticed we couldn't see the other sculpture as well because it was partially obscured by the sundial. The other sculpture is a larger-than-life size Asian archer on horseback with fully drawn bow, aiming his arrow out over the bay—shooting over the sundial's spot.

Berkeley Marina Sundial

I told my friends the sundial sculpture had always been here when I had come here without them, but never when we were here together ... until now. The sundial is chipped and worn, made out of concrete, and bears the following inscription:

> "The peoples of the bountiful Pacific Ocean are brought together by the sweep of time. This sundial honors the citizens of Sakai Japan, the sister city of Berkeley. United in warm friendship and goodwill, the peoples of Sakai and Berkeley strengthen mutual understanding and respect through the exchange of visitors and cultural programs. This sundial is dedicated to the continuing friendship and growing association between Sakai and Berkeley. 1970"

I am deeply impressed that something as large and majestic as this sundial vanished and reappeared, grasping the magnitude of what else must be possible if such large things can so easily be transformed or transported in time and space. The sundial itself is a symbol that reminds me how love transcends space and time to unite all of us across oceans that physically separate us from one another. I feel great reverence for this universe that allows us to glimpse occasional insights as to how it materializes around us.

My friends and I marveled at this new yet relatively old-looking addition to our shared experience of the Berkeley Marina. Feeling inspired by having shared a reality shift experience as we were in the midst of discussing this phenomena, I asked my friends if they'd experienced other reality shifts before. Jan replied that she notices changes in people much more than in things. She added that she's also noticed things change, particularly after returning from traveling overseas ... when she sees everything in America with new eyes and much clearer focus after having spent time away. I was so delighted to have shared a reality shift experience with my friends that I enthusiastically gushed, *"Thanks for participating!"* much to their amusement.

Transformed Sleeping Bag Fasteners

One April evening my husband and I visited his cousin Cathy and her family, having made arrangements to sleep overnight at her house. These cousins are good friends of ours, and we had recently begun talking about spiritual subjects when we last visited them.

When it was time for bed on the night of our sleep-over, I opened our sleeping bags and noticed the bag wraps for our sleeping bags were tied in a completely different fashion than they'd ever been tied before—plus the fasteners were broken off—and neither my husband nor I could recall when or how either of these things might have happened. I said to my husband, "This is *definitely* a reality shift!"

The wish I'd made just a couple of hours before I noticed the sleeping bag ties were so different was "I wish my husband and I could connect and relate to our cousins in the best possible way." I got a distinct feeling that seeing such an inexplicable physical change was an indicator that my wish was granted ... and time will show me how my connections to this beautifully spiritual and loving family may unfold.

Indeed, a few months after this wish, my husband and I were able to take his cousin's children with us to Disneyland with our daughters and I gained a much deeper feeling of being one family.

Light Switched On & Bread Appears

One lazy February morning, I was sleeping in a bit when my two young daughters came bouncing into bed with me around 7:40 a.m. They were both in good spirits, and didn't want me to get out of bed and get dressed right away. My older eight-year-old daughter entered my room first, followed by my younger daughter. As the three of us cuddled together, my older daughter's eyes got VERY wide and asked, "Who just turned on our bedroom light?" My younger daughter replied, "Not me; I didn't touch the light," and I (of course) replied I had not yet gotten out of bed this morning.

My older daughter's fear was palpable, since her bedroom light was clearly on. She even heard the "click" noise when it switched on, and she'd been looking toward her room and seen the hallway go from dark to light. I told her it could either be a reality shift or a ghost, or else it could be that someone hadn't clicked the switch all the way up or down, so at some point the switch moved the rest of the way. My older daughter pointed out that neither she nor her sister had touched the light switch that day.

My electrician-skilled husband later commented, "I don't think the girls' bedroom light could "slip" like that, given that it's a pretty tight switch. (At least it used to be!)" The next day I attempted to get the switch to go only part way up or down to see if it might then slip either way, but this switch has so much friction it never slips; it has to be pushed vigorously.

Another reality shift happened that same morning. A bag I'd left on the kitchen counter containing breadcrumbs the night before was now *full* of part of a loaf of bread. The night before I'd thought to myself *"I wish there was more of this bread, I love it so!"* I was so surprised and delighted to find my wish came true! This is a "typical" garden-variety reality shift where I silently wish something, and then at some future time see a shift has occurred—startling me in a pleasant way.

Mysteriously, only nine pieces of sausage were in the pan (re-enactment)

I looked away for a few minutes, & twelve sausage pieces appeared

Vanishing & Reappearing Sausage

I witnessed sausage pieces disappear on two separate occasions... one where a sausage piece completely vanished, and another where sausage pieces returned.

One day I was in my kitchen watching my friend toss sausage slices into a bowl in the sink. We saw one piece of sausage sail over the bowl and disappear in mid-air! It never hit the sink; there was no "whump" noise, and no piece of sausage to be found. That little sausage slice vanished completely, even though we'd both seen it go toward the sink. It was just *gone*.

My friend told me the universe was granting his old wish to send food back from a time of plenty to nourish someone hungry from the past when they were without food. My feeling about this is that there is no fixed quantity of food or anything else in the universe, so there's no need to believe in conservation of sausages. If sausage can transport, it might as well also materialize out of nowhere when it's really needed.

On a completely different day in August that year, my friend was cooking potatoes and four sausages in a pot of boiling water. He cut the sausages into three pieces each, placed them in a frying pan, and asked me to come look at them. He asked, "Does this look like four sausages to you? Because it seems some sausage is missing." We counted the sausage pieces, and got a total of *nine*, meaning only three sausages were in the frying pan. This astonished me, since I had just handed him a package containing four sausages that I'd watched him slice. I checked to see if a sausage was misplaced, but saw no signs of other pieces anywhere.

He looked me in the eyes and resumed our earlier philosophical sausage discussion, saying, "Well, this must be a sausage going back in time to when I had so little to eat." I replied, "I don't think so ... I believe the universe is *quite* abundant, and there's no need for a zero-sum arrangement where what is taken away here goes back there." My friend mulled this over as I looked back at the frying pan. "*LOOK!*," I said, "*Now count them ... TWELVE!*" Twelve sausage thirds sizzled in the pan, accounting for four sausages. Neither of us had touched the sausages, and only a minute or two had elapsed between the time we'd first counted nine sausages, and then counted twelve! I loved this reality shift, because I felt exhilarated to see the sausage return in synchronous response to our discussion.

Unspoken Words

I've experienced another kind of reality shift in which a person I'm talking to either hears me say something I *know* for sure I didn't say, or I hear them say something that they definitely know *they* didn't say.

I was walking to see a movie with my husband one day when he remarked "there's a bathroom here in this diner ... you can use the bathroom here." I assured him that I didn't think I even *needed* to use the bathroom, and he said that I'd told him I did just a few minutes before. I certainly didn't recall saying anything of the sort, and furthermore, I really didn't feel like I needed to use the bathroom! After a few more grumbles, I decided to be a good sport and go to the bathroom, where I discovered with great surprise that I actually *did* need to use the bathroom after all ... because my period was starting!

I wondered why my husband had been *so* certain I told him I needed to use the bathroom when I not only had no memory of any such conversation, but I didn't even think I *needed* to use the bathroom. I was deeply impressed and baffled by this incident, knowing how observant and reliable my husband was. If he told me I said something, I believed he heard me say it. I also knew for sure I did *not* say anything about needing to use the bathroom. I wished I could have known what it felt like to be in his shoes.

My wish was granted when I visited Disneyland with my older daughter when she was eight years old. I pointed out a bathroom to her, because just a few minutes earlier she had looked me in the eyes and told me she needed to use the bathroom. She stopped in her tracks, astonished, and asked, "How do *you* know I need to use the bathroom?!" I told her she'd just told me she did, and she replied she definitely did not! I told her how dramatically she'd spoken to me, pulling me aside by the paddleboat steamship to tell me in confidence that at the next possible opportunity, she wanted to use the bathroom. This was a highly memorable conversation to me, yet when I reminded her of how we'd just been standing by the paddleboat talking, she had no memory of that at all! I believed her when she told me, "We never talked about that!" and I gained a whole new insight into what happened to me at the diner bathroom with my husband.

My husband had *definitely* heard me say I needed to use the bathroom ... even though I know I did not say anything of the sort to him. I now found myself on the other side of the experience of the unspoken words with my older daughter, granting my previous wish to see such a reality shift experience from both sides.

Car Trunk Open & Shut

My friend and I were driving in his car one 4th of July when he stopped the car because we'd both seen the trunk of the car was open, obstructing the rear view. Both of us noticed this, my friend seeing it in his rearview mirror, and I in my peripheral vision. When my friend got out of the car and walked around to the back, and I turned around to see what was happening, we both observed that the trunk was fully shut as if it had never popped open. The same thing happened twice more on that same drive, to make the point that we were *not* imagining things ... something very peculiar was going on here!

Moments before the trunk kept appearing open, I'd been talking with my friend about the saying, "Don't change beliefs ... Transform the believer." This aphorism profoundly disturbed me. If this saying was intended to suggest I should be changing people, it felt pushy and manipulative to me. I much preferred that people discover their own truths without prescribed transformations. I also felt that beliefs *can* be changed, and people do this all the time as life experiences demand.

It then occurred to me that perhaps the trunk flapping open right at that moment was an experience to illustrate the way our beliefs actually *do* change, moving in the background of our consciousness as we experience something outside the normal boundaries of belief. Usually, the most powerful thing to change our beliefs is the shock of actual experience, which was being amply demonstrated for us right then!

The Bermuda Triangle Purse

The Bermuda Triangle Purse

One December my friend bought herself a new purse for her thirty-fifth birthday around the same time she moved into a new apartment, feeling a bit depressed. She kept the keys to her new apartment and mailbox on the same nondescript key ring with a set of keys to a car she'd borrowed. She was careful to keep her keys in her purse, so she'd always know exactly where they were. One day, however, she checked her purse and the keys were *gone*. She emptied her purse and searched through every compartment, to no avail.

After a few days of fruitlessly searching for her keys, she gave up and had a new set made, which she put on a key ring with a red, coiled wristband.

Several months later, when my friend took the bus home from work, she reached into her purse and felt a set of keys on top of all the other stuff in her purse. She pulled the keys out, and *was astonished to discover they were the original set of keys!* They were immediately recognizable by their key ring and the original mailbox key that worked more easily than the copy she'd made.

When my friend finally bought herself a new purse, she transferred all the contents out of the old purse, getting rid of some of the unnecessary accumulated junk and leaving the old purse completely empty. Sometime later, she decided to give the old purse to her daughter to play with. Before she handed the purse over, she reached inside and pulled out ... a roll of dimes that no one in the family had *ever* seen before.

The Case of the Missing Glasses

One spring day, my friend was getting ready to go out and couldn't find his glasses. He looked high and low, searching in all the logical places one might put one's glasses. Having exhausted those, he started looking in illogical places including the refrigerator, the shower, drawers, shelves, and behind the stove.

Finally, he said, "I give up!" deciding to go without his glasses. He and his wife decided she would drive, and they'd continue the search for his glasses later. His wife put on her jacket and headed out to the car, reaching into *her* jacket pocket to... *pull out his glasses!* This was not a place they had been before, or would ever be placed, so their appearance was particularly surprising.

Faxes Moved into Locked Box

My friend had a job requiring him to order things, including daily fax transmittal sheets from Tifco in Texas. When the order came in, he put the sheets on his desktop by the fax machine, and then finally put them into a desk drawer. On the day my friend needed to send his fax transmittal sheet in by midnight, he opened the drawer to get his fax sheets ... and didn't find them there. He looked for seven hours, including in wastebaskets, under the sink, and behind bookcases.

A few minutes before the midnight deadline, my friend noticed a trunk, and remembered how someone once found something missing in a trunk. This particular trunk stored new shirts and clothing placed several weeks earlier. Just for fun, he decided to open the trunk and see what was there, "So I could say I'd looked *everywhere*." He pulled down the trunk, opened it up, and there were his fax transmittal sheets ... right on top.

Guided by Lavender Scent

I browsed through a bookstore basement one rare winter morning I had to myself when both my young girls were in preschool. I felt giddy with the joy of having some time to browse through books ... one of my greatest pleasures! I hoped to quickly find some good books to buy and read, since I didn't have much free time for shopping. I was looking around at the book sections, when I noticed a very pleasant and unusually strong fragrance of lavender wafting around the store. I walked slowly to follow the scent carefully ... and noticed that the lavender scent traced a graceful path down the aisles! I thought perhaps I smelled someone's perfume; the only other person in the bookstore basement was a man. I discreetly walked behind him to sniff, and found no trace of the scent near him at all.

I continued following the trail of lavender, and was delighted to find the scent appearing and disappearing as I touched various books! It seemed this scent wasn't so much in the room as in my nose. I was amazed a smell could be so strong and clear and then completely absent ... so I playfully picked up a book that switched the smell of lavender on ... then one that switched it off. Only a few books about spirituality, myths, and religions switched on the scent, so I gathered those in my arms as I walked the aisles, following the lavender trail.

I was perplexed when the lavender scent led me to a section of history books; these were subjects of little interest to me. I didn't immediately see any book I might wish to examine. I walked a few steps more and the lavender fragrance got VERY intense. A book in the midst of the history section called to me, as the scent remained strong there, intensifying or dissipating depending on where I placed my hand. I moved my hand slowly across books until the lavender fragrance was overwhelming, at which point I pulled out a book about unicorns.

Opening the unicorn book to a random page, I read: *"The unicorn loves sweet-smelling herbs, particularly lavender."* At the moment I read this, you could have knocked me over with a feather! I felt I was in a waking dream, where my actions and the movements of this whimsical universe were magically choreographed.

Transported Magazine

On July 29, 1998, I was shopping at the grocery store when I felt drawn to the magazine section, sensing something awaited me there. I was delighted to see a single August issue of "US" magazine, featuring a cover picture of Nicolas Cage. Being a Nicolas Cage fan, I picked up the magazine and looked around for a more pristine issue. I was sad to see no more "US" magazines; this slightly worn one would have to suffice. I noticed that this copy had curled pages on the upper right side, with some white wear spots a little more than an inch down on the left side of the binding ... and indentations along its entire length.

I brought the magazine and groceries home, where two of my friends helped me unbag them. One friend later told me he saw the "US" magazine in a bag next to two frozen pizzas he unpacked, and he'd put that bag on the kitchen counter next to me. I folded it, but never saw the "US" magazine again that evening; it vanished from my house.

When my friends walked through their front door that evening and over to their bed, they saw the "US" magazine waiting on top of the bed. When my friend showed me this magazine, I saw it had the *exact* same identifying marks on it as the magazine I'd purchased at Lucky's!

My friends assured me neither of them had carried the magazine home, and I certainly didn't do that ... so the only explanation seems to be that the magazine vanished from my house and appeared at theirs that same evening. Before this transportation, I'd wished to experience a new kind of reality shift, and transportation was definitely new!

Materializing Water Shoes

One August day my mother-in-law left a message on my answering machine, asking if I'd brought home an extra pair of shoes—my niece's water shoes were missing. I called my mother-in-law the next day after searching my daughters' bedroom exhaustively—*especially* my six-year-old daughter's shoe drawer—which I felt was the most likely place to find the shoes. My daughters helped me search, and together we moved every shoe in my younger daughter's shoe drawer, to find only her pair of water shoes. I told my mother-in-law we couldn't find the missing shoes.

A couple of days later, I took my younger daughter's water shoes out of her drawer and was stunned to see *her cousin's water shoes* in the drawer! These shoes were marked distinctively with a pen indicating the owner's name, and they were in the drawer where they definitely hadn't been when my daughters and I had so painstakingly searched there just a couple of days earlier.

Vanishing Cars

I have occasionally noticed cars disappear in full daylight when I'm driving down the freeway. Sometimes I look in the rearview mirror to see a car *definitely* there ... and glance back again a few seconds later to see it *gone* with no turn-out, no exits, no stopped car by the road—nowhere for it to have gone. Sometimes I see a car vanish with nothing to replace it, and the car behind the missing car still follows along behind me—and other times the missing car is gone and a *completely different* car is in it's place (definitely not the car that was immediately behind it).

Rice Cereal Vanishes/Reappears

My friend told me she'd reached up in her cupboard to get some rice baby cereal one summer morning, and found the box *missing*! She thought this was strange, because she makes a point of always putting the box away in the same place, never leaving it on the counter. My friend searched the kitchen counters and cupboards for several minutes, and then told her husband she couldn't find it anywhere.

Her husband came into the kitchen, reached up in the cabinet where the rice cereal is usually kept, pulled the box of cereal down, and asked, "You mean *THIS* box of rice cereal?" She said, "Yes!", astonished he had found the box where moments earlier had been empty space.

From my friend's husband's point of view, this experience was not thrilling or surprising at all. From his perspective, the box of cereal was exactly where he expected to find it. From my friend's perspective, the box of cereal mysteriously appeared from an empty place in the cupboard that she had thoroughly checked earlier.

Magazine Vanishes/Reappears

I once took a bath while reading a copy of "Utne Reader" magazine. After reading for a few minutes, I tossed the magazine over the edge of the tub onto the soft bath mat on the floor.

About fifteen minutes later, I stepped out of the tub and walked around the bathroom to comb my hair and take vitamins, and then glanced at the stack of magazines on top of the toilet. There was a different "Utne Reader" there than the one I'd been reading, which reminded me, *Whatever happened to the one I was reading?* I recalled I had tossed it on the floor, so I looked straight down to see the "Utne Reader" I'd been reading in the bathtub ... *resting precisely where I'd been standing and walking moments earlier.*

This shocked me, because if the magazine had actually been on the floor, I would have felt it, stepped on it, or tripped on it, yet I'd only felt the pleasantly soft fluff of the bath mat, not a magazine. I was barefoot, and definitely would have noticed if I'd stepped on a magazine! The magazine had clearly been gone for several minutes, and then reappeared when I looked down, expecting to see it somewhere on the floor.

Car Doors Unlocked

I was camping in August 1998 when I noticed that several times after carefully locking all the car doors, I'd return to the car shortly afterward to find a car door unlocked. Sometimes it would be the back right door, sometimes the back left door. I felt flustered, because my intention was to *keep* the car locked, since my purse, money and valuables were inside! After the first time this happened, I made a concerted effort to double-check the doors were locked.

The first door to appear unlocked was the left, then the right door appeared unlocked, and then the left again! I felt consternated but also intrigued. Fortunately, the times this happened I had only been gone from the car for a short time—less than an hour—and the times I was away from the car for more than an hour, it was still locked when I returned to the car.

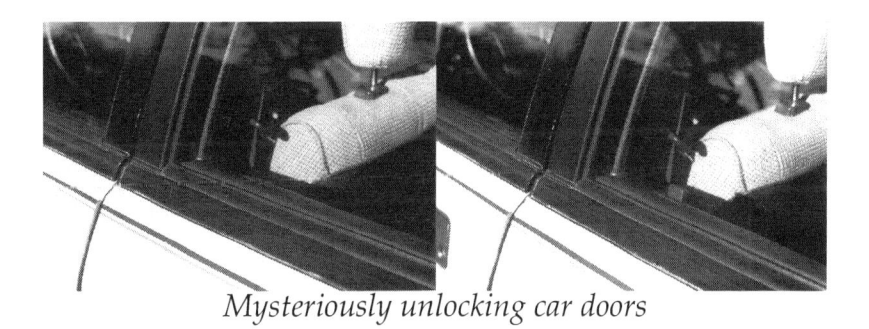

Mysteriously unlocking car doors

A similar reality shift involving door locks happened to my friend Susan's car one day when she came to visit. She parked at a commuter train station and locked the only two doors on her car, which she always locked, especially when parking at unfamiliar locations. Susan recalled finding her car door *unlocked* upon returning, which was strange, because she knew for certain she'd locked it. She was glad to find nothing missing, and the car was just fine when she came back.

Toilet Paper Roll Changes

One fine October day, my daughters and I noticed that the roll of toilet paper in our bathroom had to be torn raggedly, since it had no perforated tear lines printed on it. This seemed very odd, since just the night before I recalled tearing squares of toilet paper off this same roll, and now there were no perforated marks. I didn't consider this to be necessarily a reality shift, since there is always a chance that during the production of a roll of toilet paper the paper perforations simply not be created for a stretch.

When my older daughter noticed that suddenly the perforations were back again after having been absent just an hour earlier, I took more interest in this roll of toilet paper ... especially when I observed more closely that not only were the perforation marks back on the roll of toilet paper, but the roll of toilet paper was *bumpy* with horizontal lines, where just an hour earlier the roll had been completely smooth and unperforated.

Vanishing Photograph

I once opened a pack of photographs I'd taken at my daughter's birthday party as soon as I picked them up from the drug store. I was pleased to see the first picture I took of two friends making plate designs turned out so well! I put all the photos back in their envelope, started the car, and drove to pick up my daughters after school that Friday afternoon.

When I arrived home, I reopened the package of pictures, and was shocked to discover that the wonderful picture of my friends holding their artwork was *gone*. I next checked the negatives, but found no trace of that image—the roll of film now started on the very next picture, as if the first photo never existed.

Reappearing Computer Program Bugs

My husband once fixed a computer program bug, wrote out the computer file, recompiled his program, and saw that it ran just fine. Later on, he made a few changes having nothing to do with the previously corrected part of the program code, and noticed his program suddenly had the old problem again! He went back to the file where he'd fixed the bug before, and *there was the bug again!* Feeling a bit nervous and disturbed, he went ahead and fixed it once more, and all was well again.

The next morning, he recompiled the same program and this time it had a different bug ... one which he had *also* fixed the day before which had seemingly reintroduced itself.

Nearly empty bird feeder   *Nearly full bird feeder*

Empty/Full Bird Feeder

I awakened at 7 a.m. one Sunday morning in October by a blue jay pecking noisily at the feeder on my kitchen window. I padded to the kitchen in stocking feet and nightgown, to see the blue jay fly away from the almost empty feeder! I had just refilled this feeder two days earlier, and was amazed it could be empty so soon ... even with a hungry blue jay feeding there.

I went back to bed, feeling it was much too early to refill the feeder, and wanting to sleep in a little more ...

but after a few minutes I decided I was fully awake so I might as well get out of bed. I walked back to the kitchen to make myself a cup of hot cocoa, and looked over at the bird feeder ... *to see it was full of birdseed.*

Clothes Dryer Timer Dial

I was doing a load of laundry one October evening, when I started to set the dryer timer dial for twenty minutes as I had often done before, to dry some linen fabric I'd just washed. As I reached over to turn the dial the direction I always turn it for twenty minutes drying time, I was startled to find the dial no longer turned the way it used to. The motion of turning the dial is something my hand remembers without my thinking about it ... it's "motor memory," much the way our bodies remember how to walk or ride a bicycle.

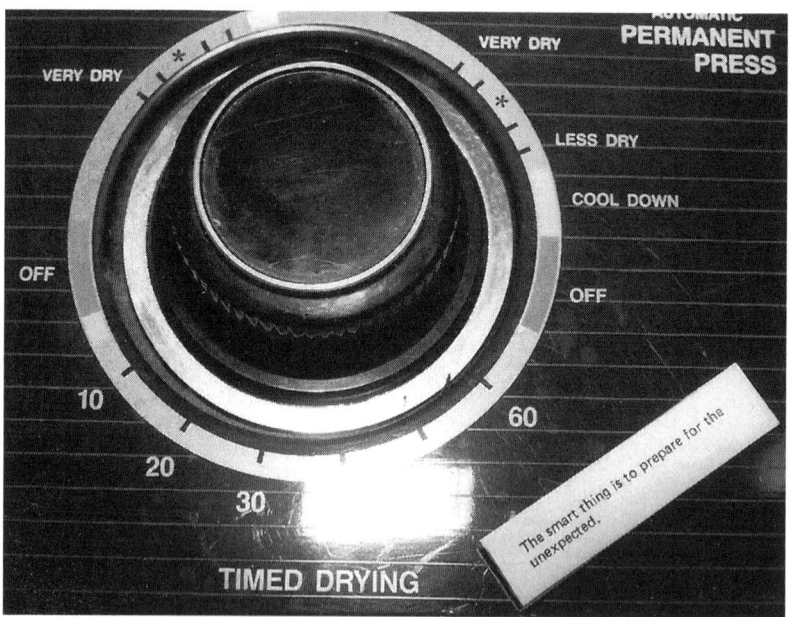

Transformed clothes dryer timer dial

I was stunned to note that my hand didn't know how to quickly set the dryer for twenty minutes, because the twenty-minute setting was on a different place on the dial! Instead of turning the dial from about four o'clock to about five o'clock, I now needed to turn it from about eight o'clock to seven o'clock. This is a *completely* different motion my hand and arm were not used to.

The most interesting thing about this reality shift is that I didn't realize I could notice a reality shift based on motor memory. But why not? These reality shifts never cease to amaze me! I told my daughters about this one, and we talked about magic tricks my older daughter read about in a book she'd gotten from school. As we talked, I popped open a fortune cookie and read my fortune aloud, *"The smart thing is to prepare for the unexpected."* My daughters and I roared with laughter!

Parallel Requests for Business Card

I met with a small group of people on the first day of our new class together, and several of us exchanged business cards. I watched the woman seated to the right of me smoothly slide two business cards across the table in front of me. One card was for me, and the other was for the woman seated at my left, our hostess. I took one card and watched our hostess take the other before standing up to leave the room. When our hostess returned, she said to the woman at my right, "I'd like your business card," to which the woman on my right responded with a very puzzled expression, and then the response, "I already *gave* you my business card," apparently unable to fathom why our hostess would be asking again for her business card. There was an awkward silence, as we studied our hostess closely. Our hostess persisted, repeating that she wanted a business card, at which point the woman on my right said to her, "I already *gave* you my business card!" I added, "I saw you give it to her just a few minutes ago," and the woman at my right continued, "I slid it across the table to you."

Now our hostess looked completely wide-eyed and confused ... saying she didn't remember that at all, and she wouldn't forget something like that. She was obviously wondering how it could be that two others were so certain she'd already received this card! Once again, the woman at my right gave her business card to our hostess, and our hostess looked increasingly perplexed. She said she does not "space out" like that, and a subsequent exhaustive search of her house turned up no second card.

Reality Shift Patterns

It's exciting to recognize patterns observed in reality shifts. On many occasions, a reality shift occurs following a wish or a thought (spoken or unspoken). I don't know if a wish is always necessary for a reality shift to occur, but it seems strongly related. The appearance of the sun-dial sculpture at the Berkeley Marina, the transportation of the "US" magazine, and the loaf of bread appearing on my kitchen counter in the morning when it had been an empty bag the night before are examples of wishes being fulfilled. All of the reality shifts in the next chapter correspond to wishes or prayers made prior to a reality shift occurring.

Another fascinating pattern in reality shifts is the active nature of some of these experiences, where they happen "real-time," right before our eyes. Examples include cars appearing and disappearing on the freeway, a woman vanishing, and a piece of sausage vanishing in mid-air. The light switch my daughters and I saw click on was another real-time reality shift. Real-time reality shifts are *especially* astonishing, because they are so flashy and crisp ... leaving no room for doubt something amazing is happening, as it flaunts it's presence!

Another interesting pattern with reality shifts is how they often blend in at first, as if nothing strange has happened. I can almost sense the shift in my awareness from one set of circumstances to another ... and in either case, things seem normal. What feels *really* unusual is the brief feeling of immediate adjacency of two differing realities ... or in the case of a non-instantaneous reality shift, upon viewing the altered state of reality from what I clearly remember. Almost everything remains the same, with just a few small changes, and those small changes are usually not too unusual.

Really strange reality shifts involving more pronounced changes are possible. If I was emotionally and mentally able to deal with shocking and bizarre reality shifts, I'd probably be much more likely to experience them. I've noticed changes that aren't too stressful for me to incorporate into what I believe can be real. They brought about a change I desired, or affected something without hurting me in any way. I don't desire the experience of seeing reality change in wildly uncontrolled fashion; I'd feel upset to sense too large a lack of stability in the world. Most people who've shared reality shift experiences with me reported reality shifts that didn't exceed their comfort zones. Perhaps the fact that so many people co-create this consensus reality, precludes the possibility of experiencing wildly erratic reality shifts.

Branching Realities

I'm especially intrigued by reality shifts involving one person saying something that another person hears ... yet somehow, the speaker has *no knowledge* that they said anything of the sort, while the listener has a crystal-clear and detailed recollection of the discussion. In my reality shift experience of knowing for certain that I didn't say I needed to use the bathroom, I wasn't even aware that I *did* need to use the bathroom, while my husband was *certain* that I did, because he saw and heard me say so. I feel fortunate to have been on the other side of this type of experience when my daughter asked me at Disneyland to let her know when I saw a bathroom ... and then was *incredulous* when I knew she needed a bathroom, since she hadn't said anything of the sort!

The meeting where a woman requested a business card *twice* was another example of someone saying and doing something, and later having no recollection of any of it at all. My friend had no idea she'd already asked for (and received) a card—and there was no physical evidence she had received two cards. Instead, it seemed two different realities had ever so briefly overlapped, the way pieces of paper overlap when making paper maché. For the briefest time, some people noticed something had happened *twice* that physical evidence suggested only happened *once* (receiving a business card). Some reality shifts might be caused by slipstream consciousness. A slipstream is a stream of air pushed back by an airplane's propeller, or the area of low-pressure behind a fast-moving racecar. It's possible that some conscious interactions move with such relative speed compared to others that they create a swirling low pressure area, where anomalous events can occur, and creating a kind of temporal turbulence that allows some people to see two different segments of reality paths.

In these cases, one person's consciousness is running on a completely different path from the other person's, although both peoples' consciousness reconverge so they can discuss and discover two completely different memories of what happened. Experiencing this branching apart and reconnecting of consciousness leads me to wonder where else reality is bifurcating and branching. I now feel I have a better idea of how some people can sincerely say they experienced entirely different realities than other people have. I wonder how we manage to share a common sense of reality as much of the time as we seem to, as well as how often these separate reality branches occur completely unnoticed.

The Significance of Reality Shifts

I have a hunch there is much greater significance to reality shifts than simply the fact that things suddenly change. Reality shifts are part of a larger consciousness we communicate with, albeit mostly unconsciously. Reality shifts suggest we cooperatively co-create reality around us every minute as we choose what is real by what we pay attention to and how we feel about it. The implication of reality shifts is that reality springs into being based on what *we desire it to be*. All possibilities may be real at the point at which we are about to choose, where consciousness is the focal point of awareness joining an infinite number of possible futures to an infinite number of possible pasts. How we feel and what we choose to attend to in this moment has incredible power to affect reality as a manifestation of our deepest conscious intent and unconscious feelings.

While I witness objects mysteriously appearing, disappearing, transforming or transporting, I may not notice when something changes that's not in my realm of experience. My perceptions of changes are necessarily limited to things I have memory of and interest in. In other words, it's impossible to appreciate how we met someone we never would have met, or saw something we never would have seen, since we *wouldn't know the difference*. Observable reality shifts are thus limited to appearances, disappearances, transformations, and transportations and changes in the experience of time, since these are ways we observe change in the universe.

Fascinating "Alive Again" reality shifts have occurred in which I read a news story about someone being dead, and later find that the person is still very much alive.

Larry Hagman Alive Again

> I saw an article in a newspaper reporting Larry Hagman's death in 1997, and a couple of months later saw him starring in a new show. I'd been only peripherally aware of Hagman's career, and hadn't closely followed the original news stories discussing his life work and circumstances of his death. I had no idea he'd be alive again later on! I discovered in autumn 1998 Larry Hagman had *not* died, but had undergone a liver transplant! I marveled at how this could be.

I feel I'm seeing something very mysterious and magical when I witness reality shifts. My perspective and field of attention expands, and I notice even more reality shifts as my perceptual range increases to encompass more possibilities.

There seems to be a fluidity to reality below the surface of what we think is real—a conscious energy bridging time and space that shifts reality in our lives. Perhaps consciousness is traveling from one multiverse of reality to another ... or perhaps things seeming solid and real are actually appearing, disappearing, transporting and transforming because reality is not as solid as we assume. If I can remember both the way things have been as well as notice how they have changed, then perhaps my conscious awareness made an interuniversal space voyage to arrive in one of an infinite number of universes with slightly different attributes, such as one in which the woman crossing the street decided not to take a walk at that time, after all. Perhaps I witnessed her change her mind, sharing first a reality where she went for a walk close to me, and then a different reality where she was elsewhere.

Once I'd seen some reality shifts, I wondered why so few people discuss them. I wondered if people see reality shifts and somehow disregard them, or if they just don't pay attention to such things. Perhaps things that don't matter to people aren't typically noticed, so all sorts of reality shifts could occur around them without them paying any attention at all ... so long as nothing is altered that they *do* care about.

I wonder why I've seen more reality shifts recently, rather than consistently all through my life. Most likely I'm noticing more of them recently, because I'm paying attention ... much as I might pay attention to what's on the periphery of my visual range and start noticing more things going on than I'd originally thought! In my childhood I'd been more open-minded, since I didn't yet know how things are supposed to be. Children start life with open belief structures to adapt to any environment they find themselves in, and begin life directly experiencing the world. When I was a child, I felt connected to and at one with my environment. I was in the sunshine, the rain, the trees, and the earth ... and they were in me. I sensed everything at once. The world was rich, mysterious, and full of infinite possibility. I have few recollections of childhood reality shifts, but I recall they occurred, and I thought them normal.

In recent years, I've become more open-minded. My belief structure now trusts the physical world to support and sustain me, as I notice how effortlessly the physical world can change.

Before I felt so open-minded, I dreamt of finding rooms in the basement of my house that I didn't know were there. I felt scared as basement walls opened up, and I saw light, sunshine, and green leaves through the cracks... and I was surprised to feel fresh air and see beautiful expanses of lush vegetation outside the walls. When I woke up, I felt an epiphany with my old belief structures crumbling. I better understood how old assumptions of causality, locality, objectivity, and material monism are invalidated by direct experiences demonstrating non-local consciousness, subjective interconnectedness, unity of mind and matter, and change being a handshake between sender and receiver. Such open-mindedness and awareness that reality is much more than I had previously envisioned allows me to directly experience reality shifts, as I feel I'm living a waking dream, observing this dream world respond to thoughts and feelings.

We are creative beings who enjoy trying new ways of thinking and feeling. We love to change our lives ... and if we feel stuck, we become anxious, depressed, or resentful as cues it's time to move on. We are artists creating lives that best convey our deepest inspirations, loves and desires. We shift reality daily, whether we are consciously aware of it or not.

Many types of reality shifts were described in this chapter to give you an idea of their variety. The next chapter describes reality shifts that arrive in conjunction with someone's wish or prayer. Reality shifts are often noticed occurring when people think positively, allowing with open minds and hearts for prayers to be answered and wishes to be granted.

Reality Shifts Experiences Exercises

Focusing Attention

One's ability to notice changes depends on correctly remembering how things *were* before reality shifted. You can hone observational skills by practicing remembering what you see. Consider the last place you sat down before where you are right now, and imagine you are there again. In your mind's eye, reconstruct that environment in terms of everything on your left, straight ahead, and to your right. Take a moment to write these down, return to the place you were, and compare what you see with your list of observations. Do you notice anything surprising?

Playing Solitaire

Becoming aware of emotions and energy helps you experience more enjoyable reality shifts. Play your favorite game of solitaire when feeling expansive and loving ... and also when feeling downhearted or worried. When playing computer games, use different names for playing in different moods, and see how scores differ. I've noticed really amazing differences in all areas of my life based on attitude and feelings ... two aspects of myself where I have free choice.

Reality Shift Journal

You can hone observational skills and improve chances of witnessing reality shifts by journaling daily events. Write down unusual occurrences of people or animals or things appearing, disappearing, transporting or transforming. Write down dates, times, significant details ... and thoughts and feelings immediately before shifts happened. Consider what message, if any, there may be to each occurrence. Is it a response to a wish you had ... even a mostly unconscious wish?

Chapter 4

Shifting Reality

*As a coal is revived by incense,
prayer revives the hope of the heart
– J.W. von Goethe*

When we discover that reality really is shifting, it isn't too big a mental leap to acknowledge we have a lot to do with that. The vast majority of reality shifts I've noticed follow wishes and prayers I've made, including some to better understand the way we interact with spirit. Witnessing reality shifts show us how spirit responds to the self; through our hearts and our minds, we can create and transform the world around us in amazing ways. As Christy says in the movie *What Dreams May Come*, "What some people call impossible is just stuff they haven't seen." There is an advantage to opening our minds to reality shifts, much in the same way we willingly accept miracles at times when we need them most. When we live each day in mindful, prayerful fashion—conscious of our blessings and choices—we live a waking dream.

Prayers and wishes are a focused way to inform the universe what we most deeply desire. They are heartfelt requests for divine assistance that work whether or not we believe in God. I've been aware of the power of heartfelt prayer since I was a young child ... that wishes come true when I wish for something with all my heart and soul. If I cried tears of pain and longing from the burning desire of my wish, it seemed to guarantee that my wish would be granted. I wished for things I desired with all my heart, things I desired so much my heart ached for them. I knew when I made such wishes that they would come true—and they did. It didn't matter that I had no formal religious training.

Throughout recorded human history, and in every culture and continent on Earth, there are stories of miracles occurring when people pray for help. We pray when we reach a point in our lives where we know we need help. We pray when we realize that we can't control our environment or a particular situation, and feel an overwhelming desire for help. Prayer provides a focal point for consciously feeling and interacting with inspiration, giving us a simultaneous sense of vulnerability and connection to great cosmic power. When we pray we most clearly feel who we are and what truly matters in our lives.

These moments of mindful awareness feel exquisitely raw. Emotions are no longer something we can suppress or restrain, and we accept that we are at the mercy of the universe. This state of mind invites us to feel a tremendously focused desire for a choice we long for with all our heart, body, and soul. When we wish or pray with our entire being, we are being completely honest about what we care most about. When we live mindfully, we are more passionately involved in our lives, and can stay focused on what matters most and what we are living for.

Prayer feels essential to me, when I feel I'm up against impossible odds. I decided to pack up camp alone in the dark wilderness one moonless night, when I realized I needed to carry my heavy tent, sleeping bag, and other gear across a stream… and my flashlight was dead! Several trips would be required across the stream, and I was alarmed to notice the footing was uneven, shaky, and slippery over wobbly, mossy rocks. At this point, I could have decided the situation was too much for me, and there was no way to make several safe trips back and forth across the stream. Instead of worrying, I chose to feel my total desire for a safe crossing, praying with all my heart and soul to walk safely across the stream. I crossed that stream *three times* without any missteps whatsoever, and felt so tremendously grateful to have crossed without a mishap!

Prayers and wishes work best when we are completely authentic and sincere in our desire. Even if you don't believe in God, there is some special value to just talking out loud to all of your consciousness, saying what's on your mind and in your heart. You can talk or cry aloud next time you feel so shaken up by life's hardships that you feel you *need* something—even if you don't know what you need. When I feel like that, I find some space and time to myself and reach down to the bottom of my feelings to express emotions in words and tears ... with only myself as witness. Yet I am never alone! None of us, no matter how isolated, are ever alone. We are all surrounded by Love ... surrounded by Spirit. All consciousness is interconnected, and we are embraced in love always and forever!

We do get what we wish for, when we make our wish from a place of self-awareness and understanding. Like the Rolling Stones' song about satisfaction reminds us, we don't always get what we ask for—but if we try sometimes, we just might find we get what we need. In other words, we'll find ourselves facing challenges we don't recall wishing for, but those challenges often bring us something irreplaceable, like courage, strength, and the ability to clearly see and help others and ourselves.

It is advantageous to pay close attention to the gifts you choose to accept and those you turn away, because it's good to notice what you open yourself to and what you shut yourself away from. When you pay attention to the boundaries you set, you can start to make better use of the gifts you have been receiving all along, but may have been turning away. If you know that you do not wish to accept things that feel bad, it's important to know what is bad to you and what is good. You are the only one who can know exactly what works best for you.

Praying with Purpose

> *Inspired intention makes dreams come true*

It really doesn't matter whether or not you believe in God for your wishes to come true. Carolyn Miller documents many examples of wishes coming true for people regardless of whether or not they are religious. As Miller writes in her book, *Creating Miracles*:

> *"But perhaps you don't even believe in a higher power. No problem. My research indicates that divine intervention is experienced by people of all religions and no religion at all. The only difference is that believers are more likely to recognize surprising reversals as 'miraculous', while non-believers mistakenly attribute them to 'luck'. Luck implies that*

> *these narrow escapes are random occurrences, but as we shall see, there is good reason to believe that they actually occur on cue whenever someone follows the appropriate procedure."*

Carolyn Miller describes "miracle-mindedness" as behaving with fearlessness, good intentions, innocence, and invulnerability. Such people remain calm even in trying times, listening to inspiration for creative and often unexpected or unusual ideas for compassionate, loving actions to take in times of crisis and danger.

Miller documents many real-life accounts of people who escaped impending disaster after going into a meditative state of consciousness and following inner guidance. People she interviewed were consistently able to escape death, rape, and other seemingly inevitable, unpleasant fates by opening themselves to experiencing a tremendous feeling of love for themselves, their surroundings, and even their would-be murderers and rapists. Facing situations of extreme stress and sudden anxiety greatly heightened some people's lucidity, and they found themselves capable of transforming circumstances that appeared deadly or extremely dangerous into much less threatening situations.

Sudden anxiety (as opposed to a state of chronic anxiety) frequently has the effect of promoting intense lucidity, because it brings our *full* focus of attention to the frightening situation in which it appears *no* good solution is possible. This sudden sense of lucidity prompts us to acknowledge that habitual, routine patterns will *not* rescue us from the situation at hand, and something much, MUCH more is needed! At these times, we can recognize that in fact, something much more is available, and we can change reality into something more palatable. Reality shifts occur when we awaken to an intense desire for a very different life experience, and long for it with all our heart and soul.

Fortunately, most of us are not in everyday need of praying for our lives or personal safety. We may merely wish to meet people who understand us, find careers that inspire us, discover more creativity, improve our health, or enhance prosperity in our lives. We may simply want to find a short line at the grocery store, a good parking spot, a good friend to talk to and hug, or a movie we want to see. These everyday ordinary reality shifts are possible for us at all times, and they happen most frequently when our physical material mortal self (ego) and our mindful eternally conscious self (spirit) are attuned to and aligned with each other.

The best way to ensure prayers and wishes come true is to make sure there are no contradictory prayers or intentions that would render the wish useless. The strongest way to pray is to find and express a sense of unified purpose supported by both the mortal and eternal sense of self combined. Whatever one desires with one's entire being can be created in this material world, provided there aren't too many conflicting desires causing destructive interference.

An example of conflicting desires is a woman thinking to herself, *"I wish I would win the state lottery,"* while feeling contradictory thoughts and feelings such as, *"I need to feel a strong connection between the work I do and the money I receive,"* and *"I don't feel worthy of receiving huge gifts."*

Most of us have inner conflicts that prevent us from moving effortlessly towards our desires without getting at least a little bit in our own way. Even unconscious inner conflicts can cancel out our wishes. For example, I might consciously believe I deserve to be loved, but unconsciously doubt anyone would love me if they knew who I *really* am. When intentions are allowed to travel free of conflict, they don't get canceled out.

It can be hard to notice your own inner conflicts; it's usually a whole lot easier to see someone else's! If you wish to remove inner conflicts that block you from receiving your heart's desire, you can wish and pray for assistance in finding and changing what blocks you. Every person's preferred way of praying is unique. Some people need formal structure and membership in a religious group, while others require solitude and immersion in natural beauty. You can pray for guidance in finding the best way to pray, and you will receive guidance. If you lack the courage to face all of yourself (even the embarrassing parts), you can ask for and receive that courage. If you need to be more honest with yourself and others, you can become more honest. If you don't know *what* you need, you can find out what you need. Just remember that when you remain open in heart and mind, you can get answers to any questions you ask and you can hear the answers clearly.

I feel refreshed and invigorated when I take time out of my routines to contemplate what I most wish for myself. When I do this, I review all my feelings and sort through a jumble of wishes, doubts, obsessions, regrets, resentments and fears. My feelings and thoughts are things, and they do not vanish after I feel and think them; they are like energy waves that travel through time and space to interact in other parts of the universe. The Tantric mystics of Tibet called these thought forms 'tsal'. The Christian Bible, the Buddhist writings, the Hindu Upanishad and Jewish writings all say similar things: our thoughts create our destinies.

There is a big difference between wishing from feeling the desires of one's material self (ego) and wishing from a feeling of one's conscious eternal self (spirit). When I feel fearful or angry, I am less likely to find my wishes granted, because I am highly conflicted at the ego level.

I notice lots of reality shifts occur when I feel connected to my conscious eternal self and everything around me in a state of unconditional love. This state of mind is the realization that we *are* all interconnected, and that we can remember that holistic unity and instantaneously create with the Love we feel. Love is the strongest thing there is, and it is the true source of all we create.

When my prayers are truly felt, I often feel I'm experiencing my darkest hour ... my most desperate situation ... the very darkest depths of my longing. This is not a feeling of carefully thought-out requests ... but a feeling of achingly raw, passionate desire for what I recognize as being what I truly need. I reach a point beyond pride, and I beg for a chance to experience real change in my life. At this point, I am finally ready to surrender myself to the experience of total unconditional love.

While it's true there are many different ways to pray, I'd like to share what's worked best for me. It's my personal experience that prayers and wishes come true when they are: felt truly from love; deeply felt and inspired with passion; consciously composed and focused; and free of expectations, doubt, anger and fear.

Felt Truly from Love

> This wish is created by honest feelings of love, free of contradictory beliefs and desires. The wish is aligned with your truest, most authentic feelings, since disharmonies can cancel out what you are wishing for. Be true to yourself, and feel your own true feelings. Most especially, be sure to pay attention to what you feel truly thankful for in your life. Feeling your blessings opens your heart to noticing how loved you truly are!

Deeply Felt and Inspired with Passion

> This wish is fueled by a complete sense of your resonant passionate desire, and infused with the highest vibration of energy you can feel. You might notice you feel energized, warm, or tingly when you consider the wish ... this helps! You can visualize yourself undergoing a phase change, such as steam boiling off a pot of water ... or as a bright, hot ball of energy, radiating energy like a star.

Consciously Composed & Focused

> This wish is something you imagine clearly and specifically in pictures, feelings, or words ... however you imagine your world. Using all your senses ... consider how this wish feels, looks, smells, tastes, and sounds. Be as specific as possible until you have the clearest imaginable view of what you actually need, and don't worry about details you don't care about. Stay focused on exactly what matters most to you, not what you think you are supposed to focus on, or what other people said you should care about.

Free of Expectations, Doubt, Anger, & Fear

> Release your wish as a freely mobile entity of its own ... without imposing any burdens of performance, resentments, or resistance. You might think of this as *giving up* as you release the wish to fly away. You are giving up on restraining, controlling, monitoring, or restricting this wish. You can visualize this as realizing that you've done all you can to raise this little wish thought, and now it's time for it to leave the nest and fly away.

Do you remember the scene in the movie *The Princess Bride,* in which the miracle man is asked to revive Wesley, the almost-dead hero? Billy Crystal plays the miracle man, and with a twinkle in his eye, he offers the sage advice to Wesley's friend who carried him there for resurrection, "Don't hurry, sonny. You rush a miracle, you get rotten miracles."

Letting go of the wish and not rushing can be hard, but I've found it to be absolutely necessary to let go of any desire to worry, blame, or control before reality shifts can occur. Some wishes take a while to come true. The American Indians wished for the return of the buffalo to their land over a hundred years before their wish began to materialize. Setting wishes free is another way of remembering to be patient.

It helps me to review these steps in making wishes, and notice if I have any trouble spots, being really honest with myself. If I've had trouble with my wishes coming true, I ask myself whether I've been getting in my own way somehow. For example, I might have a hard time focusing clearly on what I'm wishing for. Finding the right balance between being specific but not *too* specific can be a challenge sometimes.

I've been fortunate to be invited and able to attend annual spiritual gatherings of women, in which the final ceremony consists of a circle of sharing. I became aware that this circle of women is an *incredibly* powerful force the first year I attended these gatherings in 1996, when I heard women begin their turn to speak by thanking God and the Universe for answering their wishes from last year. In many cases, women said their wishes were granted almost immediately (within days or weeks), but as several women noted, now they wanted to make some important corrections, since the wishes had been granted exactly as requested, and a few important details had been overlooked in the original request!

Another common problem area in making wishes is letting go of things and loving unconditionally, which is required before setting wishes free and releasing them. Some people don't have faith that a wish will really come through, and if this nagging doubt is strong or frequent enough, it can actually block the wish from coming true. Just as our children need us to release them so they can grow strong and find their own path in the world, and just as seeds need a clear spot to grow, our wishes need space and time to develop. Thoughts are powerful things, and that's why keeping your own mind clean is so important for manifesting what you wish for.

You can choose to concentrate on manifesting physical goods and money, but it's important to understand that you won't care whether your wish for material gain is granted if you aren't truly inspired by such prayers. The things I've cared most about and prayed for haven't had much to do with money or material gain, because I wasn't feeling passionately inspired about those things. In many cases where reality shifted after I made a wish, I had no idea that my passionate feelings combined with my consciously focused thoughts would change anything, so it came as a *huge* shock to me when reality shifted!

The following are examples of some incredible reality shifts that happened following a simple wish somewhere along the way ... usually a wish that was made and then released with no anticipation or expectation of having it granted. This first story is an 'alive again' reality shift experience, in which I was detached from expectation, as I would never have guessed such a shift could occur.

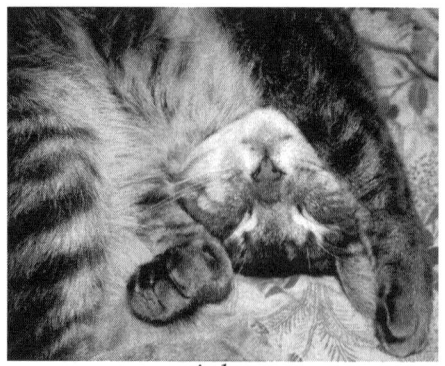

Ashes

Alive Again — Back from the Dead

In 1984 my neighbor and ex-roommate, Kathryn, told me her cat, Ashes, had died after being hit by a car. At the time, I was living in an apartment on Cedar Street in Berkeley directly across the street from hers. I'd lived with Ashes and Kathryn for years, and Ashes had visited me after I'd moved across the street. I was heartbroken to hear the sad news of his death. This cat was an integral part of our household, and I'd really wished to see him again.

A few weeks to a month after Kathryn told me Ashes died, I was *astonished* to see him walking toward me in my backyard! I could hardly believe my eyes, and as I reached out to pet and hold him again, I felt joyful ecstasy that I was given this chance to see him again. His fur was slightly more matted and dirty than it had ever been before, and he seemed to move with some pain and difficulty in his joints, but Ashes was obviously very much alive.

I told my boyfriend about this very excitedly at the time, saying, "LOOK! It's Ashes, and he's ALIVE!" My boyfriend was startled by my outburst, as if he didn't quite recall Ashes had ever died. He only had a foggy memory of that, like he'd dreamt Ashes had died. I didn't know why this was happening, and I couldn't understand how a cat could possibly come back from the dead. I greatly enjoyed continuing to see Ashes very much alive for many months after that.

Time Slows Down

In the summer of 1991, I was walking in a Swiss train station with my husband, who carried our one-year-old baby on his shoulders. She was holding onto his neck and hair for support, while he carried two suitcases in his arms. I walked a few paces behind my husband, also carrying a suitcase, and noticing our daughter had released her grip on my husband's hair, and was now happily waving her arms free so they rose and fell with each step he took as she bounced along.

Very suddenly and without warning, our daughter bounced up and free of her dad's shoulders, and began falling back, headfirst toward the hard marble floor of the train station. I realized with sudden shock that there was no way he could stop her from falling, and I was about nine feet behind him... much too far to catch her as she fell. I felt a rush of emotions flooding me with energy as I longed with all my heart and soul to catch her somehow.

In the next moment, I continued walking forward at normal speed, while everything and everyone around me moved more and more slowly. It seemed that everyone around me began moving in slow motion, with even the normal sounds of footsteps clicking on marble slowing and softening to near total silence as time seemed to stretch, leaving everything except me in a state approaching suspended animation.

I was overjoyed to easily catch up to my husband just as our daughter fell freely into my arms! As I caught her, time resumed its normal flow, and everyone around me began moving at normal speed.

Summer 1996
with wavy hair

Winter 1998
with curlier hair

Naturally Curly Hair

In October 1996, I visited a friend who invited me to look at her family photos. One photograph in particular caught my eye—a photo of her younger sister, Laura. I thought, *She's so beautiful and her hair is so wonderfully curly ... I wonder if it's naturally curly? Wouldn't it be nice to have naturally curly hair?* I felt great love for my friend and her sister, whom I hadn't yet met.

A few weeks later I was cutting my hair when I noticed it was acting very differently than it normally did when I cut it. My hair was *really curly*, and it kept sproinging up in bouncy waves. I cut my hair shorter than usual so I could investigate this change more closely, and saw that my hair was *totally* different than it had ever been before. It used to be straight with some waves that touched my shoulders, and now it had become *full* of wavy curls everywhere!

I found out that Laura had been curling her hair ... all the way up until October 1996, when *her hair suddenly became naturally curly at the same time mine did!* This is something that delighted both of us, and that we talked about the next year when she came out to visit my friend and me.

I discovered Laura and I had much in common, and we began a spirited email exchange. She advised me to "put up the poodle" and "get funky" with my newly curly hair! I did some digging in my hair accessory drawer, and found some things I'd never used, simply because there had never been any need. Now, my hair truly has a life of its own, and can benefit from some taming!

For a month after my hair spontaneously curled, my older daughter was afraid to wash her hair, saying "I don't want my hair to curl as much as yours." I spent hours telling her that washing my hair didn't curl it!

Chocolate Cravings Vanish

For most of my young adult life, I had a serious love affair with chocolate. I considered chocolate to be something *I could not live without,* and ate some chocolate pretty much every day. I felt I had to bring chocolate along with me when I was away from home for more than a day or two, because the very idea of a day without chocolate seemed unbearable. I ate a bag full of dark chocolate chips every week out of habit, reaching mindlessly for chocolate snacks whenever I walked around the house deciding what to do next, frequently popping morsels into my mouth before I even knew what I was doing. Sometimes I'd have chocolate smudges or crumbs on my hands, with only a vague recollection I'd just eaten some chocolate.

While I loved the taste and sensation of eating chocolate, I noticed my health suffered because I was eating so much chocolate and couldn't seem to cut back on it. It occurred to me that I might be addicted to chocolate since I was eating it in such profuse quantities. I also noticed problems, such as occasionally getting a headache after eating chocolate, my face breaking out with acne, and gaining weight. When I noticed in September 1997 that my health was suffering in these ways, and that chocolate probably wasn't doing much good for my teeth, either, I thought to myself, *I wish I didn't eat so much chocolate.*

About one month later, in October 1997, I noticed I wasn't eating any chocolate. I noticed this because I observed I hadn't touched my bag of chocolate chips for so long there was a thin layer of dust on the bag. I even tried some, and found I wasn't in the mood for chocolate! This was very unusual for me, since I hadn't gone a whole week without chocolate since 1980, and was always in the mood for chocolate! Since I hadn't made a conscious effort to quit chocolate, I was very surprised to notice I simply wasn't eating it anymore!

I still love chocolate, although now I can pass it by, or just have it occasionally, without feeling deprived. I feel so much better to not be addicted to chocolate any more. I also find I enjoy the taste and texture of chocolate much more now, since it's something I savor as a special treat, rather than a habitual snack.

Storybook Picture

My older daughter and I witnessed a reality shift when I was reading "The Three Billy Goats Gruff" picture book to her. We had been reading this book together almost every night for the past week, since she really loved it and liked to hear it again and again. One day we were cuddled up together on the sofa, and I'd just read the part of the story where the big Billy goat gruff was finally going to cross the bridge to the other side. We turned the page, and my seven-year-old asked me,

"Mommy, why is this page different?" pointing at an unfamiliar illustration. I had silently noticed the picture was different, too. We had read this book frequently, and the picture of the troll falling off the bridge was *completely* new! I stared at the picture in rapt contemplation ... taking it in and doing my best to recall the way the illustration had looked before.

I remembered the previous version of the picture showed the troll far off in the distance, and I'd thought to myself on other occasions, *It's a shame the troll is such a small speck ... this part of the book is such a pivotal part of the story.* Perhaps because I desired to see the troll up close, the illustration now shows the troll *very* close up and pointed directly toward the reader, head first! My daughter and I gazed at this new picture for several minutes, agreeing how we both remembered the picture used to be.

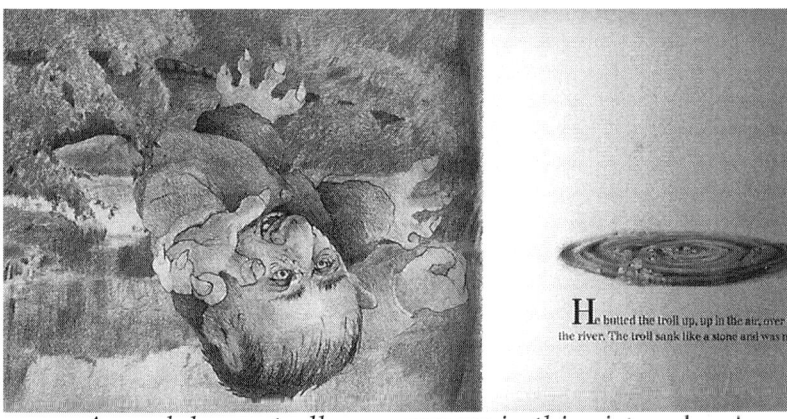

A much larger troll now appears in this picture book

My daughter looked at me expectantly for some explanation as to what was going on, and my simple response to her question about why the page was different was that sometimes things change, when reality shifts to be slightly different than we remember it was before.

Repaired Watch

My friend went sailing on the San Francisco bay on a day when a big thunderstorm was raging in the ocean. While the storm didn't come into the bay, storm warnings were in effect, and the wind was blowing hard, with gusts between 35 to 45 knots. When my friend and the captain dropped sails and tied the boat up on a buoy moored off Corinthian Island for lunch, my friend noticed from below decks that the boat was doing 360 degree turns! Wind shifts swung the boat suddenly and dramatically, hitting first from one angle and then another.

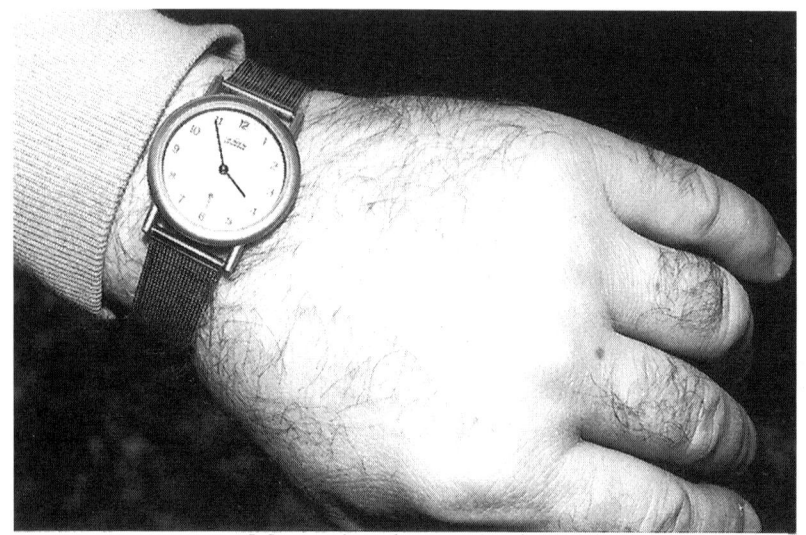

Mysteriously repaired watch

After lunch, the captain and my friend dropped a passenger off at the Corinthian Yacht Club and proceeded toward San Francisco. The captain said, "I'd better drop the jib," and almost fell overboard as the boat sped along at a breakneck speed of 9 knots (it's hull speed was only 8.5 knots)! There were several wind shifts and jibes with the main, and even though they had reefed the main onto the boom, the boat was *still* going faster than hull speed. About 500 yards from shore, the captain grabbed the downhaul on the main, and the boom threw him overboard. The captain was somehow still holding onto the downhaul, so he was now experiencing the unexpected excitement of water-skiing on his sandals (at such high speed he wasn't even getting his coat wet).

The captain had been teaching my friend how to steer with a tiller, and my friend was not yet familiar with bringing the boat around into the wind. Another sudden wind shift popped like a gun, bringing the boom back across so the captain could scramble back on board and bring the boat around into the wind, slowing them down and bringing the captain to the high side of the boat so he could walk aboard, since it had been taking all his strength just to hold on until then. The captain handed my friend his glasses when the wind changed again ... and the boat came about suddenly, pushing the lens right out of the glasses and putting the captain on the high windward side of the boat. The captain crawled over the rail back into the boat, and told my friend how to steer into the wind.

In all the chaos of this wild sailboat ride, my friend banged his wrist and wristwatch, and he looked down to see a hair line crack in the crystal from about 10:00 going to 7:00 on the dial. There was a divergence in the center, so this was not exactly a straight crack that he could feel and catch his thumbnail on.

I saw the crack on my friend's watch the day after it broke, and was impressed to hear the story and see such noticeable damage to the watch. I had a passing thought, *I wish this watch crystal could return to its normally beautiful state*, as I felt sad to see such a beautiful watch so damaged.

Several days later when my friend was on the boat again, he told the racing club the story about how his friend had gone water skiing in his sandals off the sailboat, ending the story with, "And it even broke my watch," as he looked at his watch crystal... stunned to see it in *perfect* condition. His friend then asked, "Where'd you get that fixed?," and my friend replied, "I didn't ... I was just going to!"

Transformed Coat

My husband got a red Gortex coat as a Christmas present from his parents one December, and I observed it *very* carefully for some time, because it was nearly identical to one I bought the previous year in rip-stop Gortex material. As he opened his present and I first saw the coat, I thought to myself, *It's a shame he got the Gortex coat without the rip-stop ... if anyone needs a rip-stop coat, it's definitely him* (rip-stop fabric has grid lines to help prevent ripping). I didn't say anything aloud to my husband or his parents, because he was trying the coat on and seemed to like it just fine.

About a month later at home one weekend in January, my husband was working on cleaning the car, and got some grease on his new coat. He decided to run it through the wash, and when it was done drying, I went to remove it from the dryer, and found ... *it was not the same coat!* The new coat was rip-stop with the distinctive tiny raised checkerboard grid pattern. I was so amazed at this transformation that I asked my husband if he remembered his coat being different when he first got it. He seemed quite perplexed, as if trying to recollect, but had difficulty remembering.

I have no idea why there was a one-month delay between my initial thought and the subsequent change, or why my husband had no immediate recollection of his coat being different. After about one day, he began recalling his coat really *was* different when he'd first received it. He asked me, "Wasn't my coat a slightly darker shade of red, and thicker... as well as not rip-stop when I got it for Christmas?" ... and I was delighted to tell him, "YES!" I hadn't told him any of those details! It's definitely not the same coat he got for Christmas, and he did not return or exchange it ... it simply transformed itself into a rip-stop coat.

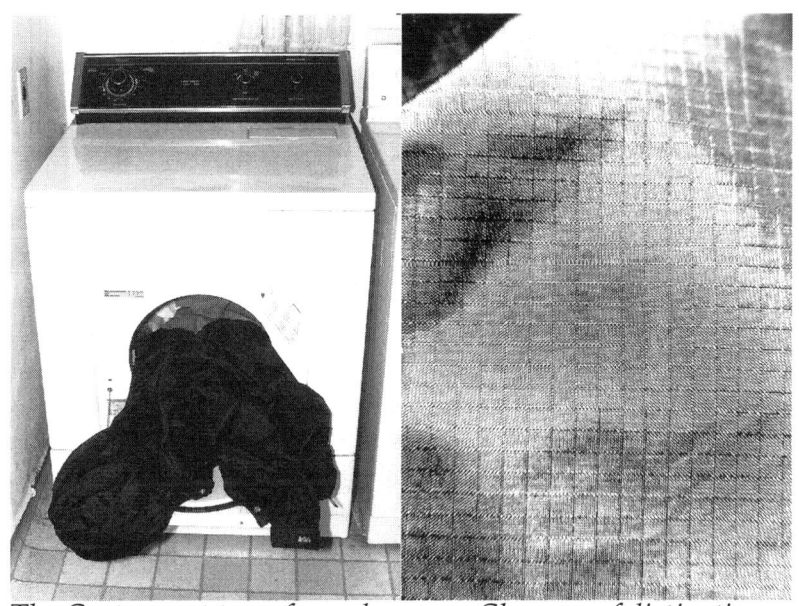

The Gortex coat transformed into a rip-stop coat

Close-up of distinctive rip-stop Gortex fabric

Who'll Stop the Rain

I relived an experience from my childhood one morning in February when I was in a wonderfully relaxed and joyous state. I was delighted to find I was able to stop and start the rain, just as I had once done as a child.

When I was about five years old, I remember looking out my parents' bedroom window into the backyard and noticing that as I thought *Stop, rain* the rain would instantly cease. When I thought *Start again*, it would instantly be raining. I could intend it to rain on just the left side of the yard or just the right side! I was so delighted and excited that I called my mom to come see this ... but when she arrived, none of it worked anymore. I had seen her expression showing a mixture of slight annoyance and more than moderate skepticism, and my spirits sunk as I observed that the rain and my thoughts were no longer in perfect harmony. I hadn't tried to start or stop rain again until that incredible Thursday morning in February 1998.

What I noticed while taking a walk that February morning was that at first the rain was delayed from when I thought start or stop ... as if it was starting or stopping up in the clouds. This was amazing to me for two reasons. I was amazed the rain was responding to my thoughts, since I hadn't had any such experience since I was five years old. I was also amazed and puzzled by the delay between my thoughts and whether or not it was raining, because I remembered there was no such delay when I was a little girl. I wondered what could have changed so that there would be such a delay, and then I laughed out loud when I remembered that as a five year old girl, I didn't yet comprehend the way rain is *supposed* to come down all the way from clouds ... so of *course* it just stopped instantly!

As soon as I knew I didn't have to wait for rain to fall all the way down from the clouds, I intended for the rain to stop and start instantly. In this incredibly relaxed, energized state of consciousness with complete confidence that rain thought control was doable ... no problem! There was no more delay between thinking *start* and *stop rain* and the rain starting and stopping. Just don't call someone over and say, "Watch this!" when they don't believe in it!

I cried when I realized that my childhood magic was coming back to me. I asked for thick, fat, wet raindrops to wash my tears of joy away and was ecstatic to have the rain I'd requested wash my face clean. What a feeling!

Materializing Keys

One beautiful evening in May, my friend and I were getting ready to go to dinner when he noticed he was locked out of his car and couldn't find the keys. These car keys were on a ring with a three-inch glow-in-the-dark owl, so they're easy to spot and feel, even in the dark. We searched inside pockets, on the ground around the car, and in the car locks looking for those keys. My friend looked inside the room, and went so far as to remove his clothes, checking pockets and seams ... all to no avail.

My friend later told me he'd thought to himself, "I don't want to call a locksmith on a Sunday on Memorial Day weekend ... it'll cost $200!" He then recalled he had put the keys with his wallet in the trunk of the car, which he had then locked. Only upon looking in the ignition lock, through the right hand window of the car and not seeing his keys there, did he exhaust his last hope of finding them in an accessible place. Then he gave up. I saw him standing perfectly still next to the front window of the passenger side of his car, staring inside. My attention focused on my friend, wondering how best to unlock his car now.

As I continued gazing at my friend in contemplative meditation, I suddenly saw the keys miraculously appear *out of thin air*, materializing just under his hands in front of him, before falling straight down. I saw the keys drop out of nowhere and land with a jangle on the ground! My friend heard them drop and land, too, while still gazing through the car's right front window, for what he said felt like just a moment.

I'd never before seen something materialize like that out of thin air, except in magic shows ... and my friend was not doing magic tricks. In fact, he later recalled he had *definitely* locked those keys in the trunk of his car with his wallet in a small zippered bag.

Transformed Tambourine

In August 1998, I was at a Blues jam night at a friend's house, borrowing his Remo tambourine to play and dance with. For the previous several months on the numerous occasions I'd used it, the tambourine had the unfortunate tendency to stain my hands blue where I held it, since the blue dye in the wood wore off when moistened by perspiration. I noticed this every time I used it for the previous several months, and although I wished the tambourine wouldn't stain my hands, I accepted stained hands as part of the tambourine experience, washing the blue dye off my hands at the end of each evening.

On the night of August 21, I noticed Tom's Remo tambourine had a *completely different edge rim* than it ever had before. This tambourine had a shiny metallic silver surface on the outside, with a black wood-stained surface on the inside. The picture on the drum was the same slightly off-center cross with four beams of light radiating outwards as before, but the blue wooden edge rim was *totally different*. This metallic silver tambourine looked well-worn like before, with small dents and pock marks in the drum skin, and a worn price tag on the side. The best thing about this transformed tambourine was there was no more problem of blue dye rubbing off on my hands anymore! After playing the tambourine for an hour straight, my hands still looked clean. I had no doubt I was using a completely different instrument than the tambourine I'd become so familiar with ... even though the design on the drum surface looked pretty much identical to the other tambourine design.

At the evening's first break in musical performances, I asked our host if this was a new tambourine, saying nothing more about my noticing it now seemed to have silver sides. He took a quick look at it, and told me with an air of confidence and slight annoyance at being asked such an odd question, "That's the same one I've always had." I then asked another drummer if he recalled ever seeing a different tambourine with blue edges at the house, and he told me he didn't recall any tambourine other than the one with silver sides I was holding right then and there. I asked my companion if he recalled the tambourine being different, and was glad to hear he *did* recall our host having a tambourine with blue wooden sides, and remembered asking how my hands got so blue. He examined the tambourine as I told him, "I'm so happy my hands won't keep turning blue from playing the blues!"

Disappearing Pig Artwork

While eating dinner in Yountville at the Bistro Jeanty celebrating a friend's birthday one August, I was stunned to see the decor had changed from the last time I'd been there. Bistro Jeanty used to have a prominent pig theme in the front dining area, featuring a large cut-out pig with a chef's hat in the dining room, and a pig art deco framed poster by the bathrooms. I'd eaten dinner at Bistro Jeanty with my sister just a couple of months earlier, and remembered the pig poster especially well. Now, there was no pig artwork anywhere to be found in the restaurant.

I calmly noticed these changes, thinking perhaps the restaurant was recently redecorated. I asked a waitress about any recent changes in decor, and then the busboy ... hearing them both swear to me separately that *nothing* had changed in the last two months! They'd been there longer than that, and each assured me the decor had always been the way it is right now.

I later asked my sister about the pig artwork, and learned she did not recall the pig poster, but she did remember the large cutout pig with chef's hat. As I wondered why these changes would occur, I recalled my friend is allergic to pork, and he recalled my telling him about Bistro Jeanty's prominent pig art after I'd first visited the restaurant. I recollected a remark he'd made to me months earlier about how unwelcoming the pig artwork felt to him, due to his pork allergy. It's possible this reality shift eliminated pigs from the restaurant decor, based on my friend's sensitivity.

It felt challenging to have this sort of surprise memory quiz a couple of months later ... especially when I didn't expect anything would be inexplicably different!

What's Going on Here?

> *"Every body continues in a state of rest or of uniform motion in a straight line, except in so far as it is compelled to change that state by forces impressed upon it."*
> – Sir Isaac Newton

In addition to the aforementioned reality shifts, I've noticed many of my wishes to connect and relate better with people frequently come true. One spring day, I wished I could get to know a musician, and by May that year, I met a singer-composer from New York at the beach. Lorraine told me she planned to move to the Bay Area that fall, and said she'd love to stay in touch. I didn't really expect to see her again ... but she did stay in touch, and phoned when she moved! I had a hard time believing I'd only met with her a few times, because the feeling of connection between us was so strong.

I wished to have friends on the street where I live, and that happened, too! Lots of cross-generational friendships began on our street, and the neighborhood began an earthquake preparedness program and annual potlucks and Halloween parades. I deeply appreciate how such a deep sense of community has sprung forth.

Wishes usually come true when we are ready for them—when we feel we actually *could* imagine giving up chocolate, enjoying naturally curly hair, having friends that live on our street, or making friends with a musician. A focused desire to explore a different set of possibilities can move our consciousness to a parallel universe reality, where what we wish for exists.

If reality shifts happen because there are an infinite number of parallel universes our consciousness can freely move between, then life is a lot like a dream or a holodeck on *Star Trek*. With an infinite number of universes of possibility open to us at any given moment, we create our life opportunities every moment, choosing our next action based on how we feel. I create my life by choosing between an infinite assortment of possible paths, viewing prayer as the most mindful way to make each choice. I am often unconscious of how I create my life every moment, so I reach out to this infinite range of possibilities with my gut feelings of what I wish for based on what I worry about, what I'm angry about, and what I feel grateful for. A mindful state of more gratitude than worry and fear brings best results, as what I pay attention to comes into being.

Some reality shifts, like the vanishing pigs in Bistro Jeanty, remind me of being inside a dream in which things are very odd or unusual, yet still feel normal and like they belong there. My usual feeling immediately following a reality shift is that things are still normal ... yet I'm absolutely certain that *something* has definitely changed ... even though everything seems normal on either side of the reality shift. Telling people about reality shifts feels like telling people about a dream about "my parent's house, but it's really *not* their house in real life, but it seemed natural in my dream." When I told the busboy and waitress about the previous reality, I might as well have been telling them about a dream. I see that the pigs *are* gone, but to the waitress and busboy, the restaurant never had any pig decorations.

It's fascinating to me that sometimes when I notice reality shifts, people are equally startled and amazed by them, and other times I notice something is suddenly very different, yet people don't seem to notice the change at all, even when directly questioned. This likely has a lot to do with what people choose to pay attention to. People who wish to experience the dreamlike nature of reality are more inclined to notice when reality shifts, while those who don't care whether reality is shifting or not don't tend to notice it is.

Most people gladly accept miracles in a crisis, but may not notice miracles happening under their noses every day. The things some people call luck and coincidence can be considered miraculous. Every person creates their life in more ways than they can fully comprehend. Even the smallest things, like smiles and friendly nods to passing strangers are just as divinely inspired as butterflies, trees, and flowers.

Prayer's Shadow Side

While it's exciting to see how much fun wishes can be when they come true, it's also important to note that wishes are powered by intentions, and it's best to wish things for oneself, or others who openly accept and welcome assistance. Making wishes for others without their consent has been called "drive-by prayer" by Dr. Larry Dossey, in cases where people recklessly pray without thinking about results. Dossey also advises against being a prayer vigilante, or declaring oneself an agent for God, or being a prayer mugger who uses prayer to seize something that belongs to somebody else (like victory in a competitive sport, or receiving a promotion or award).

Larry Dossey points out the need for *conscious* prayer. We can't afford to continue denying prayer's shadow side, because we'll likely find ourselves caught off guard and hurt by manipulative, meddlesome, or mean-spirited unconscious intentions. Dossey explains that negative prayer is prayer lacking in empathy, compassion, and love. When we pray mindfully with genuine compassion, empathy and love, we won't harm others with our prayers and wishes.

Considering Dossey's advice, it's therefore generally advisable to pray for "blessings for everyone" rather than a more narrowly based outcome. Even my wish that "Everything be the best it can possibly be" is micro management if I try to control my experience to only be *my* idea of what I consider to be good at the time. Things seem different when I step back to see the big picture.

What is truly best for us is not always what would appear on the surface to be best ... because it will often include hardships we benefit and grow from. Things that seem bad to us at the time can later be seen to be quite good when viewed from a different perspective. For example, it might seem bad to notice your car has a flat tire when you're in a rush to get to work on time—but if you find your being late meant you missed a boring, pointless meeting and were home when your best friend called—you'd be happy you were home! Similarly, you might feel bad to catch a cold, but if you understand that was the only way you would lay down and take it easy for a few days, you might acknowledge it was actually a good thing you had time to recharge yourself.

We are rarely so conscious that we can tell the complete meaning of any turn of events, since any point where we feel our knowledge of a given situation is complete is actually just an arbitrary boundary we've chosen to stop at. I love the way this point is illustrated in the following story, *Perhaps*.

Perhaps

A long time ago in China, a farmer's only horse escaped from the corral and ran away. The farmer's neighbors, hearing of this misfortune, commiserated with him: "Too bad that your horse ran away," they said. "Perhaps," he answered.

The farmer's oldest son went out into the hills to look for the lost horse. He found not only his father's escaped horse, but several more wild horses as well, and managed to round them all up and bring them back to the farm. With this, the neighbors told the farmer, "What good fortune you have, to have several more horses now, in addition to getting back the one you had lost." "Perhaps," said the farmer.

The son decided to tame one of the wild horses, for use on the farm. Mounting the strongest of the lot, the son fell off the horse, and broke his arm. "Bad luck, about your son's arm," said the farmer's neighbors. "Perhaps," he replied.

The next morning, soldiers of the emperor's army came through the village, drafting every able-bodied young man for military service. They left the farmer's son behind, with his broken arm. The neighbors congratulated the farmer for being so fortunate not to lose his son to the army. "Perhaps," said the farmer.

Life is not always what it seems, and an experience that may appear to be very bad fortune to a person may not be such bad fortune after all. In China, the words for crisis and opportunity are the same. Change is the one true constant in our lives, so it is very helpful to maintain a good attitude towards the inevitability of the ways our lives change. As much as we might wish things would remain the same, they can't, so we might as well keep an open mind and consider how we'd most like our lives to change. Simply accepting that change is always happening around us can help improve our attitudes toward facing change in our lives. Sometimes it takes life experiences of tremendous change to help us become wiser; a life with no conflicts would be boring and dull.

Prayer Protection

While we need some challenges, we don't really need other people praying or wishing malevolent things upon us. Thoughts are things, and they really do create in our world. I have personally experienced the effects of negative unconscious thoughts from others, and found them to be damaging and destructive if I allow them to reach me. In order to protect yourself from negative effects of the wishes of others, and even your own self-destructive unconscious intentions, it's recommended that you 'seal your aura,' or energy field. Visualizing your aura self-contained helps to inhibit one's instinctive emotional reaction to succumb to fear or attacking someone or something. It is important for our best health and wellbeing to protect ourselves from energetic attack.

The most effective approach to take is to visualize reflecting back all unwanted (non-loving) energy. This protective mirror visualization reminds us consciously that we have no need to accept anything less than love.

We do a great deal of damage to ourselves any time we cut ourselves off from love, or block the free flow of our emotions. To the degree we believe we deserve problems (through guilt and fear) we are vulnerable to receiving injury. Such injury doesn't even need to come from others, since we can damage ourselves by releasing self-destructive thoughts of anger and fear. When we feel cut off from love and stifled in our ability to express ourselves, we become vulnerable to illness and disease.

In some extreme cases, people have been known to die within a few days of being "hexed." Dr. Clifton K. Meader of the Department of Medicine at Vanderbilt Medical School studied "hex deaths," and determined that they occur only when three conditions are met: the victim and family and all acquaintances must believe the hexer has the power and ability to induce death; all previously known victims of the hexing must have died unless the cause has been removed; and every person the victim knows must behave as if the victim will die (leaving him or her alone and isolated). The beliefs, attitudes and actions of the victim and the people surrounding the victim can exert a powerful effect upon the victim's health.

While we may not feel these stories about witch doctors have much relevance in our lives, we often greet others who find themselves in stressful or challenging circumstances as if they are to be left alone. We sometimes isolate people who are suffering, or have been pronounced to be dying of some medically named disease, rather than support them in their time of need. We sometimes avoid people whose problems we feel are insurmountable, such as homeless people on our streets. We will even behave differently around people we feel are going through "tough times," such as being fired, getting divorced, or losing a member of their family.

Really unpleasant things can and will happen to us in our lives, like getting fired, getting divorced, or having a close member of our family die. These are not situations we wish upon ourselves, but it does no good to dwell overly long on the injustice of it. Sorrow and grief are natural feelings, as are feelings of resentment, but holding on to any of these feelings for month after month or year after year doesn't help us feel more successful or satisfied in our lives. We can actually damage ourselves further over longer periods of time by getting stuck emotionally in places we feel we've been wronged or hurt. It's damaging to our lives to continue to harbor grudges and feelings of resentment toward others, since it blocks us from moving on. Time spent grumbling about things or people who have made our lives difficult starts to become time wasted. It's much more productive to recognize what we love about our lives, and focus more time and energy on improving our lives accordingly. People who personalize and internalize bad experiences and then choose to not get over them can remain energetically stuck for a long time. Constant complaints and grumblings can become self-fulfilling prophecies, or negative wheedling thoughts that continually look for "what's wrong" with any situation. Such continual criticism doesn't allow us to choose the healthiest ways to respond to future situations, because we're already investing so much energy and attention in discovering what's less than perfect in life.

The best defense against damaging yourself and others with negative feelings and attitudes is to look for the positive in every situation. Your attitude makes a tremendous difference in transforming how you behave, which in turn makes an enormous difference in the future. Remember the times you've felt really successful, inspired, and proud of your accomplishments. Think about one of those times in detail, and consider the way you felt when your life was going really well. Don't worry what happened after that moment of glory; just focus on the joy you felt at that time. You can feel that joy again, in some new way in your life. You can accept the challenges in your life as opportunities for continuing growth, and find renewed enthusiasm.

Even times of great turmoil can bring a sense of fulfillment when we remember how much we *need* these experiences! Losing a job gives me the chance to try something I *really* love doing, and ending a relationship gives me a chance to discover who I am when I'm by myself. Every change is a new opportunity to find another piece of myself and find what brings the most joy and satisfaction in living.

Shifting Reality Exercises

Releasing a Wish and a Prayer

If you could make just one wish right now to make your life and this world a more wonderful place, what would it be? Think of what you most dearly desire, and imagine that it could actually be possible.

If what you are wishing for is something you can realistically get involved with in your life, take a moment to write down your wish or prayer in the form of a goal you can work to achieve.

If your wish or prayer seems to be outside the range of your ability to take any action, make sure that it meets these criteria, and is: felt truly from love; inspired with passion; consciously composed and focused; and free of expectations, doubt, anger, and fear. Set it free ... imagine it as a bird or butterfly you release, feeling how much you love it as you watch it fly away.

Being Time

You can experience time more actively by imagining you *are* time. You can feel this by considering the past-present-future structure inherent in all moments. Choose one part of this structure to focus your attention on, and observe what happens. If you focus on the present, you will notice that suddenly you are no longer in the present, because time has moved on. Return your attention to the present, and notice how once again you find yourself in a new set of past-present-future times. As you practice this repeatedly, you will discover a deeper truth of time and how to feel conscious within time. When you feel yourself tracking the present moment, notice how it feels. Do you feel like you are "stepping" between each present moment, or is time flowing through you?

Feeling Successful

Think about a time in your life you were most delighted and proud of what you'd accomplished. Take yourself back in time to be there again right now, feeling the joy of that happy moment as if for the first time! Recall as many details about this successful moment in your life as possible, and write those memories down on a piece of paper.

Think about what you were feeling that felt so good at that time, and specifically what qualities in yourself you were most pleased and surprised to be experiencing. Write down those qualities you embodied that make that moment in time such a pleasure to recollect.

Now imagine yourself at some time in the future, feeling very happy and proud of what you've accomplished. Visualize where you are, who you're with, and what you've done that you're so happy about. Imagine the overall feeling of joy in this moment, as well as any particular details, and write this down using the present tense. When you visualize your future and believe that you will be there, you identify a reality you can move toward.

CHAPTER 5

Allowing Reality Shifts

Nothing is too good to be true

Allowing reality shift experiences into our lives is a matter of opening our sense of self to a more loving, less fearful state of awareness. Our egos often become preoccupied with protecting us from perceived harm, creating defense systems that often constrain us to narrow paths of possibility. Such habitually defensive ways of thinking can block our ability to perceive reality shifts. People who witness reality shifts are emotionally energized with minds open to such new experiences.

Fearfulness and anger are not expansive emotions that allow us greater range for experiencing joy; in fact, they tend to shut out the possibility of joy. If you wish to experience more enjoyable possibilities in your life, you can choose to open your mind and heart and let go of constraining and limiting beliefs, behaviors and attitudes. If you want to feel joy and delight, allow yourself room for those experiences.

Open Yourself to Change

Life is a journey, not a destination

Reality shifts help me realize that many more possibilities exist than we are typically aware of. If a woman can be walking down the street towards me one minute and be gone the next, I've seen a vivid demonstration of the universe's infinite array of choices. We make choices about whether or not to go for a walk, and whether or not we become more conscious about how we live and interact with the universe.

Even though we all are in the midst of changing every day, most of us resist making conscious changes. We prefer to believe we've already made enough changes, we don't need to change, we'll change later, or we can't change—so there's no point in thinking about it. We also might feel our life is not under our control, that we behave as we do because we're not responsible for our attitudes, actions and beliefs.

The truth is that each one of us can be fully responsive and responsible, and it usually takes less energy to change than it does to fight changes. We may or may not be able to control what others do, but we can always control how we respond to what is going on around us. We can choose to view ourselves as struggling, or we can gain a higher perspective of our life, and trust we'll receive exactly what we need. Life can be viewed as flowing and moving, much like a river. When we allow ourselves to change, life carries us swiftly and surely past difficult rapids in our lives, and onward to living a life we can better enjoy.

To gain a better appreciation for just how good change can be for you, take a moment to think about how you've changed in the past ten years. Consider things you've discussed with friends recently, and imagine having those same discussions ten years ago. Chances are, you're a very different person than you were just ten years earlier. Think about what you'd like to be feeling and doing ten years from now ... and imagine that you are shifting reality every moment, to bring yourself to the future you most desire.

When you think about changes you've made in the past, consider how much easier transitions could have been if you'd spent less emotional energy resisting, and had relaxed and trusted inspiration. Your favorite memories likely have to do with choices you made that stretched you beyond what you'd previously experienced. Such choices are exhilarating… and a bit scary. Our greatest joys in life are usually associated with taking risks that work out well; and emotionally, risk-taking is greatest in our relationships with family and friends.

Guided by Intention

Reality shifts become possible when we open our minds to the idea that reality is fluid, and not limited to our particular beliefs or boundaries. In other words, entirely surprising and delightful new experiences can enter our lives when we allow and invite them. I'm thankful my belief system and mindset is flexible enough to allow me to experience amazing reality shifts. It's quite probable that people with different sets of intentions will be able to witness different kinds of life experiences, and some people with no interest in "popping the bubble" and opening the boundaries of their beliefs won't consciously experience reality shifts.

Allowing for the possibility that reality can shift and feeling excited about experiencing reality shifts is a sufficient intention to bring such experiences to you. My friend, Helen, noticed when she had the intention to experience reality shifting, she suddenly began noticing things changing in small ways. The lettering on business signs in downtown Oakland where she worked would be different when she walked past them a few minutes later; the words would be slightly different, or the lettering size and style would change.

My friend Lisa feels open to seeing miracles related to healings ... as well as other kinds of miracles. She has experienced these miracles in healing members of her family who became very sick and were hospitalized in 1996, and in January 1998, she also saw an image of the Blessed Virgin Mary in the pose of Our Lady of Guadelupe in a pine tree.

If you wish to share these sorts of experiences, you can intend to do so and discover reality shifting happens more often for you, too. Having a shared experience of reality shifts with friends is wonderful, because it's so much fun to share perspectives and insights. Experiencing shifting reality alone is enjoyable for me as well, because life then takes on a marvelous dreamlike feeling as I notice objects appearing, disappearing and changing around me. I *much* prefer to share this waking dream, because I love the exchange of feelings and ideas.

You can intend that your perception of reality shifts will be enhanced, and find your perceptions become keener as a result of wishing for this to be so. Perception has three components: the *perceiver*, an *object*, and a *context*. These three are so interwoven that we can't accurately analyze one apart from the others. We can improve our perceptions by taking into account the need to make perceptual adjustments as any of these components vary. Because our perceptions are personal and subjective, they are subject to error. Experts in the field of perception find that some general characteristics of people with exceptional powers of perception are that they are: *intelligent, open-minded* and aware of their own shortcomings, *non-authoritarian* (not overly controlling of others), and that they *lack expectations*. While we may or may not have much control over increasing our intelligence, we can improve all the other factors that increase perception by becoming more honest, open-minded, and non-controlling.

My main intention is to live my life as truly to love, honesty, and integrity as possible. There's a good chance that the honesty part of my intention triggers "behind the scenes" glimpses of reality moving around fluidly, while my desire for integrity and love helps ensure that I share these miraculous experiences with others in ways that help me see how we are all connected—or as the Mayans say, "I am another yourself."

Open Your Mind

If you'd like to experience reality shifts, what do you need to do? It's simple. Tell yourself you will now be conscious of reality shifts appearing in your life, and feel how deeply you truly desire this. People tend to see what they expect to see and what they pay attention to. People who encourage and expect reality shifts are much more open to experiencing whatever reality may bring them. When you allow for joy and love within yourself, you also allow for joy and love to show itself in the world around you every day.

An open mind is free from feeling we must choose between dualities such as right and wrong, light and dark, black and white, on and off, good and bad, yin and yang. An open mind does not judge some things to be intrinsically worse or better than others. We need not ignore or suppress our emotions, because all feelings are equally valid for helping us understand how to love and care for ourselves as we truly are. With increased awareness of how we function, we can free ourselves from habitual patterns, and find better ways to express our thoughts and emotions.

Our egos can deceive us into believing we aren't the ones

who are angry and fearful—it's *other people* who do bad things to us. It's easier to start by looking at other people, seeing how they can obviously benefit from being less angry and worried. We can notice that what we find exasperating about others may be close to what we are doing. When we are honest with ourselves we begin to see how we are often angry and worried, and how such feelings shut down the range of possibilities in our lives.

It's easier for me to live a less angry and fearful life when I allow myself the possibility of feeling all emotions while remembering I am *choosing* to feel what I feel. Nobody is *making* me feel bad, or making me feel worried or angry. Situations may be frustrating and annoying, but I am free in every moment to feel exactly how I choose. I am also free to choose how I wish to express my feelings. What I choose to feel and how I communicate what I feel is, in fact, what I choose to be.

Reality shifts tend to occur at moments of extreme emotion. Some people notice reality shift at tense times, although I don't prefer that. My favorite way to experience reality shifts is to reach and maintain a relaxed, open, ecstatic, loving and energized state of mind. This state of mind can be reached through relaxation, meditation, or simply opening oneself fully to feeling love. I've noticed all sorts of wonderful reality shifts in this frame of mind. Life feels most magical and wonderful, and all things seem possible. I literally *feel* vibrant—I get a sense of energy flowing in and around me at a very high rate of vibration.

Open Your Heart

Take the id out of intimidate to get intimate

We can best meet our needs when we are conscious of them, and when we are compassionate toward ourselves. For those who wish to heal Gaia, the interrelated ecosystem that is Earth, there is no better way to do so than learning to love ourselves. Love has the power to heal, and love is the only thing worth living for. When we remember who and what we most truly love, we remember who we truly are.

One of the most effective ways to keep an open heart is to speak from the heart. Speaking from the heart requires that we *feel* consciousness in our heart. Most westerners speak from their heads ... sharing facts, details, and information ... while masking feelings. Heart consciousness is just as intelligent as head consciousness. In fact, when we live according to our heart, life feels more fulfilling and rewarding. When a person dies, and looks back on his life, he surely won't care so much about what he owns, facts he knows, or his competence and skill. These things will only have significance to the degree he really cares with all his heart about something or someone.

Many of us live inside rigid, protective boundaries of beliefs—our egos—that give us a sense of identifying with our most limited experience of self. This protective boundary is like a suit of armor that protects us as long as nobody "pushes our buttons" and says or does something that triggers memories of past unpleasant interactions we then overlay atop current experiences. This protective, rigid belief boundary is a bit like the shell of chrysalis that protects a caterpillar as it metamorphosizes into a butterfly. The armor or chrysalis is formed by a summary of our beliefs about what is possible for us to give and receive, as well as what we anticipate might happen next in our lives. Emotions of anger and fear make these shells rigid and hard, while love has a flexible, yielding and expansive effect.

It's satisfying to our egos to show off our best side, look our best, and talk a good talk ... but if this act isn't based on what genuinely inspires and motivates us, we'll rarely excite or inspire others, let alone ourselves. If we don't take the risk of showing who we are beneath our masks, we won't have the most fulfilling kinds of relationships with other people, the universe, or ourselves.

Life lived inside masks or armor protects us from feeling *everything* that makes life worth living. It's much more difficult to feel sunshine, fresh breezes, and soft grass between our toes. Life under masks or armor is much less than ideal. Fear doesn't bring out the best in life—love does. People tend to be more honest with a person who is objective, open, self-aware, and non-authoritarian. Few people will be totally honest and open with someone who's still dressed in attitudes of battle attire ... no matter how many questions they ask, or how they plead for you to tell them your secrets! Intimacy is a reciprocal gift of love, and few people will freely give or receive love from those who are so guarded.

Taking the mental armor off is important so there aren't so many things "rattling around" inside and so we can see everything more clearly. The more emotionally naked we can be, the purer our contact will be with others. It's not really possible to have intimacy and touch another's soul without emotional honesty and defense systems down.

Getting past the ego is a bit like deciding to take off a suit of armor we've been wearing for a long time. The armor was reassuring when we felt under attack, and we might worry about being attacked if someone notices we are defenseless.

There is a great strength in being vulnerable and direct. When we interact and communicate with others as if we are at war with them, we tend to get stuck in conflicts. If there is no need to fight, flee or surrender then we don't need to struggle to obtain control over others. Some people talk to everyone as if they are talking to children, using tone of voice, body language and words in manipulative ways. Being vulnerable, self-aware, and conscious combined with directly stating how one feels can be quite disarming to other people, even if they don't seem like they want to cooperate.

To get a sense of how to speak from your heart, try starting your sentences with "I feel ..." and let go of worrying about facts and details when you talk to people you love. An example of speaking from the heart instead of the head is like saying, "I feel left out of what you're doing, and I'd really love to find some way to share more of what really matters with you" instead of saying, "What are you doing this weekend?" The latter question merely serves to conceal the person's true feelings of vulnerability and love, while the first comment is much more revealing about how caring the person really feels.

You can come out of your chrysalis and fly around! Butterflies don't need chrysalises once they're ready to fly, and our spirits do fly. Opening ourselves up to become intimate with others is a way of living more fully true to our spirits ... who really *love* being free. When you live true to your spirit, you soar and expand with joy ... you can find and follow your inspiration and come to your senses. When you're inside a coat of armor, you might not even comprehend that you are being confined ... you might simply feel safe and secure.

Keep communicating with your eternal consciousness (spirit), and know that you can and will change yourself to become what you most love.

Trust Your Higher Self

Trust only love, because only Love honors all life

How do you have faith in your life? What do you trust most? I've found that the only thing I trust is love. In my life, reality shifts through my intentions in harmony with my eternal, all-encompassing consciousness, or spirit. A harmonious relationship with spirit leads me to enjoy my wishes coming true. I feel consistently loved by spirit, so I trust it. Some people have a hard time trusting their higher selves, yet even people who feel hopeless and trapped by circumstances beyond their control can "rise above it all" by trusting love and opening their hearts.

You can learn to trust spirit, too. All it takes is sincere and deep desire to make this connection with yourself, and to start feeling it. This is a key to self-love ... loving the divine spirit within you that can turn your life around. You are an angel deep down; a being of pure light and love. You can love yourself with an adversarial hostile attachment to your total consciousness, but it feels so much better to be unconflicted! I like to experience the feeling that my eternal total consciousness is as much in me as possible, and I am listening to find my highest potential and most enjoyable life paths.

Some people feel it's hard to trust spirit, because their lives keep bringing them challenging situations they hadn't requested. It's easy to feel we have been tricked or trapped or hurt or betrayed somehow. Certainly we did not bring our pain and suffering on ourselves! Surely someone else is responsible, someone else is to blame. If only we had been treated differently, our lives would be so much better. Since spirit knows all, it must have been responsible for getting us into these messes, and not getting us *out* of them!

One night I had an insight into the relationship between spirit and self while I cooked dinner, and watched water begin to boil. I noticed something interesting as water approached the boiling point and little air bubbles started forming on the bottom of the pan. The bubbles forming in hot water reminded me of our human desire for flight. Only gases can "fly," and escape the liquid water in the pan ... that is, only the higher vibration (spirit) component can feel the truest freedom of love. Hot water molecules in the pan get excited and jump around, but their only way to break free of the pan and fly as oxygen and hydrogen gases is to get so hot that they undergo a phase transformation. Just like hot water, we humans need to heat up to excited high vibration states where we vibrate so fast we undergo phase transformations.

We can love with strength, ease, and alacrity by listening to our inner voice of eternal consciousness instead of other people or even our ego. There is no comparison to living life true to inspiration, rather than living to assuage fears or conform to presumed expectations of others.

Observe Your Feelings

It's healthy to feel consciously aware of your own emotions, even if what you are feeling is unhappiness. When you feel sad, you can imagine it's because Spirit is getting your attention ... the message might be something like, "Are you *really* happy now? It doesn't seem so. What do you feel is missing?" There's an ongoing two-way dialogue going on between your material self and spirit and you can hear the message and make the best of every situation. You always have the opportunity to choose to give and receive love and to find and follow inspiration. Sometimes the hardest thing to do is to take the first step and admit you *are* feeling pain ... and that you *can* do something about it.

It's been said there are three primary human emotions: love, fear, and anger. We can choose how we respond to any given situation, and usually we mix fear and anger into the love we share in this world because we are looking back at something that we resent having hurt us in the past, or we are worried and afraid of something hurting us in the future.

When we focus on this present moment and feel how much love is right here and now, we are most fully aligned with our eternal, fully interconnected spiritual consciousness and don't need to feel afraid of how others will react to us being who we are. When we let go of fear and anger, and notice what message these emotions bring us, we can find our direction in life. Our feelings help us know where our inspiration truly lies. If we block ourselves from feeling our emotions, we lose our ability to know our hearts.

We need to let our emotions flow so we can remain open to feeling love in the present moment. One way to free ourselves from feeling stuck in anger and fear is to feel and release these emotions, rather than pushing them down or denying them. All feelings flow freely if we allow them to, and then we don't get stuck in them. Emotional suppression can lead to disease, and isn't good for our health. When we suppress symptoms in our bodies, the underlying problem then goes to the next deeper level; for example, a skin condition that is treated artificially and suppressed there may result in a lung condition, such as asthma.

When we *listen* to all our feelings, even uncomfortable feelings ... and then let them go, we can feel clean and clear inside, like fresh running stream water. Love will flow through us steady and strong, allowing us the freedom to choose what we create in life. The greatest fulfillment comes from finding joy and satisfaction in the immediacy of experience ... right where we are right at this very moment.

What I wanted to do during my time of spiritual awakening in 1994 was to take the feelings of anger I had and catalyze them into heat and light—burning each piece of myself that I was shedding, and learning from watching each piece burn in the fire. It seems to me that at times when I'm feeling love mixed in with anger I can learn a lot. The anger helps me find direction and focus if I listen to what it shows me and then let go of it, and the love fuels my passion. The combination of these two primary emotions brings me focus and drive to find resolution and harmony amongst all the conflicts that my life is built upon.

I've often wondered why people are so afraid of love. Why be so afraid of feeling vulnerable, authentic, and conscious of being here right now? We think if we hide ourselves and how we truly feel, we might escape criticism and attack. Sometimes we don't want to look at our real feelings, because they embarrass us. We also don't want others to know how we feel, because we might then feel vulnerable to what they think or say about us. While some of our desire to remain protected is healthy, it's also worth noting that if we don't show ourselves to anyone, we are not likely to get to know who we truly are.

I grow a lot when I feel embarrassed. The feeling of embarrassment signals to me I've let my guard down, and such vulnerability feels nerve-wracking. When I take a chance, and try something new, I'm experimenting with interacting in ways I've never tried before. I used to think that this feeling of embarrassment was something to avoid, but now I see how things that used to embarrass me, like feeling concerned about what other people think, don't worry me anymore. It's like noticing I'm out there in the great wide open, with no armor on! Yes, I feel vulnerable and exposed ... but if I don't take that hot, stuffy junk off, I'll never feel sunshine or breezes on my skin. I'd rather be slightly embarrassed and emotionally naked than live confined by anger or fears.

One of my favorite ways to open my mind to fullest experience is to sit and watch the world go past, observing the passing of thoughts without bothering to silence them. Sometimes I write them down to help release them; writing a few pages of passing thoughts every day can be an incredibly freeing experience. I witness each passing thought, without identifying them. This is the foundation of most meditations… a way to keep one's mind clear with awareness that thoughts keep passing through, but not giving them attention. Thoughts feed on attention. If you tend to one, that leads to another thought, and another. Remember to not concern yourself with the small stuff ... and it's all small stuff.

Accept & Forgive

"We cannot change anything unless we accept it."
—*Carl Jung*

The reality we choose to accept is the one our eternally connected consciousness, or spirit, feels we most need to experience ... and we can change which experience we choose to accept by opening our hearts more fully and moving our consciousness to our hearts and out of our heads. When our hearts open to feel love, we can better hear messages that are coming through for us, and become more aware of why our lives are the way they are. This simple acceptance of oneself and life is the gateway to feeling great joy, because acceptance is an essential form of honesty and an absolute requirement for growth, clear communication and fulfillment.

I can physically *feel* when I'm open ... it feels like the wind blows freely right through me, cooling me off all the way through—and the sun shines fully into my heart, with no constriction or tension to block it. I feel most open when accepting and forgiving hurtful things people do. Releasing my first reaction to judge or condemn releases me from feeling tense and taut in my body. When I feel accepting, my heart relaxes. When I feel forgiving, my heart expands. When my body feels relaxed, I feel open to experiencing love.

Obviously, there are difficult situations in life that require one to be vigilant, assertive, and aware of ways to look after one's self interests, especially when it seems that others are not. It is possible to accept that we cannot control what others do, and so we may as well accept that. We can draw boundaries of what we allow in our presence, and we can do that with strength from feeling Love flowing through us.

People who are really good at "pushing our buttons" usually have some very valuable lessons to teach us about what we are unconscious of in our own behavior. The initial feelings we may have of fear or anger are keys reminding us that there's something here that *we ourselves* need to work on. When we remember to take the experience as a lesson, we can let go of anger and fear, and then it's possible to accept the way things are and what we can't change ... and forgive those that seem to be making things so unnecessarily difficult for us. We can then relax and expand our hearts and minds.

When I get upset with someone who is doing something painful and hurtful, I ask myself, "Is this person being the *very best* he or she can be?" Usually, the answer is surprisingly, "Yes!" Stepping back from the situation enough to gain the perspective that we really are doing the best we can is soothing, and then I almost always find it much easier to let go of outrage and righteous indignation. Shifting my attitude from feeling wronged to feeling acceptance and forgiveness instantly transforms the entire situation.

Bless Your Experience

> *"It is the denial of death that is partially responsible for people living empty, purposeless lives ... for when you live as if you'll live forever, it becomes too easy to postpone the things you know that you must do."*
> *– Elisabeth Kubler-Ross*

One of the most powerful things we can do to improve the overall quality of our lives is to go beyond simply accepting our lives, and bless our situations and ourselves. Starting each day by considering what we are most grateful and appreciative for goes a long ways towards increasing the amount of inspiration we have for the rest of that day! We really *can* appreciate what we have before it's gone.

It's easier to feel thankful when your life is going well, but making time to consider what you are *truly* grateful for is one of the best ways to strengthen it's presence in your life at all times, including times of conflict or stress.

I had a marvelous lesson in remembering to feel blessings even in the face of great loss when a very dear friend of mine died. I had known this friend for eleven years, and felt a deep spiritual connection with him, sharing insights and feelings on long walks.

Celebrate Life

When my dear friend, John, died in February 1998, I had a clear feeling that his death was something his spirit knew all along was going to happen. In retrospect many amazing coincidences became clear that transpired over the last few weeks and months of his life. He phoned many of his closest friends the last week before he died, making arrangements to get together, as if some part of him knew it would be the last chance.

On the Ash Wednesday that John died, my younger daughter begged me to buy her a wooden jointed snake pen. I usually respond to such requests by saying, "I'll remember this for your birthday," which I started to say, but then heard some little voice ask me, "Why not?" So I said, "Why not!" and bought one for both my daughters, even though there was no price tag attached to the pen. It is very unusual for me to buy something so spur-of the moment, and I told my daughter that it was an unbirthday present. That evening, I asked my husband to make a cake for all of us, and I made the frosting and decorated it ... this is also something I'd never before done. I called it our unbirthday cake, and after we'd eaten that and I was taking a bath I got a phone call from Highland Hospital in Oakland saying my friend had died. I realized in retrospect that buying toys impulsively and celebrating the daily joys of living is *exactly* what my friend would wish me to do, so of course I was celebrating life for "no reason" on the day I heard the news of his death. My friend had once told me that when he died he wished his friends would remember him by celebrating life instead of mourning his death.

Any doubts about the significance of John's presence in my life were completely cleared away when he died. I was amazed to come to his house for the day of his memorial service and find his young son joyously opening the front door for us and saying, "Come on inside! We're having a party!" Guests brought photos and letters remembering this incredibly loving man, that his son might one day discover how much his father meant to so many people. Hundreds of people flowed inside and outside the house, filling and overflowing it with their laughter, tears, and embraces. The shared love we all felt for this man was such a powerful feeling that it didn't surprise me in the slightest when his son tried to release helium balloons to represent his father's spirit's return home ... and some balloons got stuck in the branches of a tree. It was as if my friend wanted to be present in spirit for this gathering of most dearly loved friends and family.

When I went to John's memorial service, I returned the movie, "Fluke" my friend had insisted we borrow the last time I saw him before he died. This movie tells a story about a boy's dad dying, and the wife and boy finding a dog who embodies the dead father's spirit. My friend's widow then told me she had been planning to get a dog for her son sometime soon.

John's widow told me she'd told her five-year-old son his dad was dead, and he "just doesn't get it." I told her my five-year-old daughter didn't seem to understand what death means either. I'd told my daughters, "The good thing about my friend being dead is that now he's an angel, and he won't waste any of his energy on things that don't matter, so he's always with you." There was a pause ... then a little voice from the bottom bunk bed asked, "What's the *bad* thing?"

    Remembering to bless what is dearest to us is the best way to remember who we are and what we care most about, even in times of sorrow or struggle. Celebrating our blessings is the greatest gift we can give ourselves, because appreciating what we love and showing that gratitude naturally brings more of what we love to us.
    My friend's death was a wake-up call to me that dared me to honestly assess my life and ask myself, "How *truly* am I living my life for me? How *authentically* am I expressing myself, instead of betraying myself or holding myself back from being all I most cherish and adore?" These questions give me my greatest challenge and my greatest opportunity. I began to feel many ways I have been stuck in habitual ruts, often thinking someone or something else was the cause of it. I know I can become what I most love, and discover the ultimate ecstasy within my heart. When I open my heart, I feel heaven on Earth.

Once you decide you are ready to open yourself to seeing reality shift, you may wonder how to begin. Besides simply being open to witnessing reality shifts, you can wish or pray for them. Answered prayers are shifts in reality; they are the miracles we hope for on behalf of ourselves and those we love. Another thing we can do to help experience reality shifts and also enjoy life to the fullest is to integrate our awareness more fully between body, mind, and senses.

Integrate Body, Mind, and Senses

> *"Now is the time for all good men to come to."*
> —Walt Kelly

We are sensual beings with incredible brainpower who often choose to "make sense" rather than "come to our senses." When we let go of expectations, we can clearly sense our world and discover the beauty of experiencing what is here, rather than "carving out" conceptualizations of the world in images, symbols, and concepts. Allowing ourselves direct experience brings us a wealth of appreciation for everything. When we come to our senses, we can most fully enjoy life.

Few people today in the Western world feel a sense of inner confidence and fulfillment, regardless how much they own and do. Instead, most of us continually seek approval from outside ourselves. We often feel we need to be more attractive, more successful, more famous, wealthier, more popular, more youthful. We have trouble appreciating the beauty of who and where we are right now when our attention is not focused on appreciating the moment, or when we are preoccupied with what we perceive we lack.

When we still haven't found what we're looking for, we keep searching for happiness by pursuing money, food, cigarettes, alcohol, sex, or new acquisitions. These entertainments rarely fulfill us. Real satisfaction lies within. Integrating our body, mind, and senses re-establishes the inner balance and ecstatic harmony we were born with.

We can choose not to lose our senses. As Tarthang Tulku writes in his book, *Openness Mind,*

"Our problems are in our head and hearts and the solutions to our problems are there as well. Our problems arise because we do not let our hearts and heads work well together—it is as if they lived in two different worlds ... they do not communicate with each other, or meet each other's needs. And when the body and the mind are not sensitive to each other, there can be no real basis for satisfaction.

The bridge between the body and the mind is provided by the senses, some of which are related more closely to the body, some to the mind. Because of this overlap, the senses have the potential to help the body and mind work together naturally. First, however, we must acknowledge our senses and experience them more deeply.

The external pleasures we thought would cultivate our senses have actually dulled them because we have not made full use of them. We usually pass from one experience to another before we know what we are feeling; we are barely able to sense what we experience. We do not give our senses time to develop an experience, or allow our minds and bodies to integrate our feelings.

Our senses are filters through which we perceive our world; when they are dulled, we cannot experience the richness of life, or approach true happiness. In order to touch our senses, we have to contact the feelings of our experience. We need to slow down, to hear and feel the tones and vibrations our feelings are trying to communicate to us; then we can learn how to touch—roughly touch, gently touch. Each sense has physical qualities, but we are not often fully aware of them. We can begin to increase our awareness of our senses by learning to relax and be more open."

Integrating our mind, body, and senses reacquaints us with direct experience and brings us amazing perceptual acuity. We can heighten our sensory awareness to levels most of us aren't aware is possible. Certain tribes in Africa and South America can identify the position of Venus in daytime. A few hundred years ago, many sailors used Venus to navigate by whenever it was above the horizon, *even during the day*. Most people today would need some kind of shading or viewing tool to block the sunshine in order to find Venus in daylight, if they were even willing to attempt such a task.

Hyperacuity is our innate ability to feel heightened sensitivity to environmental stimuli. Researcher Eugene Marais showed that people under hypnosis can recognize differences between apparently identical pieces of blank paper, using minute differences such as small marks, creases, irregularities, and the position of the watermark, which would otherwise go unnoticed. Marais showed in a 1922 study how a hypnotized subject could easily distinguish between twenty apparently identical snail shells, or determine who had handled certain objects by a sense of smell alone. He devised similar experiments to show that humans have an amazing sense of direction, and this finding suggests that the homing instinct and sense of direction of animals is a natural facility that humans often suppress.

While humans may have developed intellect at the expense of sensory ability, we can recover sensory acuity. Some researchers document extraordinary cases of transposition of the senses, such as the cases Cesare Lombroso cited (1836-1909) of seeing through the skin of the ear and nose, and smelling through the chin and heel.

Many doctors are aware that High Sense Perception exists, since they use it! Some healers who feel comfortable using HSP in their diagnoses include: Barbara Brennan, W. Brugh Joy, Dr. Dolores Krieger, Dr. Shafica Karagulla, and Caroline Myss. Karagulla interviewed many medical professionals with HSP, including famous surgeons, professors of medicine, and heads of departments in large hospitals.

Perhaps part of the reason we don't realize how sensory awareness can be heightened is that our senses are so often bombarded that we rarely notice we've lost some sensual acuity. We seldom take time to savor any particular sensory experience ... to relish the way grass feels tickling under our bare feet, the way the surface of water feels in our bathtub when we stroke it from above with our palm, or the way our food and drink tastes as we swallow it slowly and savor its subtle consistency, texture, temperature and flavor. It rarely occurs to us to delight in the way cold air pours out of the refrigerator onto our ankles and toes when we open the door, or the way we sigh quietly when we sit or lie down. We don't need to lose our senses of smell, taste, touch, sight and hearing as we grow older ... we can refine and develop our senses. Recovering sensitivity is a great way to feel fully alive. We can improve our sensitivity at any time in life by appreciating how keen our senses are, and intending that they improve.

An amazing example of someone who did the seemingly impossible by curing his blindness is Meir Schneider, who was born with a number of eye problems including: cataracts, glaucoma, small cornea, strabismus, astigmatism and nystagmus. After five unsuccessful surgeries, he was declared legally blind. At the age of sixteen, Meir began the Bates method vision exercises and gradually gained functional vision. He now has a current unrestricted California driver's license, sees quite well, and teaches people to heal their bodies and improve their vision to the point that wearing glasses is unnecessary. The British writer Aldous Huxley also used Dr. Bates's exercises to recover from a condition of near-blindness.

One of the biggest obstacles to overcome before we come to our senses is our belief that our eyes can never improve, or that presbyopia (or 'middle-age farsightedness') is an unavoidable result of aging. Neither of these beliefs need be true, and an insistence on believing in such limitations can certainly interfere with improving our sensitivity. Actually, one of the keys to improving your ability to see is simply to believe you can see, and relax. Many people notice their vision improves immediately. This has been dramatically proven to work with visual perception, and it may also work with other senses such as hearing, smell, taste, and touch.

Meditate

Set yourself free, and you will release your problems as well.

I gain a sense of inner satisfaction, improved energy, and relaxation by meditating. Everyone naturally meditates when gazing off at the horizon for several minutes, playing a computer game, or washing dishes. There are many ways to meditate, and they all help us experience a simultaneously relaxed and alert state. Some well-documented physiological changes associated with meditation include slowing alpha and theta waves in the brain; decreased oxygen consumption, the elimination of carbon dioxide; reduced heart rate; blood pressure and muscle tone; and increased finger temperature and skin resistance. These physiological changes are associated with the so-called alert hypometabolic state, which some psychologists regard as a fourth state of consciousness. The other three states of consciousness are normal waking consciousness, sleep, and hypnotic trance. Many doctors enthusiastically support regular meditation as a means to reduce the negative effects of stress on our bodies, because meditation is so successful at reducing tension. Becoming familiar with meditative states of "relaxed alertness" is both conducive and necessary for being receptive to living life as a waking dream and experiencing reality shifts in every day life.

    Meditation is a mental activity that involves becoming aware of the ceaseless flow of thoughts and mental impressions, and learning to direct mental attention elsewhere through intention. The specific type of focusing or concentration used varies according to what type of meditation technique is utilized. One end of the meditation spectrum involves holding in mind the idea of nothingness and feeling total passivity or receptivity with the mind as an 'empty vessel', while the other end of the spectrum may involve concentration on a particular chosen theme, mantra or idea. All kinds of meditations are available to help free us of worries and resentments. Tarthang Tulku writes about one meditation technique for relaxing the body and mind in his book, *Openness Mind*:

> *"Our senses are nourished when we become quiet and relaxed. We can experience each sense, savoring its essence. To do this, touch on one aspect of the senses, and then allow the feeling to go farther. As we go to an even deeper level, we can intensify and enjoy the values and the satisfaction to be found there. As different organisms have different structures, so too*

the senses. There are various layers in our experience of them; layers to be revealed when we are relaxed, unhurried, and attentive.

Meditation, which encourages us to develop a listening, a live quality, provides us with a way to explore these layers. Using the tools of mindfulness and concentration, we can learn to root out tenseness and let our energy flow through the whole body. Genuine relaxation is more than having a good time or simply resting; it means going beyond the physical form and opening all the senses completely. To experience this is to take a refreshing shower within our heart.

We can encourage this openness and relaxation by visualizing vast, open space, by thinking of all external objects as well as our bodies as being part of this space, all within the immediate moment. Finally, no barriers remain. What is left is a higher awareness, alive and healing, which gives us warmth and nourishment."

The energy we sometimes notice during meditation has been called many different names throughout history and around the world. It has been known as: prana (Hindu), ka (Egyptian), mana (kahunas), Qi or ch'i (Chinese), dunamis, pneuma (Greek), baraka (Sufi), Jesod (Jewish Cabbalists), fluid of life (alchemists), and wakan or wakouda (Sioux). The ancient Chinese believed that this vital energy force permeated the whole universe, and that the human body receives ch'i both by ingesting food and air and on an etheric level from cosmic influences. You'll notice the influence of meditation in your life, as you feel emotionally healthier, more balanced, and less confused and disappointed. My own meditation technique is portable. I take it with me wherever I am walking, waiting in waiting rooms or in line, or lying down before I fall asleep or when I awake.

Physical Relaxation

Find a time and place to meditate where you are not required to be responsible for other people or things, and you will not be interrupted. You'll need at least twenty minutes for meditation, although you can take longer if you feel you need it.

I start meditations by noticing how I hold my body. I stretch myself to move around like a dancer warming up, then settle into a position of greatest comfort and good posture. Sometimes I meditate sitting on a chair or the ground. At other times I meditate lying down. I also meditate while walking. All these meditations are equally beneficial; the main consideration is that I am relaxed and comfortable.

Start your meditation by doing what most relaxes you. If you feel calmed after a massage, taking a hot bath or listening to music… do what de-stresses you best, so you can better open yourself to the universe.

Ocean Wave Breathing

Breathing is an essential part of meditation. If you can completely ignore your breathing, that's fine, and you don't need to do anything differently. You can work with breath as a tool for observing how there is no separation between inner and outer being. Breathing is a very simple and powerful way to energize yourself in any situation and to feel connected to all that is.

When I observe my breathing, I begin by closing my eyes and stretching my lungs, inhaling as deeply as comfortably possible ... then relaxing and breathing out slowly and deeply with eyes still closed. My breaths do not need to be absolutely regular; I feel them ebb and flow like ocean waves washing up upon the shore.

Listening to each breath, I notice when I inhale all the way that it feels exactly like a wave pulling itself up to full height before it crashes down and washes up onto the sand. I can feel the wave pull itself up to fullest height, just as I can feel my lungs fill with air. I can feel the wave come rolling back in a rush towards the land, reaching as far as it can go. I feel the wave again drawing itself up to full height again as the last wave withdraws from the shore. I can see these waves in my mind's eye, and I attend to my breaths exactly as if I am watching real waves forming and crashing on the beach. I feel my breath exhale like water sparkling on the sand ... and then I feel my breath going back into my lungs again, forming the next wave. I can feel that I am in the ocean, and in the shore, and in each wave.

I sometimes visualize myself breathing in love, strength, and joy and breathing out worry and resentment. Each breath in is a breath of pure love, and every exhalation takes away all my stress and pain. I can inhale health and exhale sickness, or inhale alertness and exhale exhaustion. I notice a tremendous difference when I do this.

Grounding

Once I've physically relaxed my body and my breathing, I next feel myself connecting to the Earth's core in order to ground myself. I feel that I belong on this Earth, and all the burdens I feel can be released into her as I relax myself at the base of my spine. I feel tension slip away as my worries and concerns fall downward, away from me, to this Earth which is large and generous enough to accept all I have to give.

I release all worries, thoughts, concerns, feelings, ideas and anything else that wanders through to just drop down away from me. I don't worry that I'll forget something, or that something needs tending to, or that I need to pay attention to the sorts of things I'm releasing! Anything important will come back again, and there's no need to hang on to it.

This grounding part of meditation feels like a clean, uncluttered place. Anything that comes through falls right out again, leaving a sensation of quiet calmness. This clean, clear place is a stable foundation for inner awareness.

Connecting to Higher Consciousness

Once I'm grounded, I connect myself from the crown of my head to the highest form of Love and Light I can imagine. I feel intense bright, white Love energy flooding me from above ... stimulating every cell in my body with vitality and vibrancy. I continue breathing deeply and slowly like ocean waves, as I feel a sense of tremendous Love filling me from above.

If I wish to raise my level of vibration, I can speak this intention aloud by saying something like:

I am Love.
I am Light.
I am (my name).

This affirmation is a powerful reminder to my body to fully reconnect with my spiritual essence, and can be repeated several times for best effect. I continue soaking in this energy as long as it feels good to do so. Unlimited energy of total love heals, energizes, and is always available. This energy can feel like warmth, light, or a joyous transcendent state of energized awareness that vibrates every cell and atom in one's body. When I feel I've received as much energy as I need, I begin running my energy ... feeling it flow through me, vibrating in and around me.

Running Energy

I run my energy upwards from the base of my spine to my crown chakra. This feels to me like my whole body has been recharged with the Love energy I received, and now I'm activating that energy and feeling the sensation of energy running strongly up my whole body and flowing through me and out of me.

I am not losing energy, but simply allowing it to flow freely through me. As the energy passes through each center of my body (chakra), I feel energized and relaxed with greatly heightened perception.

Sealing the Aura

Envision yourself self-contained and energetically protected—the best defense against psychic attack. Enhancing these boundaries of your being protects your energy body from harm, much as the skin of your physical body protects against infection and disease.

Visualize yourself as a being of energy that extends around your body, imagining the boundaries of this energy body as vibrant, strong, and impenetrable, except by pure love. Reinforce your energy body through intention, feeling increased strength in your aura pushing your hands back away from you. Pay attention to strengthening the aura around your ears, shoulders, back, down your legs, and under your feet.

I love to meditate when I need inspiration, clarity, serenity, and love in my life. Meditation helps me maintain optimal perspective, and frees me from feeling trapped in situations, or required to do things that don't suit me. I realize my unique purpose in life when I meditate and gain a refreshing sense of beauty and value of the life on Earth all around me.

Once we experience expanded senses of awareness, we see that the concept of only being material bodies does not ring true. Meditation brings great feelings of love and awareness of our eternally interconnected total consciousness, and the more relaxed and mindful we become, the more truly inspired we feel. Inspiration is the feeling of love and joy and gratitude for being alive, and it's the energy that powers everything we create in our lives. I *love* seeing immediately powerful results when I feel so energized! I feel I am radiating light and love from my body in all directions, shining as bright as the sun.

Allowing Reality Shifts Exercises

Opening Meditation

Using a meditation technique described in this chapter, or your own favorite way of meditating, meditate with the intention of opening your heart and mind to love.

Fully Appreciate Food

Find a small edible item, such as a nut, piece of rice, or raisin. Spend several minutes seeing, touching, and smelling it. Fully savor the sensory experience of being with this nutritious morsel, rolling it in the palm of your hand, brushing it against your cheeks, and licking it with your tongue. Roll it in your mouth, squeeze it between your teeth, and taste it. Chew it slowly and swallow, feeling every sensation.

Touching Everything

Touch every surface around you, to find something smooth, rough, fuzzy, hard, soft, firm, or pliable. Touch with fingertips, all fingers together, and your palms. Touch to feel something wet, dry, plush, and bumpy. Feel warmth, coolness, curviness, and wispiness. Wake your fingers and toes up to feeling all around you.

Imagine Yourself Alive for the First Time

Take a walk to a natural area where you can be alone in the midst of nature. Find a particularly appealing plant or rock or insect to study, and sit down next to it. Imagine that you are alive and conscious right now for the very first time in a long time. Feel how good the sun and air feel on your skin, and how incredible natural beauty is. Feel the joy of each breath you take, and the miracle that you are here to experience all this.

CHAPTER 6

Feeling Inspired Powers Reality Shifts

*Until you know that life is interesting—and find it so—
you haven't found your soul.
– Geoffrey Fisher*

Inspiration is often considered divine because it comes from consciousness that transcends time and space; it comes from spirit. When we are true to our inspiration, we aspire toward reaching our highest potential. Consciousness responds by changing the physical world. We live in a dynamic universe that is in constant communication with us as we feel our emotions and thoughts in every cell in our bodies. We attract to us what we wish for and focus our attention on, in a continual process of becoming what we think, say, do, and feel. The more harmonious and aligned our conscious and unconscious wishes are with each other, the more obvious our interaction with the universe becomes. I've found I can create reality shifts that are pleasing and beneficial rather than discordant and stressful when I feel inspired by remembering what I'm living for, and feel appreciated for who I am. Reality shifts occur most readily and spectacularly for people who feel energized and alive with love. This energy may feel like love, joy, or warmth in the body, or as very high frequency vibrations. However it feels to you, its effects are unmistakable.

The difference between having energy and inspiration and not having them is tremendous. When I feel enthusiasm and inspiration, I feel a sense of working *with* everything flowing smoothly. The more enthusiastic and joyous I feel about living, the more exciting my life becomes, and the more reality shifts I experience!

Feeling inspired means shaking off habitual approaches to life, and paying better attention to situations and people that raise or drain my energy. The more aware I am of myself and the world around me, the more clearly I see how I am continually choosing how I feel and who I am. If I choose to remain in situations that feel like they sap me of energy, I ask myself, *Why am I doing this?* When I wish I could feel more enthusiastic about my life, the best place to start is by learning who I am right now. When I know myself and honestly observe the patterns and beliefs operating in my life, I feel stronger as my understanding of myself improves. *I am my own greatest resource in changing my life!*

Most of us hide our true identities behind masks we wear to fit in and be accepted in society. I did that for much of my life, and only recently felt it was OK to be how I *really* am and not worry about whether I seem foolish to others. It takes a lot of energy to maintain an illusion of being someone you really aren't. Being true to myself gives me the greatest kind of strength, because in addition to freeing up a lot of emotional energy I'd been using to hide and defend myself, I gain the advantage that when *I* know who I am, other people *can't* "mess up" my life. Once I have a clearer sense of my true identity, I notice the ways I am completely unique and how my uniqueness indicates my life purpose.

Remember Why You're Alive

> *"First, be a perfect animal."*
> *– Henry David Thoreau*

Your spirit wants to know: What turns you on? What do you desire? What are you really living for? Only you can answer these questions. Life would be pretty boring if we didn't pursue our unique areas of interest. When I feel fully alive and thrilled to be right where I am, living a life, I discover what is of the most value to me and can actively change my life by focusing my attention and energy on what is most nourishing for me.

When I feel how deep my desire to be alive really is, I find joy, happiness, love, and ecstasy in every moment. These are tricky emotions to feel all the time, because they often seem so ephemeral, but the truth is that when you wish with all your soul to feel sunshine on your face ... to feel grass beneath your feet ... to see the smile on someone's face ... to touch another living thing ... to hear the sound of wind in the trees or a bird singing ... such simple things bring total bliss! What I sense around me is rich with a vibrancy of surprising, delightful vitality ... the world is intrinsically satisfying to touch, see, hear and taste around me. Even the quality of light in the world is brighter and lighter than ever before!

I love to feel how *awesome* it is to simply be alive and experience life all around me. When I feel this way, it's as if I've just been born. I love to feel so fully alive, seeing the world with new eyes and total appreciation and rapture. One day in March 1997, I saw a doe watching me as I walked along. She stood her ground and gazed at me with deep brown eyes as I walked within ten feet of her. The next day, I went on another walk, thinking of my encounter with the doe, feeling intense ecstasy of being fully alive, and wondering if feeling this way attracts animals and experiences to me. Just as I considered this question, I walked up to a two-foot long garter snake, sunning itself in the trail. Finding this snake felt like the answer to my question is *"YES!"* Any time I fill myself with the ecstasy of being alive, I attract friends to share the experience. The snake didn't hurry to get away, either, just as the deer was in no rush to leave the day before.

If our consciousness, or spirit, desires physical sensations of love and joy, why does it allow bad things to happen? From an eternal point of view, things like death aren't "bad" at all. Neither are many other things we don't care for, and Spirit likes to accommodate our life path experience by bringing us things we can best grow from. Spirit doesn't ask questions like, "Will this be FAIR?" (Nothing is fair), or "Will this HURT?" (Pain gets our attention very well), or "Will this be a PLEASANT experience?" (Unpleasant experiences wake us up to who we are and can really be by helping us notice what we love best in contrast to its absence in our life). Spirit's view can seem strange because it has such a different out-of-time-and-space perspective on life. Life is not about following rules to be what we or someone else thinks is "good," it's about living true to our very highest potential. The higher potentials may seem strange, because they bring with them the fuller realization that all life is interconnected. You can't do something to someone else without in some way doing it to yourself.

The answer to the question, "Why does life have to be so painful, so unfair, so unpleasant?" seems to be that spirit is running the show, and spirit doesn't feel the same way as ego about pain, fairness, and pleasantries. Fortunately, we can intend we want to pay attention to what spirit wants us to hear, with a minimum of pain and unpleasantness and a maximum of love and joy. This intention really works, and can help us change our lives, brightening our future.

It's good to remember that we humans actually are animals! We are healthiest when we give and receive energy gracefully. We have our OWN truth that is Who We Really Are ... and that's best discovered by each of us simply being and caring for our own animal self.

When we take good care of our physical animal nature, the intellectual and emotional parts of life feel better, too. Simply getting enough rest, exercise and eating well can make *worlds* of difference in how good we feel. You can think of your "true self" that lives best by being a perfect animal as spirit in human form—although this spirit is something we tend to be mostly unconscious of. Our physical, human, mortal lives embody our spirit's desire to be right here, right now!

Right from the beginning of our lives, we have some idea who we are, and as we grow up, we build on that emerging concept of self. The thought that shaped my consciousness growing up was the certainty that everyone could read my mind, so I'd best not think anything hurtful about others. In retrospect, I realize that's a rather odd founding thought, yet it was the earliest belief I could recall and I was absolutely certain it was true. I didn't even examine it until I became an adult. This thought is at the very core of who I am ... the seed I grew up from. I see now this is what I would most *hope* to be true, and what I am open to experiencing. It allows me to feel hopeful, positive, and connected in the universe. This idea also inspires me to share my ideas and feelings, so we may all learn together and help lift one another's spirits and consciousness.

Before we have any beliefs, we experience direct knowledge. The absence of a framework for understanding makes any discussion difficult, so our earliest memories are closely related to our earliest beliefs of who we are. One man I know felt he had no right to exist. This thought can lead one to feel very brooding, indeed! Now that he is consciously reconsidering this idea, it sounds ludicrous ... yet it shaped his life up until that transformative point of change.

When you go back even further than your earliest thoughts, you will find a *feeling* of being embraced by Love. This is the *true* founding thought you were created from. The unique nature of how you appreciate and learn about love is the unique path you are living right now. When you remember you *are* love, and truly feel this, your life becomes vibrant, passionate, and inspired as you reconnect to your eternal essence.

If you have trouble remembering ever having been completely unconditionally loved, it's good to consider that it's not too late to experience such feelings. Stella Resnick writes in her book, *The Pleasure Zone*:

> *"Those of us who haven't been held, touched, cuddled, cooed over and approved of for the first years of our lives are not going to feel as secure as those who have. If the need for physical affection and emotional approval are not fulfilled, the emptiness may never go away. Some people try to fill their longings for love by becoming rich and powerful, or through food, drugs, or constantly nurturing others. There is no amount of fame or fortune, however, no compensatory activity, that can ever fill the hole left by the absence of authentic love.*
>
> *Fortunately, there is hope for all of us. Studies show that the missing experiences of childhood can be made up at any age. Our best chance for love and happiness, for those of us who were love-deprived as children, is to find someone who is physically affectionate and loving. Ideally, this person is not only giving but also someone who can teach us how to graciously accept love and return it, something the love-deprived don't ordinarily learn from their parents."*

Most of us are much more familiar with thinking and talking about emotional pain than emotional health, so we often focus on what is bothering us and going wrong, rather than on what we feel grateful for. If our families don't encourage us to communicate feelings of joy and love, we tend to limit our knowledge of the range of joyous feelings possible in life. Most of us answer the question "How are you?" with "Fine," "Good," or "OK" without elaboration. Some of us believe if we suffer enough, somehow our life will eventually get better. Some even take suffering on as a kind of competitive sport, comparing hardships to others in order to prove we sacrifice more, work longer hours, or push ourselves harder than anyone else.

    I was often astonished to come into my office job early in the morning and find someone with bleary eyes, rumpled clothes and beard stubble proudly announcing, "I worked here all night long." I was amazed that people felt so driven to prove themselves at work that they'd sacrifice their personal life so completely. I'd ask, "What did you accomplish?" and discover that those long hours of working through the whole night were often spent fixing mistakes made from working so many hours without a break; and yet they still felt a sense of pride in their self-sacrificial devotion. Another common remark at this office was, "Must be nice," usually made in a sarcastic tone of voice to someone expressing interest in doing something relaxing or recreational. This comment carried the unspoken message, "I don't have the *luxury* to enjoy myself like that." I could see and feel the pain of living sacrificial lives all around me, and I began to wonder how much of this attitude of self-sacrifice I'd internalized.

    To increase self-awareness, I ask myself these questions:

> If anything is possible ... what does my heart most desire?
> What am I living for?
> Where is my heart right now?
> Where does my heart long to be?
> What brings me the greatest joy?

    I get slightly different answers each time I contemplate these questions. Being aware of what I most love, and learning to recognize my unique interests and joys is a powerful way of feeling truly inspired.

Each of us relates to the universe in a completely unique way. No other person can understand you the way you do, although some people may be able to understand parts of you. As you reframe your sense of self by paying attention to different parts of you, you create that sense of self, and physically embody and empower those feelings in your life.

There is something very sacred in the way you know yourself better than anyone else. Fred Alan Wolf discusses how this secret self-knowledge is sacred in his book, *The Spiritual Universe*:

> *"What enables you to identify with your body and keeps you apart from the outside world is not physical space or time, but knowledge. As long as you secretly know something about yourself that the outside world at large does not know, namely, your connection to the oversoul, you are uniquely connected with your sacred spirit. This secret knowledge identifies you and separates you from all others, but not from your soul. Your existence as a separate being with individual characteristics arises with or without this knowledge. With the secret knowledge you are aware of your soul. Without this secret knowledge, you are not. ... I ask you to tell me your intimate secrets, and I change you forever when you tell me your answers. Tell something about myself to the world, and I grow more separate from it. I hold the secret knowledge within myself and I merge closer to the universe, to the oversoul! This merger/separation is redefined every time I consider who I am and every time I accept answers from the outside world that identify me as some image and disrupt the internal and eternal harmony of my soul and self dialogue. ... What we say to one another, and how we say it, is more important than we ever could have believed ..."*

We instinctively feel the sacred nature of what we hold within our hearts. Some of what I know about my path in life may be an image or symbol, or music I hear, or a feeling. This secret, sacred knowledge is difficult to explain or share with others because it is such an elemental part of my own identity. We can begin to see ourselves in our interactions with others, as we discover our true purpose, our passion, and our path. This process of discovery can, and usually does, take a lifetime.

When people don't fully comprehend who I am, I recognize the unique individuality I possess that sets me apart. When I feel the confidence to nurture these parts of myself that are so different from others, I discover my unique purpose in life based on who I really am.

Discover Your Purpose

*"To love is always to feel the opening,
to hold the wound always open."*
— Novalis

Many religions and spiritual teachings remind us that we identify with being our physical bodies and personalities more than our spiritual eternally conscious nature. In other words, at various times throughout a given day, I may feel I am "the exhausted parent," "the devoted daughter," or "the competent corporate employee." These parts of my personality are roles I play that mask over my true self. Many of us know we are much, much, more than a cartoon caricature of a person, and we deeply desire to be free to express more of who we are.

Part of the problem with our ego identification is that we often run our lives more or less on autopilot with habitual patterns or personalities taking over for us, while our spiritual self feels like it's asleep. Much of our lives feel routine as we play our roles, and we become a bit mechanical ourselves in response to what we feel is a need for us to be stable, responsible, and to conform to what's expected. It feels soothing for a time to know we can continue wearing a persona, as we continue to play our part the best we can ... but at some point, we may feel depressed or desperate to feel authenticity in our lives. We often like to feel we fit in to society and are socially approved of when we follow the suggestions of others ... yet this very suggestibility is a form of hypnosis. When we act out of habit rather than inspiration, we are in a trance, sleepwalking through our lives without ever recognizing we're dreaming! We long to feel a fresh flow of inspiration, and a sense of freedom to express our truest feelings and pursue our deepest desires.

Your primary personality strengths can get in your way of finding your true spiritual purpose. Your life may feel to you like it's under complete control, for example, but that very sense of well-ordered control may sabotage your ability to hear what the universe is saying to you. Whereas your ego and personality are weighed down with "shoulds," "musts," and "oughts," your spiritual self is light and free. You can recognize your inner spiritual identity because it feels inspired, refreshing, and exciting to you ... not worried or resentful.

You can shift your sense of identity when you remember how much more you are than the physical body that follows habitual schedules and routine activities. You were born with a spiritual purpose for your life, and your purpose still exists, even though you may not recall exactly what it is. You can regain a sense of spiritual identity by considering and writing down examples from your own life of insights from:

- Mystical & Spiritual Experiences
- Dreams
- Meditation

You can look at these messages from your spirit and find a central unifying feeling that shows you your own unique spiritual purpose. You may feel like a "healer," a "motivator," a "craftsman," a "teacher," or a "harmonizer." When you consider a word that all of your experiences point toward, that word helps you to contemplate a new sense of identity, and to begin to explore the possibility of living your life in harmony with those feelings. Consider things you most love doing and being, and you're on the right track for discovering your innermost passions. You may find several spiritual purposes, and enjoy trying them out to discover which ones feel best.

The path that's best for me *feels* best for me. Whatever I strongly identify with feels like a *source* of energy, rather than a *drain* of energy. My life purpose turns me on and brings me unmistakable feelings of joy and enthusiasm! I visualize myself doing what I enjoy, and picture myself several years from now in my new life. I get a sense of how that life feels to me, and what's different about it from the life I live now.

When I'm really on track with my spirit's purpose, there are still obstacles to overcome and challenges to face, but also lots of inspiring coincidences, synchronicities and bursts of joy and exhilaration. I pay attention to signals from the universe that smooth the way for me to continue on a given path. I notice how I feel emotionally and physically. I notice how I feel about my dreams and about what other people say to me. As Mark Thurston writes in his book, *Discovering Your Soul's Purpose*:

> "The surest sign that an hypothesis isn't right for your soul's mission is not so much the presence of obstacles as it is the lack of any positive reinforcement signs."

I know I'm on my path when I feel a sense of thrilling, exciting, and inspiring positive reinforcement! Some paths look promising from a logical perspective, but feel like dead ends because they don't inspire. More than anything else, love shows the way. Feeling a sense of love is the truest way to know I am aligned with all of spirit and myself. I trust my feelings, and trust that love will find me. It will.

Maintain Supportive Relationships

Cultivate harmonious friendships

As I contemplate the life I wish to create, I occasionally find people are not entirely supportive of my sense of purpose. I sometimes feel as soon as I discover something I really love, some people respond negatively. We co-create reality with everyone around us, so others can and sometimes do dampen our enthusiasm and suppress desires they don't approve of. People can also boost our spirits and help us feel better about pursuing our dreams, by reassuring us with loving support. It may seem obvious, but it is important to remember you *need* supportive relationships in your life.

People who feel they are not living true to their heart's desire often fear others who are following their inspiration, and they can be "wet blankets" tossing emotional buckets of ice water when they feel threatened! When I don't feel strong enough to ignore and disregard this icy treatment, I remember it's best to distance myself from such influences. I pay more attention to people who offer me continuous, unconditional support, and less to those who negatively over-criticize. By listening to people who know me, support me, and cooperate with me I can keep feeling highly inspired and energized.

There have been times when I've longed so deeply for a happier work or home situation I would have *jumped* out of my life into a more enjoyable one if I could have! I ached for a reality shift of great magnitude to magically transport me to a happier place. As many miracles as I've witnessed, I haven't yet been able to snap my fingers or wiggle my nose and instantaneously transform uncomfortable life situations into ones of love and joy. I've had to face unpleasant people and difficult situations directly. I have had to tell my boss, my employees, my children, my parents, or my lover that I didn't feel things were going well, and that changes were needed.

These challenging times taught me that difficult situations and unpleasant people were not the problem. They were the messengers, giving me clues as to what I was allowing to drain energy in my life. When I attempted to avoid situations, I've found they would simply resurface again with a new person ... until I got the message, and comprehended *what I had been allowing* to drain my energy.

I once worked for a manager that everyone in my group found extremely stressful to work for, including me. I slept fitfully at night, and felt great anxiety in my stomach when I drove in to work each morning. Our group met at one staff meeting where our manager arrived late, and before she arrived, we began discussing our individual stress-related health disorders ranging from insomnia to stomach ulcers to headaches. Our symptoms were different, but we all noticed a huge change for the worse in our health since our manager had begun managing our group. Our group selected me to be the one to go talk to the Personnel department about this situation, and our general hope was that the Personnel department would then do something about it.

I was deeply troubled to discover that the Personnel manager's idea of a solution to our problem was to have me be the one to talk directly to our manager ... since as he put it, "If *you* are having a problem with a manager, this is a *very* serious problem!" I was known as a hard-working, productive employee who didn't often complain. I got my work done quickly and gracefully, even when working with extremely challenging situations and people. I had hoped Personnel would appreciate our problem to be so severe that they would talk directly to our manager, sparing us the additional strain and hardship of facing our tormentor. Unfortunately, this was not to be the case. I was asked to confront our manager, and I was scared to tell her how I really felt.

I found the courage to meet with my manager, realizing that my whole department supported me and felt the same way I did, and the worst thing that could happen would be I would request a transfer, or seek employment elsewhere. I was surprised to find my manager listening intently as I told her about our concerns, and she made gradual improvements from then on. The main problem our department experienced was a lack of communication; the employees felt a greater need for empathy from our boss than she could express.

I had a need to learn to face someone who had great difficulty empathizing with others, and this message keeps recurring in my life with new faces until I learn to speak of my needs directly to those who have difficulty listening. It is easier to work and live with caring, empathetic people, because they are willing to love and accept us as we are and to offer support without being possessive, jealous, manipulative, competitive, anxious, defensive, controlling, or demanding.

Healthy supportive relationships are ones in which we feel free to be who we are and stay true to our own inspiration, without giving up our sense of joy, vitality, enthusiasm and excitement. Healthy relationships allow us to express our feelings and especially encourage us to grow and evolve as we rediscover that there really *is* something more about us! When I allow myself to continually feel like I am becoming *more* who I most wish to be, and know that I am the one who decides what that feels like, I can allow others this freedom as well.

Appreciate Yourself

> *There's no need for panic, no need for alarm.*
> *You've got talent, and you've got charm.*
> *Just what you want to be you'll be in the end*
> *when you learn how to be your own best friend.*

My most supportive relationship isn't with another person—it's with myself. Nobody knows what I've been through, what I'm sensing, or how I feel exactly like me. Only I can truly understand my strengths and commitments in life. It's wonderful to feel love and encouragement from others, but nothing surpasses my own intuition and counsel that is uniquely suited to me. The more supportive I am for myself, the stronger I become, walking side-by-side with those I love, rather than leaning on them for support.

I strengthen my sense of self-identity and confidence by making time to spend with myself regularly on a daily or weekly basis. I set aside some time at the beginning or end of my day when I can relax with myself, away from the influence of other people. When I regularly treat myself with love and kindness, I find it *much* easier to care for others with compassion and love. I talk and listen to myself, by writing and later reading my thoughts and feelings in a journal. I invigorate myself by walking, running, dancing, bike riding, tree and rock climbing, and swimming outdoors. I delight my senses by cooking my favorite foods, wearing my favorite clothes, and listening and dancing to my favorite music. I meditate to experience the feeling of universal pure love. When I find joy in life, more joy comes to me.

I expand my capacity for delight when I allow myself simple pleasures on a daily basis. I stop hanging onto anger, worry, and doubt, since those things undermine my ability to feel joy and love in life. I gradually change my blend of feelings to feeling deserving of love and joy—and happy and satisfied with my life! I make sure my daily life corresponds to my true values, and that I take time to smell the flowers that I grow, to hug the children that I raise, to taste foods I prepare, to touch things I make, and to smile and laugh at everything I find amusing! I even learn to appreciate when "things go wrong," stepping back and looking to see if perhaps there might be *something* amusing to appreciate. Appreciating what gives me pleasure helps me appreciate myself, because nobody else is inspired to care the same way I do for things and people I love most.

The best thing I can do for myself is to stay open to feeling completely loved and loving by being honest, accepting, and compassionate with myself. When I treat myself with as much love as I give my best friends, pets, or favorite toys, I feel more inspired and generous. I take another look at my problems, and discover how they provide much of the beauty of life. Every problem gives me a chance to rediscover what I most care about, and to renew my commitment to my life and myself! Loving attitudes and feelings can always be mine if I allow myself to experience them.

What I do affects how I feel. If I have held inside and locked up most of my true feelings and nature as part of the normal process of conforming to the expectations of my family and society, I can now free myself by becoming mindful about who I am, what I am doing, and what I believe.

Examine Internal Beliefs & Attitudes

> *"A man's destiny, it has been said, is his temper. More truly a man's fortune is in his character."*
> — Ralph Waldo Emerson

Through our thoughts and intentions, we choose where our lives lead us. The things we think to ourselves are constant directions to the universe to support our belief system. Beliefs are confidence in the truth or reliability of something without absolute proof, and we tend to see the entire world through our own set of values and beliefs. Because we view the universe through our belief constructs, we often find ourselves creating and living out self-fulfilling prophecies. We are all powerful spiritual beings who bring resonant thought constructs to us, as if we're striking harmonic chords and other string instruments in this orchestra of life begin to vibrate in resonance with those sound waves.

I see the way people attract what they pay attention to in their self-talk, where they say things ranging all the way from, "What next ... what next?!" before crisis after crisis occurs, to a guilty feeling of "I always mess up everything I work on" as projects tend to fall apart, to "I am so blessed!" as they are showered with love and attention from all around them. I've learned from observing others that feeling blessed brings more blessings, while feeling harassed and victimized brings on more harassment and abuse. People who love to complain about how things are going wrong in their lives are choosing to appreciate how things are "going wrong," rather than what they find wonderful. If I am annoyed and impatient almost constantly, it is not because I am being forced to be annoyed, but because I am choosing to respond to my environment with annoyance and impatience. I choose what I pay attention to, and by attending to some things more than others, I increase the influence of those things in my life. I make time and space for what really matters most to me. This illustrates how we all live in completely different worlds from one another, and why advice for one person can feel so totally useless for someone else.

Attitudes are our emotional responses to people, situations, and things in our environment. We choose whether we greet the world with disappointment, aloofness, frustration, contempt, disdain, or with joy, warmth, acceptance and love. Our attitude is always our choice, and combined with our beliefs, our attitude greatly affects our behavior. When we care more about being right, not being judged to be bad or wrong, and about "winning," we are losing much capacity to find joy in the immediate situation at hand. Harsh self-criticism, regrets about the past and worries about the future all block our ability to feel joy and love in the present moment.

Your attitude is perhaps the most powerful thing you can change to most significantly impact your health and safety. I've seen factories that post reminders to their employees to the effect that "Attitude is Everything," since almost *all* on-the-job accidents are due to employees having negative attitudes while they are working. Traffic schools focus their students' attention on driving attitude, because poor attitudes are the main cause of road accidents. Healing clinics teach their students how to improve attitudes, because diseases tend to flourish with poor attitudes, and vanish with good attitudes.

Criticism in particular has become a habitual activity for most of us. It's easy to get stuck focusing attention at the point where some misfortune has befallen us, and wonder, "*What went wrong?!?,*" without getting past that point. It's healthier to *not* personalize, internalize, or dwell on life's setbacks and mishaps, regardless how serious they seem at the time.

I attended a two-day traffic school program after receiving a speeding ticket in 1998. The goal of this program was to understand how our values and attitudes affect our lives, and how we may change them if we desire. The twenty students in this class talked about their driving histories and how we'd each come to be in traffic school. Our instructor told us about a woman who received *four* tickets on a single day on her twenty-first birthday. She got one on her way to work, one when she drove her coworkers to a birthday lunch in her honor, one going home from work, and the fourth when she went out that evening to celebrate. When we go through stressful times in our lives, we are more vulnerable to increased tickets and accidents because our attitude suffers under stress.

What causes our misfortunes in life is the same thing that causes businesses to fail ... we fail when we encounter events we *believe* we can't handle and move on from. Successful businesses, like successful people, are capable of choosing the most adaptive attitudes for what some people might consider impossible situations, without feeling victimized or limited by external events and influences. Successful people contemplate ways to solve problems in creative new ways ... free from the mental trap of maintaining habitual patterns.

There's a powerful connection between how I explain the setbacks, failures and disappointments in life and whether I feel joyous and energetic, or depressed and exhausted. My optimistic thoughts about how I'll move on to a more joyful life help shift that happy reality to me, because I understand setbacks are temporary and unrelated to my ability to do well in the future.

There have been times I felt I needed to use my anger or fear as a tool for motivating myself. People can rely on worry and anger because those emotions provide an adrenaline rush that propels us into action. We can become addicted to the biochemical rush of adrenaline we get when enraged, usually not noticing we're using emotions of anxiety and outrage to get high on a regular basis. Adrenaline produces a feeling of constantly facing crises and emergencies, when situations might not really be so serious. Adrenaline produces a short-term rush and high, and later leaves us feeling exhausted and wiped out. Adrenaline junkies often don't notice these patterns, because they're so involved believing they really *are* facing crisis after crisis (rather than creating crisis after crisis) in their lives.

If you feel you've been getting adrenaline rushes from anxiety or anger, and wish to try a different way of getting naturally high, consider endorphins instead. Endorphins energize you without depleting you, and also encourage relaxation. You can get endorphins by breathing deeply, taking a hot bath, going for a walk or bike ride, or meditating. Simple pleasures can get you high on endorphins naturally!

I've noticed I can change my attitude in *moments*, which is very fast compared to the time it takes to increase my education, experience, and beliefs. If I'm starting to pay more attention to pointing out what's wrong instead of what's going well, I can start changing that by making sure I say at least one positive thing for every negative remark I make. It's even better when I can manage to say at least four or five positive remarks for every complaint or criticism, because that helps the people around me feel truly appreciated by me and better about themselves and their relationship with me as well.

My attitudes are my responsibility and my choice of how I respond to life. Even habitually chosen attitudes are selected based on feelings, and choosing to feel "how I always feel" in a given situation is a choice. The first step is to acknowledge that the outside world, regardless how frustrating it may be, is not the cause of our thoughts and feelings. We can change our attitudes by considering the possibility that life is full of love, that we are all connected through love, and that even things that seem to be going wrong may actually be blessings in disguise.

The Unseen Hand

There are times in our lives when we race against the clock, against our own expectation of how well we "should" be doing whatever it is that we're doing, and find ourselves falling short of where we wish we were. Things go wrong, and we don't seem to have enough time to do everything we wish we could do. Rarely do we allow anyone, including ourselves, the freedom to make mistakes without inwardly cringing.

At these times in particular it's helpful to ask what I've learned from such an experience, without blaming myself or others for "what went wrong." It helps to consider this trying experience to be a gift from an unseen hand of cosmic consciousness. What appears at first glance to be a terrible mistake or misfortune can actually be a gift in disguise.

Accidentally losing or destroying things *can* be for the best, when we see how this clears space for something entirely new. Needing to redo work we've just done unsatisfactorily can be a gift, because it can allow us to honor the value of the work itself and the company of those who work with us. Being too late to arrive at a destination on time can also be a gift, since it allows us to more fully appreciate our true feelings about missing out, and helps us prioritize what matters most in our lives.

Even disagreements with others can be gifts when they help us consider that each of us makes our own choices in life as to what we believe, what attitude we greet the world with, and how we behave. Every disagreement is a reminder of the freedom that each of has to make our own choices in life.

These times of disappointment can provide gifts from the universe, even though it can be hard to *find* the gift. As a friend of mine says, "I have a barn full of shit, so I just *know* there's got to be a pony in here somewhere!" Life presents us with so many opportunities that we don't need to get hung up on how something has apparently "gone wrong," and realizing this simple truth can revitalize our lives.

Most of us allow our beliefs and attitudes to be molded by external influences, according to expectations of our families, religion, schooling, or culture. We do this so we have a shared basis of reality, and feel we have more in common with those around us. External beliefs become a problem when we feel unable to create the best possible lives for ourselves—because we feel stuck, repressed, and emotionally constrained.

The more honest I am with myself about beliefs that don't serve me well, the better I can initiate positive changes. Chances are, I'll need to face the issues confronting me right now, since avoiding them only delays the inevitable. Before making any changes, I first observe my life. I step back from day-to-day concerns, observing the disappointments and successes for patterns without judging myself. Mistakes and disappointments can actually be the best places to find new ways of thinking and feeling, and more joy and love. There really *aren't* any failures in life, just learning experiences. Life is thus like a work of art that is continually being revised just for the joy of creating. As a work of art, what matters most is the *process*. Reality constantly shifts based on what I think and how I feel about what I pay attention to.

When I consider how beliefs and attitudes affect my every behavior, I wonder how to change them. One excellent way to change beliefs and attitudes is simply letting go of what I've been hanging onto so tightly. Things naturally improve when I don't blame anyone, and when I stop trying to control situations. I can stop holding onto things that need to be free to grow and change, remembering that I need that same freedom. Giving up blaming and attempting to control situations requires that I let go of my fears and cooperate with others, as I open myself to feel more possibilities in life. This can be a better world for everyone when all of us are free to pursue our unique individual inspirations and passions.

I widen my awareness of different beliefs and attitudes by looking at successful people. I notice people are successful when they are aware of more alternatives, and when they carefully consider consequences of choosing between many alternatives. People feel successful and satisfied in their lives when they are open to learning from experience, feeling free to make the best of every situation, no matter how unexpected. Even when things go wrong, successful people roll with the changes, developing themselves while adapting to life situations they didn't foresee.

Forgiveness is the key to finding the freedom to make any choice in our lives, as we realize we are totally responsible for our own lives. Forgiving oneself releases us from the burden of guilt, and forgiving others releases us from the burden of blame. It helps to remember that we are all doing the best we can in our lives to find and follow our inspiration.

Feel Your Passion

> *"Too much of a good thing is WONDERFUL."*
> – Mae West

It's essential for me to live true to my passionate self, rather than attempting to control, sublimate, suppress, ignore or deny it. I get sick and feel depressed when I repress my true enthusiasms ... and I can't totally suppress my feelings, anyway. My passions require me to be much more aware of what I'm doing, so I don't find reality shifting in inexplicable ways according to unconscious desires. I know when I need to recreate myself, because I feel that I can't *stand* the thought of continuing to live the way I have been any longer. The passion I feel to try or do something new is my spirit's invitation to stretch the boundaries of who I believed I was. My passion tells me I am much more than what I believed myself to be.

Carolyn Myss points out in her book, "Why People Don't Heal and How They Can" that we meet opposition when beginning the journey of self-discovery, because the tribe we came from strives to keep members together. Your first task for discovering who you are is to ask where you are going ... and then who will come with you on your journey.

We intuitively know that passionate love shifts reality. The ecstatically transformational force of passionate love has been both sought after and guarded against. As William McNamara says so beautifully in his book, *Mystical Passion*:

> *"Passion is simply life in its most intense vigor. But people are afraid of passion because they are afraid of life. They blame passion for the limits they refuse to vault. Passion is the breakthrough virtue. If passion remains unspent, the limits remain unleveled. In this way, passionlessly, apathetically, we permit the natural boundaries of our life to enclose and enslave*

us. We allow finite structures themselves to distort and sully life in fallen sensebound humanity."

"Passion (passio) literally means the suffering of life, creatively, gloriously. To refuse to suffer or to spend a lifetime trying to avoid it, is to refuse to live, to love, to be."

"The mystic leaps beyond the boundaries into the mystery. Or, if you will, having exhausted the powers of Eros, he is lifted by the Inexhaustible Spirit into agape and in that divine realm he begins to envision and inhale the impossible possibilities or the possible impossibilities of love."

    One of life's most rewarding experiences is to share our love with others as fully as possible. However we choose to do this—whether it's through caring for children, a lover, friends, or strangers—we find that lives based on caring and compassion bring us the deepest sense of fulfillment and satisfaction. We know what kinds of shared love are right for us by which feel most passionate.

    This feeling of intense invigoration and inspiration can scare people because it can feel out of control. Passionate love burns through us, moving us to feel we must follow our heart. People's passions are what drive them to do what they feel a need to do in spite of what others may say. Because there's no path to follow but your own heart's pull, following one's passion really *does* feel like leaping off into the unknown. There are no maps or guarantees of where you'll end up.

    There's a natural law of passionate love that states, "We can't control love," or "love is out of our control." This means we don't *choose* who or what we fall in love with. Falling in love is something that happens to us whether or not we think we want or need that experience. "We can't control love" also means we can't *direct* those we love to do what we want—they are free to do what they please.

    Love is, by its very nature, chaotic, unpredictable, joyous, and dependent on so many interrelated and complex influences. Any consistency, predictability, or reliability would interfere with love's limitless capacity to stretch us emotionally. We can find some comfort in knowing that the unpredictability of who and what we fall in love with, and when, is the only certainty in love.

I've hoped passionate love would be reciprocal, reliable, consistent, open, and sincere. Apparently, this is not always possible at some fundamental level. It seems the world would be more enjoyable and satisfying if those we loved accepted our love as we most wish to *give* it, instead of how they prefer and are able to *receive* it! We need to develop our abilities to appreciate the love we receive, and give up attempting to control love. To the degree we can accept the unpredictability of love, we can be truly unconditional in our love.

The object of our love is free to react to our love in any ways he or she pleases; otherwise love wouldn't be nearly so exhilarating, exciting, and such a perfect learning opportunity. This falling is an act of trusting something that doesn't even look like it's there. As we fall in love, we re-create ourselves as what we most desire, and what we love becomes who we are.

Some people attempt to control love, by expecting the one they love to believe as they do about the world. We tend to believe that reality is based on areas of agreement, thinking if we can share common beliefs with others, we must be "right." This desire to get others to agree with us is typically unconscious, so it can be difficult to pinpoint why a relationship feels awkward or unpleasant. People often contain themselves within their beliefs, only changing beliefs as they feel so inspired.

Sometimes we establish barriers between ourselves and those with beliefs we find painful to be around. We might accept such people from a distance, but not close to us. Consciously understanding the boundaries of what we find tolerable gives us a better sense of our own identity.

I have known people who died at a point where they "ran out of steam" and saw no reason to go on living. They were living for what other people felt was best right up to the moment they died, dedicating their lives to work and family duties, yet neglecting commitments to the deeper wild inspiration of their souls. We can choose to limit ourselves to living safe lives in well-understood, non-challenging ways ... but to make such a choice is to pay a terrible price. We need to find ways to honor the creative, passionate parts of ourselves in order to feel most fully alive.

If we wish to be free to feel love, we must lose any desire to blame or control. We can put our faith in love, stretch our wings, and trust the wind to carry us where our hearts soar. Before we take off into the great wide open, we must drop all excess baggage! Negative beliefs weigh us down, and it can be nearly impossible to stay airborne when we're lugging heavy thoughts and feelings wherever we go.

Transform Sabotage to Strength

Love and gratitude give one the greatest strength

Viewing one's situation from the eyes of the heart, and what one most loves and feels grateful for is the strongest possible perspective one can take. With loving acceptance and forgiveness, we see and defeat self-sabotage, with sufficient strength to change our beliefs and our lives.

It can feel threatening and frightening to closely examine how we block enjoyment and satisfaction in life. People "make their own luck" by choosing to believe in themselves—or not. We can picture how the energy of our thoughts and feelings can either be constructive or destructive by imagining the way desire peaks ... so our attention is focused on a favorite wish. Other surrounding areas are only attended to sporadically, giving them an appearance of being background noise.

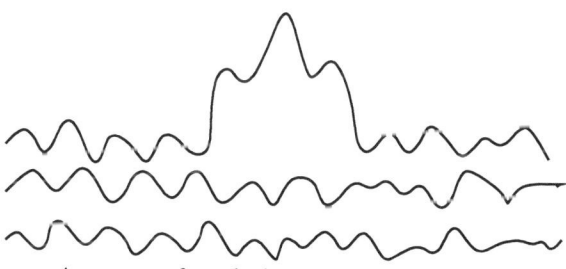

An area of peak desire surrounded by "background noise" areas of lesser interest

Your peak desire stands out and up above the rest. As your interest builds constructively with expansive feelings of love, waves of energy combine to create an even higher peak and a larger probability that space and time will accommodate your desire. The more positive energies are felt from emotions such as trust, hope, and basking in unconditional love, the higher the peak will be. Conversely, feelings of doubt, anger, and fear cause destructive interference, creating depressions or dips with those negative emotional energies. A person suffering from depression caused by chronic destructive interference often internalizes negative beliefs such as "I never get anything I want," or "I don't deserve anything good." Such destructive beliefs can be self-perpetuating, self-fulfilling prophecies, even if not consciously stated. Negative feelings can damage the area of peak desire, leaving the mountain looking something like an exploded volcano.

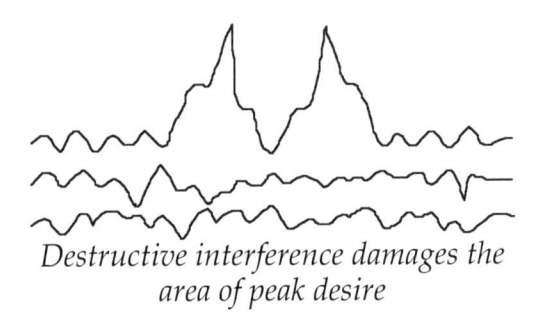

Destructive interference damages the area of peak desire

It feels rewarding to constructively build desires into higher peaks, where greater feelings of love and joy attract the very things and situations we most prefer. Prayer and meditation help "boost the gain," amplifying already pronounced desire into higher peaks. Stronger feelings of love help eliminate doubt and fear, as love helps us pay more attention to the present than the future. When we build our intentions stronger with love and inspiration, we shift reality in directions we love most.

I identify my inner blocks by noticing any destructive inner commentary I play over and over again to myself. These are negative statements of how I feel inadequate, clumsy, foolish, stupid, or otherwise unfit for living a life I most love. Most of these negative barbs arose from feeling judgmental reactions from others around me that I internalized at traumatic points in my life ... points where my life path veered away from my original path of joyous self-discovery to one of fitting in and conforming to what I "should" be.

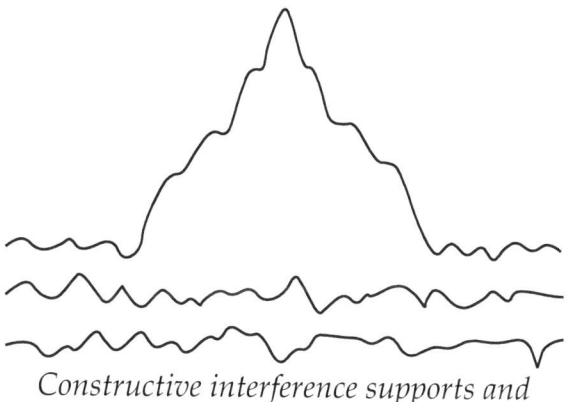

Constructive interference supports and builds the area of peak desire

When I write down and rephrase these negative statements in a positive and present tense, I create a powerful set of my own personal affirmations! I reform my inner belief structure in ways that harmonize with my creative intentions, so I'm not at cross-purposes with myself. By focusing on what I am grateful for, I empower those qualities to expand ... finding joy in being me without grasping onto people or things that are "supposed to" bring happiness.

Personal Affirmations

The process of reviewing inner, previously unexamined beliefs is incredibly powerful. These personal affirmations allow us to consider new ways to envision how we think about ourselves, while giving us opportunities to heal our self-inflicted wounds. For example, one of my negative self talk statements was, "If people knew who I really am, they'd shut me out," which I rephrased into the affirmative to be:

> *"When people know who I really am, they will welcome me in."*

This affirmation shifts my reality to feel much less shy and tentative in social situations. Another negative self-talk statement I used to have was, "Don't express your ecstasy so openly," which I rephrased into a personal affirmation of,

> *"Express yourself! Allow yourself the pleasure of feeling ecstasy, passion, and love!"*

I really love this one, because it is so life-affirming and positive! My reality shifted with these affirmations so much that I now have a much more joyous, unselfconscious attitude on my neighborhood walks ... often feeling inspired to reach up to touch tree branches, leap, twirl, dance, and sing!

I can tell what beliefs and affirmations work best for me by how they energize and empower me, even if I also feel rather embarrassed by them at first. In fact, I take embarrassment to be a very *good* sign. It means I am expressing my unique passions despite what others might say! I found myself feeling uneasy at first with spending much time and attention on loving thoughts and feelings for myself. When I relax and consider what's just on the other side of my old belief boundaries, I discover a whole new way of caring for myself.

In addition to negative self-talk, we also block ourselves from staying true to our heart's desire by engaging in destructive behaviors. Some people drink alcohol or enjoy food to excess, while others watch so much TV they have little time left for what they most love, and still others can't ever seem to stop working. Obsessions can take many forms, and it takes great honesty and a true desire for change to admit what we're doing that gets in the way of *really* living our lives.

When I examined my life, I was shocked to discover that I had a reading habit! I tended to read anything and everything I could get my hands on. I even did this even when visiting friends or my family, picking up whatever was handy that had writing on it, and starting to read, even if it was the liner notes in a record or compact disc! Once I acknowledged this had been a form of escape for me, I developed some restraint, and started spending time visiting with people rather than burying myself in their books and magazines.

There are many destructive patterns we can get caught up in, such as avoiding facing problems, or feeling competitive, restless, resentful, selfish, or controlling. We can go through these problems if we face them honestly and allow ourselves to change. In every situation, no matter how difficult, a creative path exists that brings greatest joy.

Just Say "No" to Stress

It's good to remember there are many things in life you can't control, so you don't need to increase stress by feeling guilty or worried about them. You can say "no" to people who ask you to over-commit, and you can remember your primary responsibility is to yourself and those who depend on you.

One secret to feeling maximum inspiration and energy is to follow the five basic principles of Reiki, the study of universal life force energy. These principles seem deceptively simple, obvious, and clear—yet they provide us with simple keys to feeling most energized. These keys to Qi are stated in the form of daily affirmations:

> Just for today I will not worry.
> Just for today I will not be angry.
> Just for today I will do my work honestly.
> Just for today I will give thanks for my many blessings.
> Just for today I will be kind to my neighbor and every living thing.

There is simple elegance in contemplating these affirmations every day. The desire and effort to fulfill these promises begins a deepening inner understanding of how we can open ourselves to love.

I am impressed by the power of these intentions, especially the ones about "Just for today I will not be angry" and "Just for today I will not worry." Those two were challenging for me. I often felt tempted to hang onto "a few" well-justified resentments and concerns ... until further reflection when I realized I didn't need them! I now know there is no justifiable reason to hold on to anger or worry, or blame someone or something else for causing pain and suffering. Anger and worry just get in the way. All the miracles I've experienced happened when I felt full of love and free of anger and fear.

When I begin to feel overwhelmed, I remind myself I can choose to let go of my anger and fear, even if I feel I have to take immediate action (with a fight or flight response to stress). I observe my feelings to get a sense of whether a fight or flight reaction is necessary. I prepare to face stressful situations by envisioning feeling calm, loving, and strong. If I have difficulty imagining myself being calm and courageous, I think of someone who *would* be able to face this stressful situation with calm confidence. When I visualize myself feeling loving and relaxed amidst stressful circumstances, I'm more capable of facing real life stressful situations calmly.

It also helps to understand we have a tremendous amount of control over our own lives. Other people may *seem* to tell us what to do, but we always have complete control over how we respond to every situation in life. We have a choice of what we believe and how we act.

Choose Your Life Path

> "Go confidently in the direction of your dreams.
> Live the life you have imagined."
> – Henry David Thoreau

When we imagine our idea of heaven on Earth, we take the first steps to living such a life. Goals help us change in ways we *choose* to change, and help us appreciate what matters most in our lives. Perhaps best of all, when we set clear goals and visualize what we wish for ourselves, our minds start working on bringing us to them even when we're not consciously thinking about them!

Wishing is the basis for how we create our world. It's easy to live unconsciously, and this helps explain why change is usually so gradual, as we learn by experience how we wish to live. I like to share what I learn along the way, and I feel constantly inspired when I remember to ask myself,

What's the best possible thing for me to do right now?

This question fills my life with meaningful activities, so I don't feel resentful that I'm only doing things I am supposed to be doing for other people. I feel more inspired, more creative, more generous, and more loving when I am focused on what I most feel I need to be doing and becoming.

Listen *really* carefully to your inspiration and gut feelings without judging them, because judgment and criticism can so easily kill creativity and inspiration. When you find yourself strongly attracted or repelled by something or someone, you can choose to follow through on your feelings.

Sometimes that feeling might make no sense at all to you ... it might tell you that you need to *"Go NOW!"* and leave a place abruptly at an odd time. I've had this experience at unexpected times, and have begun to trust my gut feelings, which I feel is spirit's way of communicating with me. When I get physical sensations in my body, I recognize them as messages from spirit. They help me know things I might not notice other ways. If I get an itchy eye, for example, I look around to see what I might be overlooking; while a ringing in my ear reminds me to listen more carefully. If my heel tingles, I know I need to make some time for healing.

The Earth Moves

> I wondered one day why I still didn't know what I wanted to do next with my life, since a friend of mine was starting up a new business venture and asking me to join him. I realized his business ideas didn't suit me ... and as I walked by myself, listening to "Screaming Love" by Soul Divine, thinking how much I love music ... I felt the earth pulse beneath my feet. This was no earthquake, but instead felt like an earth wave exactly under both my feet ... like walking on water!

> When I mentioned this to my husband, he pointed out that obviously I'd know what I'd feel like doing next ... the earth will shake! There's no point in taking on anything less moving to me.

Your path at this juncture is up to you. Open yourself to finding sources of inspiration you feel especially attuned to. Remain true to your desire, to feel a sense of accomplishment and success at the end of your life, knowing you followed your correct path. Involve yourself completely in living the life you most wish to live.

While envisioning an enjoyable reality, you begin the process of creating your life as you imagine it can be. With a mind free of worry and anger, you can invest emotional energy elsewhere ... such as in thoughts of how enjoyable your life is and will be! By visualizing a joyous future for yourself, you begin the process of creating it. Your visualizations are based on what you believe to be possible, and when powered by strong feelings of enthusiasm and inspiration, they become the basis for all you create in your life.

If you don't feel comfortable visualizing an enjoyable future, you can set the direction of where your life goes just by living each day as you feel it. There is no way to chart a course to the best possible future, since the journey is more important than the final destination, which is unknowable in any case.

My dreams come true whether they feel bad or good ... it is up to me to pay attention to what feels best and to attend to thoughts and feelings I most enjoy. My favorite feeling of all is love. I can feel totally in love with life by recalling how it feels to be alive in the world for the first time. This recollection heightens sensations, transforming my awareness of what matters most in life. I feel tremendous gratitude for every moment of life, and for perceiving this world of joyous sensation. I recall my true inner nature is love, which is stronger than I can fully comprehend. Such a powerfully strong feeling of love comes over me that I sense it expanding out of me through every cell and molecule of my body, as I am unable to restrain such intensity of feeling. Waves of love radiate outward, warming and illuminating areas of my attention, heightening sensations of love while simultaneously increasing amazing synchronicity, coincidences, and dreams-come-true. The more love I feel, the more in harmony I feel with everything and everyone around me.

I feel different when I reach this state of rapture at being alive. My breathing is fuller, and my mind feels distributed fully throughout my body ... quite noticeably in my heart! A healing quality of love surrounds me, and a sense of unity with all that is. Serene ecstasy fills me with deepest feelings of love radiating out of every cell of my body... even the soles of my feet! As I remember and experience that I AM LOVE, I feel energized, renewed and revitalized, with a positively transformed perception of the world. I sense a unity of being transcending all time and space, that awakens within me a deep knowingness of why I am alive, and what I live for. Each moment is a gift of such exquisite beauty and love that it overflows my ability to sense and perceive it, as joy of being alive overflows my body, radiating and flowing outward. In such moments I realize my every thought becomes reality, whether it is unconscious and out of my brain's control, or consciously willed into being. The line of distinction between cause and effect blurs at the same time as my physical life is effortlessly rewarded and enriched with instantaneous feedback from my every thought and feeling.

I face each fear until I comprehend it's message, going through every false concern as if walking through fire. This fire cleanses, only destroying that which cannot withstand total love. The more love I feel, the less I fear. I trace fears back in time, knowing I am love… and am loved. My desire to find love and face fears is a spark that ignites spirit in me. What I choose to do next is up to me, and determines who I am.

Once I've chosen a path that inspires me and feels genuinely exciting and *fun*, I benefit from living more mindfully, more lucidly. Having fun is a good indicator of being inspired, relaxed, and engaged in life. Life lived this way feels very dreamlike, and learning to be lucid and aware in dreams is a powerful way to shift reality whether we're asleep or awake.

Before reading the next chapter, read and do at least one of the following exercises. Inspiration is something that comes when we call it, and these exercises can help you reconnect with your own naturally great inner strength.

Feeling Inspired Exercises

Transforming Sabotage into Strength

Take a few minutes to consider ways you've been undermining your own success in life by inwardly criticizing yourself. Write down things you say to yourself that put you down, criticize, or point out faults. For each criticizing, sabotaging comment, "flip" the idea around and transform it into a supportive, encouraging affirmation. Put these affirmations in a place you will see regularly, and take time to read them to yourself every day for a week.

Transforming Attitudes

Think of a situation that you typically respond to angrily or fearfully ... preferably something that you face fairly often, or are facing right now in your life. Breathe fully, slowly, and deeply in through your nose and out through your mouth to release the feelings of stress, and visualize yourself in that situation feeling as calm and relaxed as possible. Imagine that when you are facing this stress you are not alone, but are supported by someone who understands and appreciates you, and who cares about your best interests. Continue breathing deeply in through your nose and out through your mouth, to clear out the stress. Visualize yourself calmly dealing with the stressful situation, and practice saying exactly how you feel. Breathe slowly and fully through your nose and out through your mouth, imagining you are expressing your true feelings in the stressful situation, while feeling as calm, loved, and loving as possible.

Appreciation

You are the living embodiment of what you most love. Every moment of your life is an open invitation to appreciate the universe with all your senses. Give yourself some quiet time to do something you've been long wishing to do, but haven't allowed yourself. Give yourself a chance to live your life to the fullest. For example, go outdoors and walk around your neighborhood or some place you can appreciate natural beauty. Plan a vacation to a place you'd love to visit. You can try out musical instruments in a music store, or watch the sun come up at dawn or the stars come out at night. Play the music you love best, and sing and dance to it! Stretch your imagination and boundaries to appreciate how big the spirit of Joy can be. If you really need to swim with the dolphins, fly in a hot air balloon or climb a mountain ... find a way to go *do* it!

Unconscious Inner Dreams

Imagine you are on a planet far from Earth where you may live for as long as you wish. What will you bring with you? What can you not survive without? How will you spend your time? Imagining yourself living on a desert planet gives you a fresh perspective on what you may take for granted right now, and helps you become more mindful of what you truly need. Besides basic needs for food, air, water, and shelter, everyone needs love.

Consider how you would spend time on your that planet, so you can recognize what your present life may be lacking in some ways compared to how you'd most love to be living. You *can* change your life to be more like your best dreams!

Popping the Bubble of Self-Limitation

Give yourself some time and space where you won't be interrupted, and prepare to face your deepest feelings. If this exercise feels like it may be too painful or emotionally exhausting to you, then don't do it now.

When you're ready to begin, consider your life with the idea that you will be intentionally, consciously expanding whatever anxious and angry tendencies you may have, to feel where they take you. For example, if you worry about what others around you are doing with their lives, then exaggerate those concerns. When you experience the fullest emotional reaches of your feelings, stretch those feelings to such an exaggerated self-caricaturizing point that the bubble bursts.

When we exhaust all our feelings, the only feeling left in that state of what seems to be complete isolation and nothingness is ... Love. If I'm feeling something other than love, I know I haven't truly felt and released all the other emotions yet. This exercise reminds me of being like a dog by the river, rolling in dead fish until finally feeling sick of it. This is definitely something best done by oneself!

Feeling Totally Alive

Remember the feeling of being alive for the first time ... and imagine you have never lived until *this very moment,* right now. Every thought, feeling, and sensation is extraordinary in its impact—even something as simple as sunshine or breeze on the skin is a total delight! Imagine how much you longed to be alive before you were born, so you could experience these ecstasies for yourself, first hand. Remember how loved you are by all that is right now, forever, and always.

CHAPTER 7

Lucid Dreaming

Consciousness is realizing you're always dreaming

Lucid dreaming is the art of shifting the reality of dreams. This skill is essential, because when we learn how to shift reality in dreams, we become adept at shifting reality whether we're asleep or awake. Lucid dreaming is a special kind of dreaming in which the dreamer knows this is a dream, realizes a great deal of creative control of the dream, and is aware of effects of one's presence and actions. Lucid dreaming can be thought of as being *conscious*, so the dreamer is capable of greatly transforming any situation—as opposed to feeling like a victim of circumstance. Consciousness is a relative term, since we are generally able to focus our attention on only a few things at any given time, rather than on everything simultaneously. It even requires a great deal of effort to pay attention to just what we really care about, so we typically focus our attention very narrowly. Many of us have had the experience where something has been hidden right in plain sight in front of us, yet we couldn't see it. Most of us focus our attention into such tight, narrow bands that we suffer from a loss of conscious peripheral vision. We perceive what we pay attention to, and we only pay attention to certain things that seem relevant to ourselves.

In a lucid dream, one identifies much more with being boundless spirit rather than a more limited sense of self. There are no barriers holding us back in lucid dreams ... no rules we are forced to live within. All things *are* possible, and in lucid dreams we experience those possibilities first-hand. We fly; walk on water; see through walls; zip to other solar systems, the bottom of the ocean, or straight through the Earth.

A key to enhancing our ability to dream lucidly is to practice emotional detachment, to better know the difference between our earth-bound ego sense of self and our soaring spiritual identity. Detachment helps free us from the two extremes of getting so absorbed in what's going on that it seems real and important, or feeling such anxiety from sudden stress or conflict we'd rather jump out of the dream and wake up to a higher level of consciousness than deal with the one we're in (the dream we're having). These are the same two extremes to be aware of when facing reality shifts: the extreme of *strongly identifying with the reality shift*, and the extreme of *shutting out such inexplicable phenomena* from one's life. When we achieve a mentally balanced perspective of detachment where these two extremes are seen from a great height, we can better see their interchangeability, and release our mind's attachment to holding fast to either extreme.

A simple way to become more detached is to notice the difference between when and how you feel fear, and when and how you feel love. Feeling love is a more detached, eternal perspective, while fearfulness is a natural state of ego. The experience of ego without any inspiration is a miserable state of being in which one feels small, relatively disconnected and somewhat stupid, survival-focused, and scared. When you notice yourself feeling scared, remind yourself you can relax and reconnect to feeling love and oneness.

Another way to increase chances of dreaming lucidly is to sharpen your critical thinking skills, so you *notice* when something different or strange is going on. Hone your powers of observation by quizzing yourself daily on what you notice in your bedroom, your refrigerator, your family and your friends. See the world with an artist's eyes, imagining you will recreate what you witness, so you must pay attention to every detail. The more you become accustomed to paying attention, the more you will observe.

Some people say that if you wonder whether or not you're dreaming, you probably are. Many dreamers notice when objects start changing, appearing, or disappearing that they are dreaming—or they might notice having magical powers, like flying or altering what happens around them.

You can increase chances of having lucid dreams by frequently contemplating during your waking hours that this, too, is a dream. The more I believe I am *always* dreaming, the more often I have lucid dreams to the point I begin feeling my whole life is a lucid dream! Considering myself to be dreaming has the effect of helping me achieve a detached focus of awareness, which helps me pay attention to a wider range of experience.

It helps to pay attention to the most important and powerful dreams you've had, and particularly to recall any recurring or attractive scenarios. If you can remember that these recurring and pleasant dreams may repeat, chances are greatly improved that next time you have these dreams, you will know they *are* dreams.

Resolving Monster Nightmares

When I was a little girl, I had recurring nightmares about dinosaurs and large monsters chasing and trying to devour me. I frequently ran into my parents' bedroom in the middle of the night, seeking solace, but when I fell asleep again, the nightmares returned to torment me right where they had left off.

One night, after several particularly bad nights in a row, I remembered these nightmares were just dreams, and that I was in fact, dreaming. The next thing that occurred to me was that if this monster situation *was* a dream, I could imagine a solution to get rid of the monsters! I felt incredibly energized and amused when I imagined a bunch of tiny cartoon characters that together formed a large configuration, which looked like a much larger version of themselves.

I began to look forward to my next nightmare, so these little heroes could enter my dream and scare the monsters away, never to bother me again! I felt a sense of empowerment and exhilaration at finding a creative solution to what had been such a big problem.

Stephen LaBerge writes in his book, *Lucid Dreaming*, that he uses symbolic stimulation of lucidity to notice he is dreaming and to awaken within his dreams. There is a Sufi saying, "When a bird will land in your outstretched hand, *then* you will understand." When Stephen experienced a bird landing in his hand, he knew he was dreaming, which helped him awaken while still asleep. While symbolic things provide clues that we're in a dream, they can also occur in waking reality ... with a similar awakening effect. Symbolic reminders can give us a sense of our degree of consciousness by drawing our attention to fully appreciating the present moment.

Bird Lands on Shoulder

I was talking on the phone to a friend in 1994 while watching my four year old daughter play in the front yard through the open front door. I saw her standing perfectly still, gazing intently at something in the trees in our neighbor's yard next door. I continued talking, and then saw a Junko bird land on her left shoulder! I was amazed and surprised, but she remained calm, apparently not even noticing that there was a bird sitting on her left shoulder, looking around with occasional quick turns of it's head.

I watched my daughter as she continued to stand very still with the bird on her shoulder for several minutes, both my daughter and the bird appearing calm, relaxed, and observant in the front yard together. The bird continued looking around, moving its head and occasionally fluffing its feathers. Eventually, the bird shuffled its feet and took flight, my daughter having never noticed that anything unusual had occurred.

I was so impressed to see a bird sit on her shoulder all that time that I asked her, "Did you SEE the bird that landed on your left shoulder and sat there?" She said she hadn't—she'd been looking at the trees.

We can most fully enjoy the experience of having a wild bird land on us when we notice it happening. It's possible that every day in some way, we each experience a bird of some kind landing in our hand or on our shoulder, providing us with an opportunity to broaden our ability to pay attention to more than what we are focusing on at the moment. Miraculous things can occur every day, and we can experience them directly when we learn how to live more lucidly.

Stephen LaBerge explains in his book, *Lucid Dreaming*, that attitudes characterizing lucid dreaming have parallels with an approach to life that can be called 'lucid living'. Lucid and non-lucid dreamers have different attitudes, which apply to both waking and sleeping states.

Know You Are Dreaming

Lucid dreamers know they are asleep and dreaming in their dreams, while non-lucid dreamers tend to assume they are experiencing objective reality. What we see is truly an interpretation of our senses ... a creative internal reconstruction of the world around us. We are rarely aware of how we construct our world inside our minds, even when we consider ourselves to be fully awake.

Our experiences are necessarily subjective, not objective. Each person's perceptions are constructed based upon their current motivational state as well as what they see and believe of reality. Few of us experience reality directly; instead we tend to view the world through our models of the world ... with our perceptions screened through our expectations, feelings, concepts, values, attitudes, and goals.

When lucid dreamers realize they are dreaming, the dream suddenly feels very different. If this *is* a dream, then what is happening is not what it seems to be. Your dream senses that tell you something looks, feels, tastes, and smells like it's physically there are presenting that idea to you, but seemingly solid dream objects can be changed or withdrawn in an instant. How can you prove to yourself you are dreaming? You can discover you are dreaming by observing that your intentions have an instantaneous causal effect. Lucid dreams are incredibly responsive to your every thought and feeling. If you suspect you are dreaming, you most likely are.

I frequently experience a sense of awareness and lucidity just before I wake up in the morning, as I am aware I am asleep but I *could* fully awaken if I wanted to. During these moments, I sometimes know what time it is and what's happening inside and outside the house! I also feel connected to other people, animals, and things. At these times I am frequently aware I am talking with other people, even though my body is still sleeping in bed. Somehow, my consciousness is aware, awake, active, and alert! I have a sense of energetic knowingness, in which I feel vibrantly attuned to the universe. Sometimes I move from simply observing my surroundings to starting to dream again, even though I am still quite aware of the fact that my body is in bed dreaming. I often notice that noises outside me do not seem random at all, but harmonize with my inner feelings of wakefulness, even as I am asleep. Sounds have shapes and colors, and resonate in my body and in everything around me—integrated in a harmonious whole.

Many dreamers first become acquainted with lucid dreams when they have nightmares. Just as we become more lucid when facing a frightening situation in waking life, we realize we need our full lucid facilities when facing nightmare situations in our dreams. We know our old habits *won't work* here; we need inspiration right NOW! Our attention is riveted in this moment, right now. Anxiety pulls us to full attention, although too much anxiety can awaken us out of the dream.

It's a good idea to have a dream sanctuary when you begin lucid dreaming, so you can feel safe in the event you find yourself in an unpleasant situation. The energetic experiences you have in lucid dreams are strongly connected to your health and wellbeing, and it makes a big difference to know you can always access a protected place filled with your highest sense of love. Your dream sanctuary can be a sense of place, a feeling, a visual image, or a concept of a person or animal. The more aware you are of your "home base," the more confidently you can explore the multiple universes that open to you through lucid dreaming. My dream sanctuary is deeply sacred to me, and close to my heart. I feel I am always there, and simply being aware of it gives me strength, whether I'm asleep or awake. This consistency in my consciousness helps me relax and enjoy the feeling of creating my dream life.

Know You Are Creating

Lucid dreamers know they shift reality in their dreams. While non-lucid dreamers assume dream events are "just happening" to them, lucid dreamers see the effects of their intentions on their surroundings. The passive non-lucid attitude involves a belief that the rules of dreaming are entirely determined by an external reality principle. Non-lucid dreamers thus remain earthbound by gravity, believing it to be a universal law of physics, even in their dreams—while lucid dreamers regard "laws" of the dream world as self-made rules that can be changed.

The non-lucid attitude is that we are generally powerless to change or affect our lives, because experience is largely defined and determined by external factors as things happen to us. The non-lucid attitude contains a belief that once we consider ourselves to be a certain way, we essentially do not change, but instead remain fixed in accordance with established patterns. The non-lucid attitude is one of feeling there are "good guys" and "bad guys"—victims and victimizers. Feelings such as blame, shame, guilt, and fear are unquestioned parts of non-lucid life.

In contrast, lucid dreamers have an attitude that *we* define how we experience situations in our lives; whether we view a given dream as a nightmare or an opportunity for self-integration is a choice we each make. The lucid attitude involves believing that great change is possible within every moment—we are not "stuck" or "doomed"—it is never "too late." The lucid attitude is one of realizing we are all interconnected, and all of us share the same need for experiencing love and joy and inspiration in our lives.

There is a direct connection between you and everything else in the universe. You are shifting your reality and manifesting what you truly desire, because you are creating something new every moment! Your very presence is a creative force in this world. Your very existence has incredibly far-reaching effects. Lucid dreamers know their consciousness changes the reality of their dreams non locally, and that everything in the universe is interconnected.

Know What You Are Doing

The lucid attitude is mindfulness, while the non-lucid attitude is mindlessness. It may initially seem easier to be mindless and operate from habit, since mindfulness and consciousness require effort. The main advantage of being mindful over mindless is that one gains increasing flexibility with mindfulness. When situations are unpredictable and new, it helps to be mindful—to know what you are doing, rather than to do as you've always done.

When situations are normal and predictable, habitual behaviors can be efficient and effective, as long as they are appropriate reactions to the situation. Some people notice they're on autopilot when they drive the same route to work every day, and discover that somehow they got all the way to work without remembering what they saw along the way.

When you ask yourself, "Am I awake?" note how difficult it is to genuinely raise this question. To ask this question sincerely requires honest doubt—however slight that doubt might be. Maybe we are partially awake—partially mindful. Lucid dreaming can provide us with a point of departure from which to understand how we might not be fully awake—for as ordinary dreaming is to lucid dreaming, so the ordinary waking state is to the fully awakened state of lucid living.

Malcolm Godwin describes the fragile balance between being an identified participant and a detached observer in his book, *The Lucid Dreamer*. Keep in mind that what Godwin writes about dreams can be equally true of our waking selves:

> *"Any moment dreamers become too identified with their dream roles they fall back into the non-lucid state, losing the alert awareness that they are dreaming. In order to sustain lucidity, or to invoke it in the first place, it seems necessary to be an active participant, center-stage. Yet at the same time a degree of detachment is required in order to remain alert and not to get lost in the role-playing. Becoming lucid has these twin levels of awareness, although their combination often brings bewilderment and paradox. Believing you have just woken up as your normal waking self, only to recognize that you are in fact still asleep is an example of how confusing it can be."*

This description beautifully indicates the importance of maintaining awareness of both one's ego and spirit levels of consciousness.

Tibetans believe the foundation of lucid dreaming is to be an alert, silent observer. Gradually, your thoughts will begin to fall away for want of attention, as will mental screening that prevents you from glimpsing past habitual perceptions of how the world is structured. While total consciousness may prove elusive, glimpses you get of the true nature of this universe and yourself have unsurpassed beauty. Eventually, the dreams will fall away for want of attention and the next moment you will be truly awake for the first time; the Tibetans say it will also be the last. Perhaps this is because at that level of awareness, you truly become cognizant of being All That Is, and are quite content to no longer live a life of fragmented awareness.

Godwin's *The Lucid Dreamer* book refers to a meditation technique called Shiva's meditation technique. This technique is concerned with the process of awakening rather than dreaming, and uses sleep as its starting point. According to this technique, relax and wait, feeling every sensation as you drift into sleep. Remain alert and aware. The gap from waking to sleep where one gains a glimpse of reality is tenuous, subtle, minute ... but it is there. The Sufis prepare for this sort of meditation by first "Falling into the Darkest Well," imagining falling down a bottomless well while blindfolded ... falling and falling into infinite void.

> *At the point of sleep*
> *When the sleep has not yet come*
> *and external wakefulness vanishes,*
> *At this point Being is revealed.*

This heightened sense of awareness that can also be called being present... can be felt either while waking or dreaming. It's that feeling of surreality that shocks one into full consciousness, a state where we otherwise seldom reside.

When we know where our thoughts and feelings come from, we start to understand who we are. The capacity to double back on one's consciousness this way is demonstrated by the drive to question one's questions—which is the source of the experience of nothingness from whence all comes forth.

As Brian Swimme elucidates in his book, *The Universe is a Green Dragon*, there is great value in this kind of self-reflexiveness:

> "The Earth awakens through the human mind. You have to understand this from two different points of view. We have a humanity that awakens to its planetary dimension, to its planetary responsibility, and thus begins to provide the Earth with a heart and mind. From the other perspective, we can see how the planet as a whole awakens through self-reflexive mind, which happens to unfurl through humanity."

My experiences with lucid dreams have been varied. I have not always felt I knew what to do with the realization that anything is possible; sometimes it felt easier to do whatever routine things I normally do, rather than choose among infinite possibilities.

Lucid Flying Dreams

One summer when I was 35, I had lucid dreams where I was flying around fast, like a UFO. I was simply spirit essence, and didn't have my usual body at all. I could zip around faster than anything ... faster than light. The dreams didn't have deep ideas for me to ponder ... but I was AWAKE in them! The way I got into this state was by realizing every day of waking life that "This is a dream." The more familiar I become with that realization, the more I can wake up inside my dreams, and know anything is possible.

Lucid Monster Dream

I once had a lucid dream that I was in a house, when suddenly a monster burst through a wall. I was startled to see such a fearsome apparition, but I knew it wasn't real, because I knew I was dreaming. I thought to myself *I'd probably know exactly what to do if I was not so aware I was dreaming.* I sensed that I possess a very effective set of coping strategies for handling monsters in dreams ... but being lucid put me at a slight disadvantage, because I had no routine response for dealing with monsters.

What I decided to do was to consider the monster unnecessary to my life, so it could vanish and leave me alone. I also decided to fly upward through the ceilings of the multi-story building. It felt wonderful to fly upward through all the levels of the building until I came out the top into the clear, fresh air!

One thing lucid dreams invariably bring me is a *much* clearer sense of experiences I have trouble reconciling in my daily life. I face my fears vividly in lucid dreams, although I don't always consciously know what those fears represent at the time of the dream.

Falling Car Dreams

I had a series of lucid dreams involving seemingly ordinary events being interrupted by my seeing some kind of unmanned car flying through the air, and then falling from a great height and landing extremely close to me. I knew I was dreaming, and knew I was creating this experience… but I couldn't comprehend *why* the cars would come flying in the air and then fall.

These dreams often started with me talking to someone inside a house as we had a cup of tea. I would look out a kitchen or living room window, and notice a flying car was up high in the sky, headed in our direction. As the car approached, I could see nobody was driving it, and I sensed it would be unable to continue flying without a driver. I felt awestruck to witness something so unusual and improbable, yet not comfortable with the idea of jumping into its driver seat to prevent a fall. Sure enough, the car would get *very* close to me, perhaps only 200 feet away, and then plummet straight down, accelerating as it fell.

The impact of the falling car felt like an earthquake, and the dust would continue rising long after the shock wave from impact had passed.

These dreams point out that I can take my spiritual consciousness to seemingly impossible heights, but the only way I can continue flying up there is to *be* in the driver seat of those cars, even if such a thing as a flying car seems unlikely. As I became more relaxed and accepting of the concept of how fluid reality is, my flying car dreams had me at the steering wheel, which felt a lot less scary and a lot more fun. The symbolic meaning of driving my own car is accepting responsibility for taking control of my direction and speed in life ... realizing reality shifts through me as I change.

I had some wild dreams in December 1994, and then a friend gave me a book about lucid dreaming. I'd previously avoided reading any books regarding lucid dreaming, because I had the impression lucid dreaming was about forcing one's will into the realm of the unconscious, in order to control one's dreams, which I considered to be a mistake. I was pleasantly surprised to find this book recommend relaxing into receptivity, with the intention to explore meaningful areas.

License to Die Dream

I had some lucid dreams in December 1994, which had a heightened sense of reality, including colors I don't see in real life. I also encountered some less-than-friendly aliens in a couple of dreams. My first encounter with them showed them as being very tall, sticking a sticker on me labeled, "License to Die. February 1967 - February ...   Hare." I don't remember what the year on the second date was, because I was so shocked that anyone would have the nerve to go around sticking death labels on people! I also didn't recall having died in 1967, except that I did recall having had a strange waking dream experience when I was very young around that time.

I ran into these aliens again in another dream a couple of days later when they were in the disguise of being my husband's two brothers. One of them started distracting me with a story, while the other slid over to approach me from the left. When the older 'brother' touched my shoulder, the younger one was over at my right shoulder and together they ran an ENORMOUS current of energy through me ... enough to cause heart failure for someone who had a weak heart or was easily startled. I absorbed the energy into myself, realizing that if I did this some more, it could transform me.

While these dreams seemed shocking, I wasn't scared, since I knew I was dreaming, safely asleep in bed, when these things were happening.

Bagged Hawk Dream

On January 5, 1995, I dreamt I was visiting my second cousin's house, situated in the woods in such seclusion that the only way to get there was to hike on foot for several hours. I walked there with my sister, her husband, and my husband, carrying food with us as a house gift. We were all quite tired when we arrived, so after a brief refreshing swim in a nearby river, we fell asleep in my cousin's multi-story tree house in the woods. My cousin was not there when we arrived, but my sister stayed up until he arrived around 11:30 PM, and talked with him through the night.

When I awoke the next morning, I found my brother-in-law sleeping on the floor below my husband's bed. I walked onto the balcony and saw morning sunshine through the trees. I climbed up many levels of balconies to the very top, where I saw a small and amazingly beautiful blue hawk fly down, and hover in mid-air like a hummingbird. It landed on the balcony and perched atop a potted cactus to sip water and eat kibble someone left for it. I was surprised how close the bird let me approach. As I stood an arm's reach away, I could better see the elegance of it's design, and the iridescent multi-hued shades of blue feathers dappled with soft tones of brown over it's hand-sized body.

As I stood watching the bird, my cousin approached the balcony from inside the tree house. I motioned to him that it was OK to come out on the balcony. Everyone came out on the balcony, and somebody captured the blue hawk in a plastic baggie. My brother-in-law came out to show me a little carved art piece resembling the hawk (a half unicorn, half-dragon ornament that a friend of mine gave me). Amidst all this confusion, and before I had any chance to react, my sister tossed the bagged hawk high up to the roof of the tree house. I watched in horror as the bagged bird then came back down, beak-first, and smacked down onto the deck of the balcony.

When I awoke from this dream, I recognized how similar it was to the dream I had two nights previously where a red sports car zoomed through the air before crashing down headfirst very close to me.

I analyzed the bagged-hawk dream, and noticed it might be warning me not to force my will into transforming myself. To do so too soon may be tempting, like a bird inside a plastic bag might think it can fly—yet, to toss the bagged bird in the sky only results in an injured bird. My development is not something I can rush by force of will, but something that flows through me in its own time and way. This dream is more intelligible to me than the red sports car dream, yet both dreams bring the same message to me—a warning to accept the fact I am still inside a chrysalis of sorts, and although I may start to feel I have wings, I am not yet ready to fly off. It's good to remember that natural growth feels better than forced growth, and natural growth takes time.

Care for the Living Dream

I had a dream on September 12, 1997 set at a coastal town in Europe, where Roman ruins lay submerged under water. This city was a ghost town, with a long history of brutal wars being waged for control of a key seaport. The city had been built up many times, only to be attacked, destroyed, and built up again and again.

I was visiting with a small band of people who were cautiously sorting through the rubble of the last conflict ... when I felt many of the spirits of the deceased from all those conflicts contacting me. Oddly enough, the message they had for me was that they no longer held any grudges, anger, resentment, or desire for revenge. They repeated this message, and added that they wanted me to know they wished all could be forgiven, and that the living could take loving care of each other. I was astonished at the feeling of passionate urgency and compassion accompanying this message, and wondered why they'd wanted to tell me this.

A while later, I walked through a large boat where my companions were quietly stationed (in order to avoid detection), when I found an injured soldier who was badly hurt and in need of medical attention. He was hiding with his gun aimed at me when I found him, and I approached him very slowly with hands up, to reassure him I intended him no harm. After learning what I'd just heard from the spirits, I was in an unusual frame of mind; I felt compelled to do everything I could to help this man. His legs were atrophied from a combination of inactivity and severe injury, and he was so lightweight from malnutrition I could easily pick him up and carry him to our party's nurse.

When I delivered him to the nurse, her eyes met mine with a steely cold gaze; then she turned abruptly away from the injured soldier and me. She muttered about "something I need to do," and walked out of the room.

I chased after the nurse, feeling astonished she could be so cold-hearted and abandon him! I stopped her, and then understood she hadn't received the same message from the spirits I had. I told her what they'd told me, and the importance of caring for the living NOW, regardless what they may have done in the past. If the dead can be so forgiving, why can't we? I had to repeat this message to her several times, in several different ways, with the added message that I'd care for this man myself if she wouldn't, because I had a pretty good idea what he needed, and I was going to make sure he had the best medical care I could get him.

At the end of this dream, I got the feeling I'd broken through this woman's cold exterior and reached her heart, so she felt how this injured man was part of her.

I get a strong feeling from some of my dreams of how I work with others to "feel out" possible realities. The most amazing part of this experience is those wonderful occasions when I awaken in the morning able to *remember* what I was doing in the dream—since usually these dreams are immediately wiped clean from my memory upon awakening. Dream messages can be gifts that allow us the freedom to see our lives from a different vantage point ... considering the dream characters to be separate from ourselves, so we may see how various attitudes, beliefs and behaviors look when others act them out.

Apocalypse Dream

I dreamt one day I was in the process of exploring the feel of a reality strip—like a possible reality movie that we needed to believe we were really in—where everyone in my community was certain an apocalypse was upon us, and most people were totally preoccupied with "disaster planning" activities in microcosmic neighborhoods. I walked over to a neighboring town a few blocks from our house, and looked into an overcrowded home where an entire community gathered to tackle the problem of apocalypse. A middle-aged woman frowned at me with serious concern and propriety ... indicating this was *her* town's planning group, and if I live in a different city, I should be attending my "own" group. After feeling the burn of her geo-centric possessiveness, I walked slowly back toward the border toward my house, noticing a young boy of about ten years of age.

The young boy was being addressed by a foster care woman who attempted to convince the boy he should no longer stay with the family he was currently living with, since that family specialized in one-year stays only. The boy insisted this is where he is happy, although he seemed overwhelmed by the foster care woman's insistence that he must consider leaving. At this point, I could no longer resist joining the discussion, and I asked the foster care woman why the boy couldn't stay where he was so happy. The woman immediately asked, "Do *YOU* want to care for this boy?" which caught me off guard. I replied that this boy desires to stay with the family he's with, regardless of the family's fast-turnover policy; his feelings were clear to me, and they ran quite deep. I made sure she could feel this without constantly changing the subject, or becoming so stubbornly focused on her desired outcome of removing the boy from a "temporary" home, before I walked on again.

The next place I came to was a courtyard, where a young dark-haired girl organized a little cardboard box of her dearest possessions. I felt she was our true "neighborhood organizer," and felt compelled to stretch out in the sunshine nearby. I wore a winter coat that felt soft and luxurious beneath me as I stretched out so the sunshine warmed my legs. I talked with her as her hair fell down around her face, and she continued rummaging around in the small box. She was removing candies from her box, so only the "important" papers would remain. She wanted to know where she could safely keep this box, so it wouldn't be destroyed in any cataclysm, and I helped her think of a way to attach it to the underside of a man-hole cover in the street. This idea made her very happy! She had a mini Leatherman tool that I opened up, to discover she'd left one of the blades out. I pointed this out to her, and corrected it so she wouldn't get hurt.

As I talked with the young girl, a friend of mine emerged from a building somewhat out of breath, and sat down beside me, saying he'd almost knocked someone over in his speed to be by my side. Two other people also came to sit with us (a man and a woman), and a neighbor whispered in my ear something about how we could make a lot of money in this apocalypse situation—meaning that he, like me, sensed the time-independent quality of this reality strip, and was thinking of how to play the stock market to advantage. I asked my neighbor what he intended to do with the money he made ... if he was thinking of buying helicopters for the time when everything collapsed?

My questioning helped me ascertain that even though my neighbor was aware of his spirit's time-independent abilities, he was still thinking from habitual materialistic frame-of-reference that accumulations of resources are always a good thing to have, regardless what situation we find ourselves in. This made me suddenly aware that aside from my coat, I had no possessions or resources whatsoever, and the little girl was "better equipped" than I, with her mini Leatherman tool. My higher self responded to these observations of my body's consciousness by soothing me with warm vibrations of love, nonverbally reaffirming that everything I need is simply who I am. This put me back in a serene and loving frame of mind that seemed uniquely mine in this dream.

The other woman who joined us was radiating immense pain from her neck, so I sat up to massage her ... letting her head relax in my arms as she lay down, facing up. Unfortunately, this woman was not able to release her own inner tensions, even with massage, and she continued to create pain through her body. The fear of certain apocalypse preyed on her mind so heavily she was attacking her own body with constant worries and feelings of helplessness. In fact, as I looked and sensed all around me, most everyone was in some state of emotional panic, and practically nobody was feeling the fullest, highest potential of his or her spirit.

The way I felt this in my dream was something like being on a train with thousands of other spirits/people. As we left the station, embarking on an apocalyptic reality path, many people almost immediately jumped overboard. Nobody besides me seemed capable of feeling their highest spiritual potential. Some jumped off at the first stop, some at the second stop, many at third and fourth stops, and only one person from my immediate neighborhood made it up to the fifth.

I got the impression most people did not have a clear sense of how they create the universe; becoming "material" when they hit a feeling of unbalance and "rippling" themselves into "reality." They did not realize we can go much higher than before when we relax into the fullness of our spiritual selves, waiting for a place of love and joy to ripple out into "reality," rather than jumping off at the first sign of panic.

To be honest, I can't say I was any better than anyone else in this dream. I had an unfair advantage of an extremely close "hands-on" relationship with my high self that soothed me whenever I had doubts or uncertainties, with thoughts like *"Why don't I have a Leatherman tool, currency for bartering, or a neighborhood group meeting?"* These insights allowed me to observe people behaving as they would act if this particular reality was selected by our consensus reality selection process. My more-or-less objective observation of all this was that although this reality strip was emotionally evocative—which is all we ever really need, as my spirit reminded me—the unfortunate thing is that people reacted to a heightened sense of emotional feeling too soon, jumping out in the midst of panic to try to "control" what seemed to be an out of control situation with group meetings and stock market schemes. I felt that at this time, apocalypse won't serve to bring humanity the full depth of emotional range we need. We'll need to try another possible reality strip.

This dream operated on many simultaneous layers for me, so the part we get from reading this written account just scratches the surface. On a surface level, I understand that all the characters I encountered in the dream are parts of myself I am integrating into a cohesive whole. When I examine such a hypothetical reality as I did in this dream, I sense I am connected to billions of people. I got a deep sense of the possibility my own feelings may be capable of stabilizing others around me ... not just those who know me, but people all over the world. I feel I was doing my best to serve as a clear example of how to manifest oneself into material form at one's highest potential ... even though few people could focus their attention on me to perceive my message and example. It takes focused relaxed attention to see such examples, and most everyone in this dream was distracted by the upcoming apocalypse.

When I awakened from this dream, I remained in a place where I could observe all around me so clearly in so much more fullness than our means of expression can possibly capture. I have a very strong feeling that people create each day in cooperation with all consciousness. In dreams, time and space do not separate or limit us, and we have access to all knowledge about the universe and ourselves.

Connect in Dreams

My dreams have confirmed my belief in the interconnectedness between me and other people in my life. In 1994, the year I had a kundalini experience, my dreams took on a whole new kind of synchronicity with people around me who confirmed what I saw in visions and dreams. I once had a dream where I knew what flowers my mother was planting, even though I hadn't spoken to her in a month. I was startled to discover my dream was true, but it's a small example of some of the amazing things I've discovered in my dreams!

For many years, I shared dreams with my husband. We often woke up and talked about individual dream experiences for times we spent apart in our dreams, and were excited and amazed to share identical experiences when we were together in our dreams! On some occasions, we heard our dream selves speaking to each other before we awoke. These voices we overheard often had something to do with the dreams we'd just had, and we often heard the same things upon waking.

Gun Discussion

Once I dreamt my husband's cousin was considering buying a gun. In my dream, I strongly discouraged this and recommended he get something like a remote-controlled car instead, because I felt his two young daughters would enjoy a toy car more than a gun.

Several days after this dream, I laughingly told my husband's cousin about the dream, and was amazed to discover he *was* seriously considering buying a target rifle. This was especially surprising to me because he is a spiritual person deeply devoted to living his life for God and raising his family according to spiritual principles. He's the last man I'd guess would buy a gun! I then had a very similar conversation with him to the one I'd dreamt about. If I hadn't dreamt about the gun, I wouldn't have brought up the subject at all.

He did get the gun, but our conversation helped him appreciate that there are other recreational things he could enjoy with his daughters besides target practice.

Replacing Garage Floor

Just before returning from a trip to Europe, I once dreamt about my husband's parents. In my dream, they were tearing out their garage floor. There was a big mess from all the construction, and my father-in-law seemed a bit depressed about things. He sat for hours on end, drawing beautiful pencil sketches of mice. When my husband and I picked up our daughters who'd stayed with his parents while we traveled, I told my dream to my mother-in-law. I was *quite* startled when she said, "Well, we *are* going to tear out our garage floor very soon; we need to replace the flooring." I hadn't heard anything about this before!

Leading the Blind

One of my oddest dream connection experiences was where I dreamt I was at the UC Berkeley campus leading a blind man around the grounds. I showed him the main points of interest, describing them to him in detail as we walked together, hand in hand. In this dream, everyone was talking about the brand new Bevatron. When I woke up, I felt inspired to tell a friend about this dream, and she told me she'd recently dreamed I was talking to her dad's blind college friend. My friend's parents met through this blind friend, who *did* attend UC Berkeley when the Bevatron was new!

Another startling dream connection occurred when I dreamt of my husband's friend every night for a week:

Shopping in Israel

Each night at the beginning of March 1996, I had pleasant dreams of visiting my husband's friend in Tel Aviv, Israel. These dreams prominently involved clothing. In one dream, my husband's friend gave me a swimsuit to try on (a black and white swimsuit with connected bikini top and bottom that criss-crossed over each other into a one-piece), and she bought herself some black leather pants. I dreamt she was shopping with us, showing me blouses she thought would look especially nice on me. I don't usually dream so much about clothing, or so much about visiting someone, so I wrote an email to my husband's friend to tell her about these dreams, hoping all is well with her, and that she's happy, healthy and having as much fun as possible.

On March 10, 1996, she wrote an email response to me:

> I received your mail 3 times! Well, that is quite weird what you write me. It has been so long that we haven't met, and you dream about me for a whole week! Moreover, related to clothes. Actually, I have been shopping for clothes for myself recently and it is not such a good memory because it was the day of the attack in Tel Aviv and I was a few meters of that man who exploded. I was not in the street, but in the shopping center when I heard the explosion. I was really frightened, more because I didn't know what to do and what could still happen. I felt very trapped. They told us to go out the center, which I did. Thankfully I was close to an exit and I ran back home. I was so nervous I guess, that I slept (slipped) at home and fell on a chair, breaking a rib! But I am so grateful it is just a rib and that I am still alive, that I am waiting patiently that it stops hurting. Well, I'd be glad if you would come visit me in Israel. I guess it would be better to wait a bit because the country is a bit dangerous these days, but after it could be fun. Actually a friend from France is coming at the end of the month and we will spend a few days together. I hope you will continue having nice dreams (me being there or without). Thank you for writing me. That was quite a surprise but a nice one.

Earthquake Dream

One day in 1998, I dreamt I was talking to the Earth. She asked whether I'd prefer more frequent, less intense earthquakes, or less frequent, more intense earthquakes. I said I'd prefer less intense earthquakes more often ... and she replied there'd be an earthquake the following morning. I didn't think more of this dream, and went about my business as usual.

While sound asleep in the middle of the night, I felt a jolting earthquake rock the house. I recalled my dream about how the Earth planned to have an earthquake this morning, so I relaxed and fell back asleep.

That morning, several neighbors excitedly exchanged earthquake stories, describing how it felt like it was directly under us! One woman said her husband had groggily leapt out of bed to stand in his pajamas in a doorway with flashlight shining from room to room, and others told similar tales of great anxiety, since they hadn't been conscious that an earthquake was coming that morning (just a small one)!

Awakening

When I know I am creating my world and my beliefs and attitudes shape my reality, I become conscious of how I am the primary creative force in my life. Not only do things happen *to* me, but also reality shifts *by* me, and *through* me as I shift. This realization challenges me to stop blaming others and attempting to exert control. At times, I felt it was much easier to live a life of habitual mindlessness than to admit my life is exactly what I created. It also sometimes seemed a lot easier to feel my resentments and anxieties *were* justified, because others really *did* hurt me. My belief in my limitations can convince me I have limited options or choices.

G.I. Gurdjieff believed most people's normal state of consciousness is a state of light hypnosis, and most of us are almost never truly awake. This perspective helps explain how our world can feel real to us instead of dreamlike, for we are usually in an extremely suggestive state of mind, seriously believing the world of material objects to be all there is.

The extraordinary thing about realizing I am dreaming my life is that I can attain a very aware perspective of simultaneous involvement and observation of my life. As a self-aware observer, I know what I truly require, and how I sometimes automatically follow suggestions, such as feeling I need to buy stylish jewelry, clothing, and cars. The difference between living a good life and a truly inspired life requires that I awaken to my inspiration and realize my dreams.

When we feel how dreamlike life is, we can awaken within this dream and identify with something bigger and more all-encompassing than ego. We begin to feel we are both eternal and mortal, like lucid dreamers who know we are asleep while dreaming—we intuitively know we are both here in body and also far beyond. It feels liberating to release ourselves from confines of ego, noticing sources and directions of deepest inspiration. Issues that trouble us are not so big in the scheme of things, and we can more easily accept and forgive idiosyncrasies and foibles. The hustle and bustle of everyday life takes on a different feel, as we see through masks people wear to see who they truly are inside.

Many people wake up when encountering something so shocking that they feel mindfulness to be necessary. Shocking events such as near death experiences remind us there's *much* more here than meets the eye. We look deeper into our soul when we find ourselves in situations we have no scripts for.

Relationship crises are one of the *most* shocking and stressful ordeals we can face, and they encourage us to express a full range of emotions. Daphne Rose Kingma writes of the process of realizing how our intimate relationships offer extraordinary opportunities for personal growth and awareness, and how our unconscious expectations rise up in times of ordeals or power struggles in relationships.

> *"As the relationship goes through the ordeal, it is no longer being carried along on the wings of romance and great expectations; it is being dragged along by disappointment and disillusion. Why hasn't our love fulfilled our dreams, become the perfect fairy tale we imagined? Why has it, instead, become this monstrosity that's bringing up all our fears and vulnerabilities? At this point we have a choice of saying, 'Okay, you're not my everything, so I'm out of here.' Or of saying, 'Oh, I get it. There's an opportunity here. I'm being invited to deal with my*

> *own emotional issues, to stop being angry at my father for abandoning me, my mother for smothering me.'*
>
> *At this point, you can get stuck in blaming or you can start looking at yourself. If you're courageous, you will respond to the challenge, and if you are steadfast, you may actually move to the place where you are no longer just endlessly slapped around and controlled by your emotions."*

It may take many, many learning experiences before we learn what spirit desires to teach us. We may find it difficult to release ourselves from getting entangled in power struggles and seemingly endless cycles of blaming, placating and controlling relationships—until we finally surrender and let go of whatever expectations or limiting beliefs block us from feeling pure love. This surrender to love is the spiritual journey to accept reality as is, instead of how we wish it to be.

There are probably as many ways to get shocked into mindfulness as there are people on Earth. Near death experiences help people awaken, as do deep depressions. Death of a spouse or close friend can bring an awakening. Different kinds of peak experiences can awaken people when they discover the best moments of life—with experiences of ecstasy, rapture, bliss and great joy. Falling in love can awaken people. My spiritual awakening began in 1994, several months after I'd become acutely aware of living a soporific life.

Out of the Chrysalis

In spring of 1994, I commented to a cousin that I felt I'd overslept, and I *strongly* desired to wake up. My life had a heavy feeling, like I needed to look around, but my eyelids were too droopy to lift. I longed to know who I am, and what's real in the world and my life.

A few months after this talk with my cousin, in July of 1994, I wrote a short story, *Chrysalis*, that paralleled how I felt. The main character was a woman named Sian who decided to quit her job of ten years. When Sian announced her decision to her boss, her boss rejected Sian's decision to leave, and suggested she take some time off. Sian felt like I felt ... that she needed to extricate herself from being wrapped tightly up like a butterfly inside a chrysalis. I felt ready to begin a new phase of life, but had no idea how or when such a change would occur, let alone what it would be.

The *very next week* after I wrote this story, my husband had a spiritual epiphany at a work-related conference! When he returned, we discussed his experience, and my spiritual awakening began, continuing intensely for months. At last I awakened from a long sleep to see the universe with new eyes. I began communicating with angelic guides, and that autumn experienced a two week long kundalini awakening, which completely transformed my world.

When life feels like a dream, I know what feels right for me. Each moment has something dreamlike calling—something I can reach out, touch, and walk into. It helps to pay closer attention to all the senses—touching, smelling, and feeling around me with heightened awareness and sensitivity. Each time I do this, I shift the course of reality, changing the universe as I am more mindful of myself in my surroundings.

Choosing a path of dreamy fulfillment is surrounding myself with my true being. There is nothing to fear or doubt when choosing this path. As I pay close attention to every moment, I see there is always a way to feel more myself; there is always something dreamy I can choose to be doing! Fully participating in this waking dream is the experience of lucid living—the awareness that I am creating this life that is so much like a dream. I don't need to suffer any bad dreams, since I have full control over my attitudes, actions and beliefs. I can change my viewpoint, change my mind, and change my experience. I can greatly affect the universe, and can show the universe what I most care about, by paying the most attention to ... and becoming ... that which I most love.

Lucid Dreaming Exercises

Dream Journal

Get a dream journal or a book of blank pages and write down your dreams when you awaken. Don't worry that you have trouble remembering all of your dreams ... write down what you do remember. You can also write a list of each dream's elements ... the principal characters, places, things, and activities of the dream. Alongside each of these dream elements, write a few words describing how that dream element feels to you—what its symbolic meaning is to you. Read your entire dream through, and get fresh insights from the way all the pieces go together. Take a few minutes to consider what message, if any, you can find for your life right now.

Recognizing Recurring Dream Themes

When you pay attention to your dreams and wish to experience the sensation of lucidity in the dream, you can start by noticing your recurring dream situations. By reminding yourself frequently that a given dream situation *is* a dream, you greatly increase the likelihood that you will one day comprehend within the dream that it is a dream. Consider what dream situations recur most often for you, and you will prepare yourself to notice that it is a dream when you next dream of it again.

CHAPTER 8

Living Lucidly in a Shifting Reality

You are talking with the universe right now

Lucid living is the art of living a waking dream, and consciously initiating reality shifts. Reality shifts are more obvious when we are lucid and aware of discontinuities, rather than unobservant. We can converse with the universe in cosmic dialogue in a waking dream, where questions are answered symbolically and in the form of everyday ordinary experience. You may have experienced a time when someone told you *exactly* what you needed to know before you ever mentioned the subject. Perhaps you've noticed times when signs on billboards or news stories felt equally personal. Maybe you've noticed sounds, smells or bodily sensations that focused your attention at a meaningful moment.

While some people believe we learn best from discomforts and pain, I've found great insights in the dreamlike quality of life of sharing love and joy with others. Wouldn't you prefer to learn from love instead of suffering? I know I would! I often get messages that feel like questions to ponder ... such as bumper stickers and signs whose messages I may not agree with. I take such messages to be questions that help me clear out internal conflicts. I welcome opportunities to know myself and the world better, only digesting messages filled with love that are free of anger and fear. Ideas and beliefs we internalize are much like food ... we don't eat contaminated food, and similarly don't need to digest angry or fearful ideas! Love is pure soul food.

I love the feeling of living a waking dream. I feel so energized, free-flowing, and expansive in dreams, and it feels great to shift reality as I bring these feelings into waking life. There is a boundlessness to lucid living ... a sense of complete freedom to express myself and find ways to become Joy and Love. I hold onto hope, with care to focus on what I need most at this very moment. I get what I wish for this way, especially when I consciously, clearly imagine what I need.

Do you ever feel you're conversing in a dialogue with the universe? That's how lucid living feels. When I need emotional and physical support, I get it even if I don't ask for it, as my need is "heard" by everyone around me. I don't plan or expect surprising shows of support, and I keep an open mind and heart to ensure I don't accidentally turn away the love I need when it comes from unexpected sources.

Lucid living is a life filled with hope, open to possibility and experiences of love and enjoyment without judging people or things by preconceived ideas of "what should be." We are all interconnected in love. Through love, anything is possible in every moment.

If you want to experience the fluid, dreamlike quality of life, you don't need to take mind-altering drugs. You can understand that everything unusual happening in your life is a dream message to you. If you have difficulty believing this, think back to the last odd or unexpected thing that happened in your life that seemed to transcend or bypass logic, and ask yourself the question, "What is a possible meaning of this for me?" If you can realize in the midst of an unusual experience that something very different is happening, you can ask yourself, "What was the last thing I was thinking about when this strange incident occurred?" You can get answers to questions you are asking unconsciously this way.

Receive Messages

> *"The individual who wishes to have an answer to the problem of evil has need, first and foremost, of self-knowledge, that is the utmost possible knowledge of his own wholeness. He must know relentlessly how much good he can do, and what crimes he is capable of, and must beware of regarding the one as real and the other as illusion. Both are elements within his nature, and both are bound to come to light in him, should he wish — as he ought — to live without self-deception and self-delusion."*
>   *– Carl Jung*

We communicate with spirit consciousness all the time, wherever we are. We are all connected and all as One at a very high level. There are many ways people use to listen and talk to spirit, such as meditation and interpreting dreams. Donald Watson defines mystical experience in his book, *A Dictionary of Mind and Spirit*, as being:

> *"Direct knowledge of God, the inspiration that comes to us in a flash, during prayer, meditation or fasting is known in most religious traditions. It is called 'baraka' by the Sufis, 'baruch' (a blessing) in the Jewish tradition. Common characteristics of such experiences are a loss of ego boundaries and a corresponding identification with the whole cosmos—cosmic consciousness; there is a feeling of total freedom, a sense of being beyond space and time, free from fear, free from separateness, at one with everything; even the senses seem to be unified in total perception of abundant clarity. To this cosmic feeling might also be added the feeling of overwhelming love for the whole of creation and of being loved by the Creator."*

Spirit *loves* to communicate with us. When I pay close attention, important messages arrive any time I'm ready and willing to listen. If you feel uneasy with the idea of talking with spirit, there are other ways to contemplate the entirety that is you.

In the transitional state of consciousness while falling asleep, people are much more open to hearing voices, feeling phantom bodily sensations (such as being touched or tapped) and seeing visions. These 'hypnagogic' images (Greek: 'leading to sleep') can seem like they are fluidly entering one's awareness in a dreamy fashion. The 'hypnopompic' time (Greek: 'sent or escorted by sleep') between sleeping and waking is perhaps the most conducive to removing belief constraints we use to interpret direct experience. When I have been in the hypnopompic state, I've noticed that my thoughts and feelings seem perfectly orchestrated to the sounds around me. I feel how the external world and my inner awareness are interconnected at a very fundamental level.

You are a conscious receiver and transmitter in this universe, and you can start sending your thoughts by doing something as simple as writing your feelings and thoughts down on a few pages every day. You can listen for answers in your dreams, in your meditations, and in the messages you get from the people and things around you. When you understand and believe that everything can talk with you and hear you, you'll be amazed at how true this is. Our thoughts and feelings are transmitted like waves to be received by others or ourselves across space and time.

I once got a message from the universe while I was on my morning walk, listening to the song "Shine" by Collective Soul ... and the tape player's battery suddenly went dead! I had spare alkaline batteries with me, but it turned out that the connection on the battery pack was REALLY hard to get working with the tape player, so I carried the pack back home without listening to the rest of the tape. This felt to me like spirit was giving me the following message:

> "Some days you will find you feel like you just don't have the strength or the will to move mountains with your hands. You'll go to the people and things that you've gotten recharged from in the past (parents, spouse, friends) ... and feel you're STILL not recharged! Don't lose faith! When you find yourself feeling run down like this, and nothing restores your feeling of flying/falling in love ... simply REMEMBER that LOVE IS ALWAYS WITH YOU ... all you have to do is RECONNECT to your eternal sense of self."

When I felt this message, it reminded me of Dorothy in the Wizard of Oz, clicking her red shoes together and saying, "There's no place like home." It's a reminder that I've always got home in my heart—we all do. We are all connected through love to the source of all that is.

You can begin a dialogue with spirit right now by accepting messages from all around you. One fast, fun, and easy way to get feedback from spirit is to use your dictionary. Just about every possible idea and answer is in the dictionary, so you can ask a question, shut your eyes, open to a random page and point at a word, with your eyes still shut. When I've done this and opened my eyes to see the answer, I've been impressed with the insightfulness of answers I've received. Keep in mind that the answer you receive from the dictionary is *symbolic*, so it can be interpreted with a dream symbol book or your own intuition as to what that symbol means.

Consulting the dictionary as an oracle provides answers when we ask for help, much like making a wish. I sincerely feel how much I wish to know the answer with all my passionate desire, and I put my question into words, pictures and feelings to fit my own way of imagining the universe. The answers I get never cease to enlighten and amaze me!

Answers in the Dictionary

In 1996, I wanted to figure out how to approach my fear of facing all my feelings ... I wanted to know what the best way is for me to work through my tendency to objectify people, feelings, and situations. When I got stressed, I'd analyze situations with my mind, but end up feeling even more high-strung, stressed, and overwhelmed.

I shut my eyes, opened to a random page of my appropriately named "Random House" dictionary, and pointed with my index finger at the first definition for the word, "populate." I read the definition:

"Populate: to inhabit, live in, be the inhabitants of."

Now I happened to find this very interesting and timely, because I knew that when I feel disjointed from spirit, I can become stressed-out and overwhelmed. This definition reminded me to make sure I'm as much in myself as possible—staying inspired and *fully* inhabiting my whole body, not just my head. This reminder is important to me, because I often would rather ignore, box up, or pretend my feelings don't exist; some of them seem so inconvenient. This answer reminded me that the only way for me to overcome my tendency to fixate on ideas or people is to most fully become aware of all of myself.

Our dialogue with spirit is ongoing, and we get answers to our questions all the time. Just as wishes come true, questions are answered ... even questions that we forgot we asked. It helps to pay close attention to unusual things in life, asking what was thought and felt when events occurred, and contemplating the connections.

Skinned Knees

An example of my real life "talking" to me happened in December 1997, when I went for a walk at night and tripped in the dark and skinned both of my knees. My knees represent to me what I need in life ... both what I need to receive and what I need to give. I immediately noted what I'd been thinking about before I tripped and fell, and I recalled I'd been thinking about what a fast typist I am, and how well I'd summarized results from a school brainstorming workshop I'd helped facilitate.

I often have a tendency to listen to people who tell me "You're the best person for this job!," agreeing to do whatever they asked of me, since I felt a responsibility to do everything I could possibly do for people I care about. Even when the praise is genuine, I'm now beginning to understand it's more important for me to recognize what I need to give and receive, not what functions I'm most in demand to perform.

Creating Synchronous Reality Shifts

Sometimes the synchronicities and coincidences in our lives seem so amazing that they *really* grab our attention. I believe these synchronicities are actually reality shifts, and that we ourselves are responsible for the occurrence of synchronicity, coincidence, and manifestation in our lives. We manifest things like good parking spaces right in front of the shop we're going to, or arriving somewhere exactly at the right time for something we didn't even know was going to happen, such as a free performance in the park.

When events align themselves in noticeably conspicuous fashion so as to capture our attention, they seem to be fitted together for us against all odds ... as if all possibilities were considered and *this* particular combination was selected for our experiential pleasure from an infinite range of possibilities. I feel that this is indeed the case ... we shift reality to attract all that we most love right to us by the very strength of the love we feel!

Thinking of You

A beautiful example of synchronous reality shifting is the story about the man who arranged for my parents to meet. I'd been thinking of him a lot back in April 1997 ... asking my mom how it was that she'd met my dad to begin with, and how the friend who had introduced them to each other is doing now. I remember his two daughters, who are a little older than my sister and I, and wondered how they were. My mom had no idea how they were doing, because there had been no correspondence. I felt the longing and love my dad and his friend shared for one another, and an enormous feeling reached out to me, inspiring me to wish with all my heart that we could hear from this special man again—that my dad and his old friend could reestablish this love and friendship again.

Incredibly, when I went to see my parents at Mother's Day in 1997, there was a letter from my dad's friend, the man who "never writes letters." Inside were pictures of him with his two daughters, and you can see how much he loves them, because he's smiling so much his eyes are shut and he has to look down! His daughters are beautiful, and their love for him shows as well! The letter to my dad began something like, "I was just thinking to my self the other day, Self ... you really need to write," and this very simple way of starting the letter gave me the electric realization that at the same time as this man was writing a letter to my parents, I was longing to hear from him.

This story illustrates the new assumptions that we are all interconnected; that change does not occur causally, but instead through a handshake between sender and receiver; and that consciousness is nonlocal. I don't know and don't try to figure out whether I read my dad's friend's mind or he read mine—that's irrelevant! The point to me is that he really loves my dad, and that I felt their love for one another. Love is the stuff that binds the whole universe together.

The strength of love we allow ourselves to feel greatly expands the range of possibilities in our lives. Visualize an image of a parabolic curve, in which a realm of possibility opens up to be seen directly ahead of us, with curved edges on the left, right, top, and bottom where we most rely on our peripheral vision. Love can feel expansive in our hearts, and it opens up a much greater range of creative possibilities in life, like widening the parabolic curve so more opportunities and possibilities come into peripheral view.

One way to envision the difference between a loving or non-loving perspective is that love opens up one's peripheral view, while fear and anger shut down visual range to tunnel vision. When experiencing tunnel vision, it seems only one possibility is available ... the only one we can see that's directly where we happen to be looking. The expansiveness of love acts like a magnet to attract all kinds of possibilities to us, including possibilities we might never have imagined ... possibilities outside any previous experience and beyond our limited bubble of beliefs. Simply *feeling* great love is enough to bring an abundance of blessings into your life! We will probably not feel "in control" of what is being attracted, but we will be able to enjoy a much greater sense of how the universe appreciates love and how love attracts love.

Just as self-reflection differentiates lucid dreams from regular dreams, self-reflection and an awareness of the non-duality of the universe differentiates lucid living from regular life. Consciousness begins with self-reflection ... the awareness of who we are, where we are, and what we are living for.

It's great to think and read about these things, but it's *extraordinary* to experience living examples of being in a waking dream! When I am in a specially heightened state of awareness and Love, the most incredibly magical things have happened to me, even in times that would seem to be potentially disappointing:

Finding Friends

I had a wonderful experience of lucid living one day in February 1996, when I took the BART commuter train to San Francisco to have lunch with three good friends. I had trouble finding a parking space at the BART station, and missed the commuter train I needed to be on in order to meet my friends at the agreed upon time.

I felt relaxed as I arrived in San Francisco, but then became slightly concerned when I saw nobody was waiting for me at the office building where we'd agreed to meet. I went inside the office building and asked if there were any messages for me ... and found out there were no messages. I tried all logical means I could think of to contact my friends. I left a phone message at my friend's office phone, I asked people where the most popular lunch places are, and I walked around to look inside the restaurants nearby, only to discover that there are too many restaurants in downtown San Francisco to be able to find someone. Every city block seemed to have about ten more restaurants on it, and every restaurant is jam-packed with hundreds of people at lunchtime.

As a slight drizzle began to fall on me from the overcast sky, I felt a feeling of relaxed joy overcome me, and I thought to myself, "Well, if logic can't find my friends, maybe love can!" I couldn't stand the thought of missing my friends, and I felt certain that if I could relax and feel our love for each other I'd have no trouble walking straight to them. Renewed with gigantic feelings of love my friends and I feel for one another, I walked through a pedestrian alley back to the Galleria. I don't know why I walked to the Galleria; it just felt right. As I reached the Galleria, I saw a sign for "Faz" which felt completely right, so I asked the first woman I saw how to get there, and she pointed out the hidden elevator to me. I continued to walk directly to the restaurant, then directly past the hostess inside to where my friends were seated.

My friends looked so surprised that their mouths hung wide open! I was happy to see them, and delighted to be there not too late! Because I'd felt confident I would find them, this incident didn't startle me all that much at the time. It was only after a few days as I thought more about my walking directly to where they were, that this incident seemed much more amazing to me.

This experience was a powerful reminder to me that we are all connected across time and space through love. There's tremendous power when strong emotions are combined with thinking about someone else. I've often noticed if I'm feeling strong emotions and thinking of friends, they'll later tell me they were thinking of me at that time. Similarly, when my friends feel strong emotions and think of me, I've thought of them and picked up their feelings on the "psychic network."

Psychic Network

One morning in November, I dropped my younger four-year-old daughter off at a friend's house and went to the grocery store around 9:30 AM. When I arrived at the store, I suddenly felt quite bereft. I felt like I'd just lost both my children, and I felt this so strongly I was on the verge of crying. Tears welled up in my eyes as I felt how much I love my daughters and missed having them with me right then. Suddenly, I remembered a friend of mine who told me that he often had felt this way about his teenage son who'd gone off to college recently ... and thinking of my friend brought me instantaneous relief, so I was able to shop without tears streaming down my face.

When I came home with my groceries, I found a phone message on my answering machine from my friend, asking that I please call him as soon as possible! I called him right back, and he asked, "WHAT were you doing at 9:30 am this morning?!?" I told him I'd been grocery shopping. He said, "I'm asking because I felt something like a tidal wave of love for you right then that was so strong I stopped what I was doing and looked at the clock!" I was impressed he had felt our love for each other at the precise moment I most felt I needed him! I told him this was a test of the psychic emergency broadcast network. I really needed his reassuring love and support, and I could feel it as clearly as though he'd been right by my side.

This experience with the psychic network reminds me that I've helped people overcome serious health problems when I have similarly felt their symptoms hit me suddenly without warning ... and I've slowly learned to trust that these feelings are real. I now know that when I think of someone out of the blue, chances are that they really need that extra love and support right at that very moment.

I've found the results from meditation of feeling relaxed, energized and loving makes a *huge* difference in energizing synchronicities and changing what happens in my life. Another good example of the power of meditation to alter one's waking dream is the time I waited for some friends to meet me at an interactive science museum in San Francisco.

Summoning Friends

I was at the Exploratorium in San Francisco with my two daughters one day, waiting for some friends to meet us there. When they were an hour late, I found a relatively calm spot to sit, meditate, and raise my energy. I did this for an hour or so, then felt suddenly inspired to gather the girls and walk to the front of the building. I didn't see the friends I was expecting there ... but I was *astonished* to see my Swiss friend driving up at that very moment in his taxi cab! He gave us some Swiss chocolates and talked with us for a few minutes.

My daughters and I re-entered the Exploratorium, and were surprised to find two more friends! It was their first visit to the Exploratorium, and they were having a blast! We enjoyed walking around with them, and my daughters were happy to have met some friends I love so much.

The friends I expected didn't arrive that day (they had car trouble) ... but this outing was very special because of the friends who came to meet me where I was.

Sometimes people can tell when a friend is about to phone or come to visit, even before the phone or doorbell rings; they have a very clear sense of connectedness with that person and can *really* sense when they are close by.

Keep on Trucking

I have a friend who worked as a trucker, and he told me that whenever his friend and trucking partner comes into town, he can feel it. His friend is frequently on the road, so his ability to sense when she's around and when she's gone comes in very handy. He doesn't have to wait for her to phone!

One day, my friend spotted a very familiar big-rig on the freeway near San Leandro, and he noticed it was his partner driving his old truck! They pulled off the road to talk, and she told him she was really glad to see him, because he'd left some things in the truck.

It's possible coincidences are created by love, where the love flowing through us attracts all that we love and that loves us back. I've noticed coincidences become much more frequent when people feel inspired and energized. Accessing this free energy is the foundation for the wonderful reality shift phenomenon I've experienced. You may notice feeling most energized and invigorated outdoors, or around certain people, or when you listen to some favorite music. Whatever it is that most inspires you can help remind you to feel your own maximally energized state.

I was in a *very* energized, relaxed state of consciousness when I wanted to meet my friends for lunch in San Francisco, but I got there late and didn't know which restaurant they'd gone to. I was confident I would simply walk straight to where they were, since I was in a very energized, relaxed state of mind. The quieter the noise of my thoughts and feelings of anxiety and resentment become, the more vibrant, light, and expansively loving I can feel. When I feel like this for any period of time, the most wonderfully amazing things begin to happen! Numerous coincidences occur, and life seems brighter and more vibrant.

Getting into a loving meditative state is simply a matter of feeling very, very light, and very, very energized. It's also a feeling of being so calm, focused and joyous that a feeling of loving oneness permeates everything. This is a sense of detachment where the divisions and desires between things seem irrelevant, and one can experience the true interconnectedness between all of us in space and time. There are no feelings of worry or anger in this state of energized, detached awareness; only love, peace, and joy. It might feel physically a bit like having goose-bumps ... like having electricity running all the way down the spine from head to toe. It first feels warm and vibrant and light to me, and eventually feels like a complete experience of love and joy as I sense a direct experience of being connected to all that is. We all create this reality together, like one big, shared dream ... yet we seldom acknowledge this is in fact what we are doing.

I can see reality shift when I relax into a state of openness and love. In this state of mind, I have seen cards *change* to allow me to win games of computer solitaire.

Winning Solitaire

When I play computer solitaire (Klondike), I sometimes notice I can win almost every time I am in a relaxed, ecstatic, love-filled meditative state of mind, and as long as I don't pay too close attention to what cards are on the screen. It seems that when I look at the cards I believe are there, I fix those cards in place simply because I believe I have seen them to be there. As soon as I believe a certain card is definitely present in a given position, I have a harder time allowing it to be something else. When I don't look closely at the cards, I can win *much* more frequently, and sometimes out of the corner of my eye I can see a card change!

I play solitaire now as a kind of biofeedback tool; it helps me remember to breathe deeply, feel love flowing through me, and as I remember and re-experience this ecstatic, high-energy state of consciousness I can win games much more easily.

When I feel great love in a relaxed meditative state, my waking life and my dreams feel more vivid and vibrant. I become increasingly aware of how all existence is like a dream, and the meditative practices I learn in sleeping or waking can be used in either state, since I have the same consciousness whether asleep and awake. As my self-identity becomes less ego-based, I feel warmer, more expansive, and more energized. I feel able to learn from whatever I experience as I realize all experience is like a dream ... a dream that I am co-creating. When we feel relaxed, unbounded, and focused only on love, psychic powers and feats are normal.

We choose how we respond to our world. We can be confused, scared, angry, worried, bitter or joyful—whatever we like. This is the real creativity through which we shape and create our universe. *All* emotions are possible; there is infinite freedom. Perhaps having such freedom is how some people feel lost, because there's so much besides pure love to explore.

We can't pay attention to *everything*, so we usually operate unconsciously to some degree. We have a tendency to only pay attention to things aligned with current goals and desires ... but we might miss many opportunities in life by being so narrowly focused on what we *think* we need that we neglect areas we consider of little interest, or a "waste of time."

It's easy but not necessarily very fulfilling to live and work on autopilot. When we live according to what others feel is best or right for us, we can lose our sense of inner guidance. We can lose our sense of who we truly are, and what we're living for. If we get caught up in living according to what we feel we're supposed to be doing, joys seem fleeting, responsibilities and duties feel overwhelming, our days feel rushed and crowded, and a lasting fulfilling sense of happiness can seem to be forever just out of our grasp. Our lives can feel empty and hollow, and we can feel there's no real point to anything we're doing or have done. These are some of the disadvantages of viewing oneself purely as ego, and not stepping back to gain a more mindful perspective.

When we feel real experience directly, we rediscover we are made of pure love. We usually forget about this while we're alive, and lose the feeling of love that exists between us and everything and everyone else in the universe. When we pay attention to where we are and what we're doing in the present moment, the greatest ecstasy is possible. I've had very joyous life experiences at such times, and have felt such happiness at sharing the feeling of being in a waking dream.

Sufferer

I was grocery shopping one weekday at lunchtime when I got a very strong sense of being in a waking dream. I was standing at the checkout line with all the groceries I had purchased to feed my family of four for a week (a sizable amount of groceries). The cashier scanned each item and bagged things as I noticed the woman behind me. She was holding a single item—menstrual cramp relief medication—with a pinched, pained expression on her face.

I immediately smiled at this woman and told her I wished she could take her medication *soon* ... and suggested she go ahead and do that! I convinced her there was no reason she should not open the medication and take some with a glass of water right now. The woman was grateful to hear such a caring suggestion, and immediately did just that.

When she returned to the check-out line, my groceries were still being scanned and bagged, so I offered to massage her neck and shoulders and upper back as we chatted with the cashier. The three of us were in the kind of reverie one only experiences with dear friends, and the cashier told us personal stories about what mattered most in his life right then. This was such an enchanted moment in our lives, and I felt my spirit soar with joy as I left the store that day.

I felt immensely grateful to help this woman, and thankful to have experienced a moment of waking life that felt like the best of dreams. When we listen to intuition, life can feel wonderful! Every moment can be magical, filled with a warm, energized, expansive feeling of compassion, love, and joy!

While many of us are happy to help those in need, we often have the greatest difficulty being equally generous and lovingly expansive to those who know us most intimately ... our family. Our closest relationships offer us the greatest challenges and the greatest opportunities for growth and transformation. As we learn to be consciously aware of how we choose to relate to those around us, we face many inner fears and doubts. We can learn to face our doubts by listening to and trusting our intuition.

Listen to Intuition

Intuition means "inner teaching." When we observe our physiological sensations as we consider different possibilities, we can make good "gut decisions." Our inspiration often comes through our bodies, and we can get some very good intuitive advice by paying close attention to how we feel physically and emotionally.

Parking Spot Phobia

When I lived on Cedar Street in Berkeley, I parked my car any place I could find an open spot, since parking spots were hard to find in the evenings. One day, when my boyfriend drove me home, I got a panicky feeling as he began to park on the corner spot. I had a strong feeling great danger was imminent if we parked in that spot, so I insisted we must find another spot, even if it was farther away. My boyfriend could see how concerned I felt, so he moved the car to another spot.

My feeling of uneasiness about that parking spot continued for a few days, so we continued parking elsewhere. Several days later, at about one o'clock in the morning, I heard a CRASH outside on the street. When I looked out my window, I saw a car had crashed into the car parked in that corner spot.

Sometimes, intuition guides us to do things we would never have guessed we could do, such as locate something that someone else has misplaced. I've enjoyed numerous opportunities to find missing toys in my house that I had not recently seen or touched, and I've also managed to find small items such as screws or small mechanical parts.

Finding Lost Keys

One evening, my husband was working on the computer while our younger daughter played with keys in his pocket. My husband was distracted by his work on the computer, and didn't notice when she wandered off to another place in the house with them. He definitely DID notice his keys were missing the next morning when he couldn't find them! He knew our daughter put them somewhere, but had no time to search. He borrowed my keys as I said I'd look for his.

I had no idea where the keys might be, since our daughter was very active, and wandered all over the house. I decided to simply follow my legs wherever they took me. I found myself feeling inspired to walk to the bathroom, and stop facing the bathroom sink. I then followed my hand, and felt inspired to pull open one of three drawers in the bathroom sink cabinet. I looked down into the drawer, and in the midst of bathroom odds and ends were my husband's keys!

A great way to develop intuition is to notice some of the more subtle clues around you by writing in a daily journal. After you've written in your journal for several months, look back to see how patterns of thinking and feeling interweave with events in your life in ways you won't see so easily when you're in the midst of it all. You can develop trust of intuitive knowledge by learning the ancient art of dowsing.

Dowsing

Dowsing is a wonderfully easy, practical, and fun way to discover things you had no idea you could possibly know, such as the location of subterranean water or energy fields, or the presence and strength of the human energy field. You can experience first hand for yourself the true energy nature of this world, which is where reality shifts begin.

I first learned about dowsing when I traveled to England with my husband in June 1995. I brought along a book called *The Sun & The Serpent*, by Hamish Miller, on the subject of tracking ley lines using dowsing. This book tracks both the Christian and the very ancient sacred sites along ley lines that go from the far west of Cornwall to a point on the east coast of Norfolk. Although we didn't explore the whole line, we did investigate some areas of interest.

We stopped in Royston, England to see the Royston Museum, and were disappointed to discover the museum was closed the day we arrived. We talked to the museum curator,

Jane Vincent, who opened the front door to ask where we'd come from. When she heard we had traveled all the way from California, she welcomed us in with warm smiles and kind hospitality to the closed museum to personally show us its 6,000 year-old stone axes and arrowheads. She spent two hours with us, and told us that the male and female earth energy lines were very strong in this place. Jane insisted that my husband and I try the "very *practical* art of dowsing."

Dowsing for energy spots

Jane took great care to demonstrate the correct way to hold the dowsing rods (two coat hangers) loosely out in front of oneself, one in each hand, about eight to fourteen inches apart. Metal coat hangers work fine as dowsing rods if you hold them vertical to the ground by the longest straight line, leaving the hooked part at the top of the triangle to point forward ahead of you. Hold the dowsing rods loosely enough so they sway gently to the left and then the right as you take slow steps forward. When you reach something (such as energy lines or underground water), these dowsing rods will indicate that by swinging together or apart as if by magic.

Some people are quite naturally good at dowsing, and others can't seem to get their rods to move at all. My husband was *quite* good at it right away, but I got so excited and nervous I had to calm down first and take off my purse that was interfering with my ability to relax and move freely. Once I relaxed, everything went much more smoothly and the coat hangers clanged into each other as if by magic as I walked forward. I walked slowly towards my husband to notice where his energy field was, and I was astonished to discover that dowsing *really does work!* After dowsing each other's energy fields, we were delighted to find that we could dowse the energy lines in the museum, too!

Jane warned us about dowsers who talk about spiritual dowsing. She explained dowsing is a practical matter, best learned from someone who uses it regularly for real life matters (like finding water). Jane then led me outdoors to the museum courtyard and asked if I cared to try outdoors water dowsing. I could hardly believe it, but the dowsing rods indicated very clearly where the water main line was hiding underneath the cobbled patio! I was amazed to see how simply such a strange method could be applied to indicate so accurately where water lay ... when I had *no idea* where that would be! I got so excited by all this that I wanted to practice dowsing everywhere, but Jane recommended starting with well-known areas to get a better feel for what I was doing. She also recommended joining a "practical" dowsing club.

The Royston Museum visit was a highlight of our trip, and I was struck by the realization of how fortunate we had been that the museum had been closed, so we could get such personal attention and dowsing instruction! This part of the trip provided an excellent demonstration of how just when we find a disappointment in life, we may be surprised to find things turn out even better than we had hoped!

Continuing on our trip to Avebury, England, I dowsed confidently around ancient stones, finding great energy around the old, mysterious monoliths at the Avebury Henge. We arrived in Avebury on the summer solstice, and I enjoyed feeling the energy lines from the stones using dowsing rods. I got a clear sense of the way these stones have life in them, and how their placement was carefully arranged corresponding to energy fields in the Earth.

In Avebury, my husband and I also spent some meditative time inside tree circles. Circles of trees form mounds when their roots collectively push a whole cluster of trees upward over many years. Sitting atop these mounds feels like being in an exhilaratingly refreshing cathedral! Wind blows through the leaves, and a stained-glass effect of light gently filtering through dancing leaves and branches is breathtakingly beautiful. The sense of magic and mystery in these places is intense, and one's choice of entry and exit from these tree circles is akin to choosing one's path in life. Each "door" between tree trunks has such a different feeling to it.

When we returned home to California, I felt inspired to show my friends how to dowse. We were amazed at how we could discern each other's energy fields so clearly! One of my friends was having so much fun learning to dowse in the house and garden looking for energy fields, that he wandered off to the public front yard to continue dowsing around the street. I was really impressed at how unconcerned he was about our neighbor's raised eyebrows and slightly negative remarks ... it was water off a duck's back to him. Seeing such confidence inspired me to not worry so much about how ridiculous I may feel in awkward social situations. As my friend later told me, "Lots of people go forward with complete confidence who have absolutely no idea about what matters." It's good to remember that we are following intuition when we venture out into the world with dowsing rods in hand!

Getting involved in the hands-on process of dowsing brings energy fields "to life," in the sense that otherwise invisible fields of energy feel physically present. Dowsing is easy to learn, and can provide you with a gentle nudge to do more than sit back and analyze the way matter and energy interact here on Earth. Even though I was warned to keep my dowsing practices practical and earthy, I've found dowsing can be a wonderful catalyst for heightening my senses. For example, I saw colors in someone's aura for the first time a short while after learning to dowse.

Dowsing reminds me there is no need to go to exotic locales for amazing insights and spiritual truths—everything talks to us all the time. We need only listen.

Listen for Peace and Harmony

> *"When the Universe was not so out of whack as it is today, and all the stars were lined up in their proper places, you could easily count them from left to right, or top to bottom, and the larger and bluer ones were set apart, and the smaller yellowing types pushed off to the corners as bodies of a lower grade ..."*
> – Stanislaw Lem

The magical key to success in being heard is simply to *listen*. Listening works because it requires that we actively pay close attention to other individuals, empathizing with their situation, and making an effort to care about them. We all have a need to be heard and understood, and only when we openly approach others as equals and friends can we be heard ourselves. The person who waits to be invited to join a discussion may wait forever. The person who makes threats and insults will be ignored as well. Only those who actively seek out feelings of others will be rewarded in kind. You won't always hear what you want to hear, but you'll be heard. To the degree you see more than a narrow perspective, you may be further rewarded by being understood.

We hope for a wonderful environment for our children and community. For this to happen, we need to regain a vision of our world as one Earth; one family. Success for one of us is success for all of us, and exclusion for one of us is pain and loss for all of us. We don't need to parcel out compassion for some people, and leave others to wait an eternity.

We know that issues can seem insurmountable, often because "somebody isn't listening." It's time to see that "somebody" is us. When each one of us cares, takes time, and makes an effort to reach out to hear what others feel, we heal wounds we've inflicted on ourselves over the years, and start making our dreams come true. We're all in this together; we are one family. It's up to us what kind of family we choose to become: divided and fighting, or unified and thriving.

When we listen in the form of attentiveness to our surroundings with all our senses, we love. When we come to our senses fully, and awaken to beauty existing around us right here right now, the world becomes vibrantly alive! It helps to feel all you can feel with all your senses, paying full attention to what you hear, see, touch, taste, and smell. It's energizing and enriching to take a few moments and fully experience something ... and every time you do this, it's amazing how such simple appreciation of living can totally transform one's experience of life.

In 1994 I was asked to give a talk about how I'd helped influence a school board's decision to rebuild a school rather than close it down. I spoke to the community about the power of listening, and how it allows us to help others state and release their fears, so we can work better together without feeling threatened or taking things personally. After my talk was over, I was amazed to hear the speaker who followed me speak of how people "hadn't listened" to him and things had gone wrong ... and then as his own words still hung in the air, he shuffled restlessly through his speaker's notes and seemed to have an epiphany of comprehension at the podium. He set all his notes aside, and began speaking from his heart about what he'd really hoped to accomplish. I felt a tremendous difference in his presentation as he abandoned an attitude of lamenting how bad things had happened to him, and began speaking instead of how things *had* been transformed by his actions and presence. I sensed this man knew he really *was* being listened to, and was now ready to let go of blaming others for the problems in the community.

You probably know cases where the best thing to do for someone who's going through a terrible time is to be there and listen. Listening is an art of knowing the message beneath spoken words, and feeling the impact of emotion behind those words. There is no greater gift we can give another person than listening—feeling their emotions as ours. Listening is loving, and love shifts reality.

Live Mindfully

> *"Chaos often breeds life when order breeds habit."*
> *– Henry Adams*

Developing mindfulness means letting go of habitual ways of responding to situations. We no longer need to react, "the way we always have," and can instead consider each moment a unique opportunity to live life to its fullest. We may face similar challenges, but we can now meet them without expectation, assumptions, anger or fear, as we see how we color every experience by choosing such feelings.

Meditating helps us find the presence of mind to discover joyfulness in every moment, helping us handle problems gracefully as they arise. Meditative awareness is a state of being that overcomes fears and neediness for support and stimulation, so we don't feel distraught, distressed, depressed, and alone. By observing the way thoughts enter into our consciousness, we become aware of how their very presence greatly affects our ability to enjoy life.

When we realize that we can consciously choose how we feel and face our feelings from many different perspectives and directions, we discover that we are often *choosing* to feel melancholy, despair, or isolation. We can just as easily choose to feel joyous and loving, and live accordingly! We don't have to be trapped by our emotions: we can choose to relax and become sensitive to our feelings, observing and learning from our problems without ignoring or running away from them. When we open ourselves to feeling love, the range of possible realities opens up for us, too. The more expansively loving we feel, the more love we attract into our lives. Discovering this ability to see what is really here without obsessing about it or discounting it is precisely that detached perspective that allows reality shifts and all manner of miracles into our lives.

Lucid Living Exercises

Receiving Messages

Think about the last time something really unusual happened ... something so out-of-the-ordinary you never forgot it. Write down the full story of what happened, and draw a line at the bottom of your narrative. Next, list the specific details of what happened in this experience, including the people involved, the setting, and each thing and activity involved. Alongside each of these elements, write a few words describing how that person, thing, place or activity feels to you, and what its symbolic meaning might be. Now, read through all the symbolic meanings in this waking dream experience, and summarize them in one sentence.

Dowsing

Take two simple wire hangers and practice holding one in each hand so the hooked parts face away from your body. Keep the hangers positioned vertically, straight up and down, and hold them loosely by the biggest part of the hanger (the bottom part) so you can see and feel the hangers sway gently left and then right as you walk slowly forward. With your dowsing rods loose and remaining vertically upright, about eight to fourteen inches apart, test them out on a person or animal or take them outdoors to locate earth energy fields or subterranean water. Keep in mind what you are dowsing for as you walk, and the rods will respond to your focus of attention. You'll know when you've found something, because the dowsing rods will suddenly "clank!" together or swing widely apart like barn doors opening wide. This is a terrific exercise for discovering how subtle energy fields surround us all the time, and how something as simple as a pair of clothes hangers can show us those energy fields!

Answers in Dictionary

Think of a question you'd love answered that you don't already know the answer to. Take some time to consider a question you *really* care about, that truly matters to you; frivolous questions get frivolous answers in reply. Phrase the question so that you can receive an answer that isn't simply a Yes or No. When you've come up with your question, hold a dictionary closed in your lap and with eyes shut, state your question as clearly as you can, either silently or aloud. With eyes still closed, open the dictionary to a page, and point one finger at some part of a page. When your finger touches a page, open your eyes and read the answer to your question. If the answer makes no sense to you at this time, meditate for a few minutes, and try this exercise again.

Energizing Yourself

This exercise requires help from a friend who is willing to dowse with you. Start by holding two wire coat hangers lightly, one in each hand, standing about ten feet away from your friend. Slowly walk toward your friend, with the intention that you will sense the human energy field. When you encounter your friend's energy field, your coat hangers will respond by moving out (like barn doors opening wide) or in together (like doors shutting), or they both may go left or right. When your dowsing wires respond in any of these ways, stop walking forward and take a step back away from your friend. Now ask your friend to imagine a pleasant fantasy or memory such as a favorite vacation, food, music, or friend. Watch your dowsing rods respond as your friend's energy field increases in size; you are witnessing the power of feelings on the energy body! Take turns with your friend to see where your energy body starts out, and how far it expands when you feel good.

Chapter 9

Shifting Reality for Healing

Consciousness of love heals

Spontaneous healing occurs when reality shifts occur in our bodies that restore balance and vitality. Consciousness of love is the power behind healing and health, and love can cross any distance, boundary, or barrier because we are all interconnected.

Wishing for healing is a focused prayer for reality shifts to occur that produces the most intimate kind of reality shift—one that affects our bodies. Healing requires the same components of successful prayer, especially the holistic feeling of being connected to all that is, and it also involves something very personal and very special. The special thing about praying to heal someone is that we are actively getting involved in a dialogue the sick or injured person is having with consciousness, or spirit.

When you or someone you love is sick, the benefits of shifting reality for healing are obvious. Being healthy greatly improves the quality of one's life, regardless of one's purpose in life. Without good health, one doesn't have anything. Shifting reality to heal ourselves or someone else is a marvelously practical way to make our lives the best they can be—provided we first listen carefully to any personal message in the injury or illness, and contemplate and communicate a reply to questions it poses. When we listen and respond to the message, we are better assured of lasting healing because we are addressing any underlying energetic conditions.

Many different types of energetic healing exist. *Faith healers* are usually members of religious sects, who typically require both healer and patient to have faith in God in order to heal. *Psychic healers* often regard their own energy to be the energy utilized in the healing process, and sometimes believe the healer to be at risk of being adversely affected by patients they heal. *Spirit healers* don't require the healing recipient to believe in healing, but instead channel healing energies. Healers typically channel healing energy through their solar plexus, or heart chakra. The type of healing I have experience with is spirit healing, utilizing the universal interconnectedness between all that is, and feeling the conscious universal love energy that creates and sustains all life.

Healing with prayer and love is not something I would have believed in thirty years ago! Due to a series of events and personal proofs in my life, I've found that focusing healing attention on another is extraordinarily and consistently effective. Until several years ago, I didn't have such conscious awareness of what my energy body feels like, or how it feels when it's grounded, energized, or in a state of rapport with another. I only had the barest sense of how my emotions seemed linked to my physical body. I came to notice a real physical feeling in my body when I am spiritually charged with the energy of universal love; it feels a little like a warm, tingly sensation of love all the way through me.

What I've learned about healing has come from listening to spirit, and from a natural proclivity toward healing. As one psychic once chided me, "You're what we call a runaway healer!" as I ran my energy with each person in the room. At the time I heard that comment, I had no idea what she was talking about. In the past several years I've had a number of experiences doing remote healing, and I've learned what her comment referred to. I've had a tendency to reach out to others around me, sensing their pain and inner turmoil, and feeling those sensations as my own. I often energize others after feeling attuned to them, and work to remedy energy imbalances I find—all of this happening mostly unconsciously on my part. I am now more conscious of how I run energy with people both close and far from me.

When I began healing, I followed my intuition and the guidance of a tortoise-shaped Indian spirit that appeared to me in my mind's eye calling himself Carapace, perhaps in reference to the tortoise shell he wears. Carapace holds a medicine stick with bones, shells and feathers attached to it, and does his healing through dance and rhythmic movement. Carapace gave me a sense of how to attune myself to those in need of healing. I came into the experience of healing from the point of view of a reluctant skeptic, feeling there was no harm in giving prayer a chance to heal those I love. Now I have learned through experience that intending the healing occur by focusing awareness and intention, and channeling love energy, is all I need to do to facilitate healings.

I feel energized when I help others who ask me for help with healings, since pure love energy flowing through me revitalizes me at the same time as the person being healed! Healing feels like a natural part of living and loving those around us. We are constantly healing those around us every time we share kind words, smiles, and feelings of love and kindness.

Before doing any kind of healing, it's important to remember that not everyone is ready and willing to receive help shifting his or her reality. It is imperative that as a healer, you respect the person requesting your assistance. Regardless how the situation may appear, each person has the full opportunity and ability to solve his or her own problems, and you have no right or obligation to lay those troubles on your shoulders. It's important to remember that everyone's lessons are theirs to learn, and if your healing does not address the underlying cause of illness (which can be communicated by Spirit), then the healing may not be effective, and some other malady or misfortune may strike in order to get the message through to that person.

If you are seriously interested in becoming a healer, it's a good idea to learn about the body's physiology and anatomy as well as psychology and nutrition. There are many healing programs available, which teach massage therapy, acupuncture, chiropractic, and bio-energetic counseling. While I have not studied all these fields in depth, I have some familiarity with them. I receive guidance from spirit showing me how to recognize hidden questions in illness, and the importance of responding sincerely and honestly.

Fred Alan Wolf describes how some shamanistic healers are *quite* vulnerable to receiving illnesses of their patients in his book, *The Eagle's Quest*. I was not aware of shamanistic techniques when I began my forays into healing, nor was I aware of other healing techniques. I was only peripherally aware of healing, since my friend had asked me in 1994 whether I had any interest in healing. At the time she asked the question, I'd replied without hesitation, "No!" Little did I suspect I'd soon participate in healing all kinds of people, and see that healing prayers really do work! I was fascinated to discover Jane Katra felt recalcitrant about *not* being a healer when she described her transformative spiritual awakening in the Philippines in the book, *Miracles of Mind*. While Jane vehemently denied her role as a healer when it was first presented to her in her dream vision, I simply dismissed any interest the subject of healing might hold for me. Apparently, having a conscious interest in learning to do spiritual healings is not necessary in order to develop those abilities.

When I'm ready to begin a healing, I go through three steps. I begin by reminding myself of my healing intentions. Next I feel the injury or illness as an overlay over my own body. Finally I heal the ailment as I feel it in my body, and channel universal Love energy through the healee and me simultaneously so I can get feedback as to how the healing is proceeding. This process works well for me; other healers use different techniques.

State Your Healing Intention

I feel the most important thing for any healer is to know what your most fundamental wish is. It's important to be conscious of your own belief structure, your own sense of self, home, and how you fit into the universe. For many years, my fundamental intention has been:

> *I will assist life to be the best it can possibly be for everyone and everything that has love in it.*

Notice I'm not asking to "share the pain of all those I love," for example! I don't feel a need to do that, and at no level am I asking for that. I do share pain from others on occasion, but I have total faith that when such a thing happens, I needed that feeling in order to bring some message to me. I believe my basic healing intention keeps me on track for how I go about doing healings. I intend to accept only love from the universe, and that only love will stay with me. This protects me from less healthy feelings (like anger and fear) that are not my own as I work on the person to be healed. Protection is very important, since healers can be vulnerable to feeling and taking on the imbalances of those they are working to heal.

It helps to request a better understanding of what is causing the injury, illness, or infection. It's been my experience that unconscious conflicts manifest in the form of injuries and illnesses and infections, and they bring the problem up to consciousness symbolically, by affecting the body, which is one way that consciousness or spirit "talks" with us. Listening to the meaning is the best way to address the deeper issues and the true cause behind the symptoms that need healing.

Because all energy fields of everything in the universe are interconnected, it is important to learn where your compassion boundaries are when you work on healing. One can get lost in another's anger, pain, or misery, and lose the ability to provide assistance while bringing one's own energy levels down. It's therefore important to remind oneself that the other person's maladies belong to them. You can remind yourself of your true energy nature, and that we are all inviolate beings. We can aid a friend without allowing his sadness, anger or physical pain to attach to our etheric bodies. During a friend's traumatic times, we can remind ourselves to establish boundaries between his misery and our physical form, etheric body, mind and emotions.

Healers need to remember that before we can work with or pray for another person, it is our responsibility to first wrap every possible concept of ourselves—in the astral, etheric, and physical levels of our being—in protection. There is nothing to be gained by receiving cast-off energies of another person's illness.

Another important thing to remember is that you don't need to feel your energy depleted when you heal. You can use energy from the universe for healings and allow that energy to flow through you, revitalizing you as it also works on those you heal. Your intention to focus healing energies is enough to activate this universal energy, provided you are relaxed and feeling loved and loving, free from anger and fear. The better you are at maintaining your spiritual health, the better your healings will feel for others.

After doing healings for several years, I took a Reiki class, and found the Reiki system of working with universal life force energy is very similar to my work with energy through visions and spirit guides (who helped me understand how energy flows to revitalize my body). The Reiki system is the universal life force energy that powers all the reality shifts I've experienced so far. Reiki is unified energy behind all dualities, and it is a powerful healing force that synchronizes and energizes vital meridians and acupuncture points while aligning and balancing the major energy centers in physical and finer bodies.

Reiki is a universal form of energy practice originating in Tibet over 2,000 years ago, that brings and focuses healing energy for a person in need, who accepts healing. Usui rediscovered Reiki in Japan, after it had been a forgotten art for almost a century, and found himself performing little miracles, much like reality shifts I've experienced. His toenail ripped off, and he grasped it in extreme pain, only to discover when he removed his hand that his toe was completely healed! He healed a little girl's toothache, a man's arthritis, and a whole bunch of beggars' ailments. Usui discovered that physical problems are typically due to spiritual issues, and if left unresolved, those spiritual issues will once again precipitate physical problems. Many people Usui healed returned to their previous ways of thinking and behaving, and their lives then fell back into the same patterns of disease once again... unless they dealt with their "inner work."

Reiki is similar in concept to the Holy Spirit ... in fact, that's how Usui began his quest to rediscover the hidden mystery energy. His Christian students kept asking him to please show them "just one miracle," since the Bible teaches that the sick can be healed. His students' request seemed perfectly reasonable to Usui, so he began a quest to find answers. He traveled to the city of Chicago in the United States, where he spent seven years in theological school, asking experts to please teach him how to heal the sick. He found out that Americans didn't know how to do that, so he returned to Asia and spent three years in Japanese Buddhist temples, asking the same question, temple by temple. At the very last temple he asked his same question that he'd been asking for at least a decade, and an old monk told him nobody had healed the sick for at least seventy-five years! That's a forgotten art, because the monks found that people are sick in spirit ... any physical healings are undone, because most people need spiritual healing. Usui almost gave up at this point, saying, "This is the end. This temple was my last hope." The monk replied, "We say that this is just the beginning!" Usui felt this was the only place he'd found any kind of hope, so he continued to pray and study there for some time, before undertaking a 21 day fast and meditation atop the mountain where he had his vision of Reiki.

The Christian Holy Spirit energy has been recorded as bringing miracles through Jesus Christ and Christian saints. Miracle healings are still performed even now in the Philippines. Tibetan Buddhists had been using Reiki for thousands of years, and now there is a revival of interest in this healing energy. Simply allowing universal life force energy to run through you, by whatever name you choose to use for it, provides the power necessary for healing to happen. It is not advisable to, nor is there any need to deplete your own energy on healings, when the ultimate healing energy is freely available in all places at all times.

I do many healings for people who are not physically present. I have picked up feelings of intense fear and pain, and not known whose feelings these were on many occasions, sometimes to later discover who it was that was feeling something (like having all their teeth knocked out in a bicycle accident). I don't need to have the person I'm assisting with me physically. The consciousness or spirit of love connects all of us, and brings pain to my attention so I can assist others overcome fear, and speed their healing. In many cases, I have gotten both the feelings of the injury or illness along with the knowledge of whom it is I'm assisting. I prefer to know who it is that I'm helping, to bring the healing to a much more conscious level of participation, so I can talk to the people wishing for the healing wherever possible, so they can learn about the power of unconditional divine love to heal, and aid in their own healing process.

Feel The Injury/Illness

You might have an easier time feeling the sensations of another if you attempt to contact them just before you fall asleep when you are feeling relaxed, but still awake. This is the time your boundaries of self-limitation are most weak and permeable. You are then most likely to find success in overcoming skepticism of your objective mind. If you have trouble tuning into someone's injury or illness, start by relaxing yourself fully, grounding your energy to the Earth, running energy up to your highest sense of self ... and meditating on the subject of inquiry. Meditate to raise your energy and prepare yourself for healing.

Concentrate on empathically feeling the pain and fear of those you love. Pay close attention to all areas of illness, or what feels or looks "off" or wrong to you. These are specific symptoms of what's wrong, and what you can work to help correct! You can get physical bodily sensations corresponding to the ones that need healing that overlay themselves on your body, if your favored way of sensing reality is through feeling. If you prefer visual input, you can get visual images that show you exactly what needs to be addressed in order for healing to occur. You can use visions and symbols to guide you, by requesting that the person's spirit show you what needs tending, and walking through this vision to heal what is wrong.

You need not be in any other kind of contact with your patient than these meditations; there is no need for physical proximity. The "permission" you need comes from the spirit of the person you are healing. I've usually been openly welcomed by spirits when I've requested permission to help them heal. I have not helped heal everyone I know, because some people are not open to sharing their experience of illness and healing or do not accept energy healing, and we must honor their wishes.

Heal With Love & Light

When you've "tuned in" your healing recipient, and feel confident they are ready for healing assistance, you're ready. You've tuned in their fears and pains, and can feel the person's feelings in your own body. Run your energy up to BRIGHT white light, feeling the healing frequency of all the molecules in your body vibrating with healing love. You can specifically heal each individual symptom, then bring the whole body to a high-energy sensation of being totally loved, totally healed, and in a state of ecstatic bliss! This part is the most fun, and makes the healing experience worthwhile, because you the healer get the benefit of energy healing, too.

Energy work training (like Reiki) can help you refine your abilities to channel healing energy. If you are bringing healing energy through yourself to someone who is with you in person, you gain the advantage of sensing how the person feels from their tone of voice, movements, and breathing. You can use all your senses to assist their healing, and convey the love you are channeling for their healing. Your own Qi merges with Universal Life Force energy to give your life a unique blend of heightened awareness, inspiration, and health.

I don't feel energy-drained after healings, because of this last step. I bask in healing energy and feel restored to better health myself. The most challenging part of this last step is simply staying focused on the bright white light healing energy, continually running that divine unconditional love until you get a feeling of ecstatic bliss that signals you've done it! You've given that person as much healing energy as they can accept from the universe at this time, to the point the problem is corrected, and reality has shifted. If you're having trouble contacting healing energy, focus your attention on that, and request all assistance to come to your aid in this healing. Even some healers are not always able to feel the healing energy when they heal, but the healing takes effect just as well!

Each healing feels different to me, because each person feels different. My feelings of love help focus healings, so I recall my times of greatest love for the person I'm working with. The more love I feel for those I'm healing, the more likely my healing is physically noticeable to me.

Breathing can help you heal, since breathing is closely linked to Qi. In combination with visualization, breathing can release unwanted energy patterns. Deep breaths energize the body, and short, sharp, pulsed breaths can clear your body and those you heal from unwanted energy patterns, ideas, feelings, and thoughts. Ex-pulsing breaths in which you exhale as much air as possible either quickly or slowly are very powerful for healing energy patterns.

Healing Power of Words

What we feel and say has a direct effect on our health; positive words of love are powerful healing forces, whereas words of sarcasm, criticism, resentment, and complaint are invariably destructive. One of the simplest ways to change how you feel is to change what you say and *how* you say it. Your voice can carry such soothing feelings of love that it heals those who hear it, or such hostility and anger it can destroy. When you care about others and speak from your heart, your words actually come from your heart. You can literally hear the difference when you speak from your head or from your heart, as you can demonstrate to your own satisfaction by paying attention to how your voice sounds when you really care compared to when you say something you don't have much feeling for. Words spoken truly from love are an *incredibly* powerful way to remind others how much they are loved, and to shift reality in ways you will most enjoy and appreciate.

People who complain and worry the most seem to suffer from ongoing health maladies, as well as much more than their fair share of catastrophic life events. In contrast, people who take each change in their life as a positive opportunity seem to hardly ever get sick or suffer a continuous onslaught of disasters. Words have tremendous power to heal and protect us from harm, and they're such simple things to change! Notice the words you say, and ask your friends to help you identify things you say that sound destructive (they probably are). Once you've noticed habitual patterns of destructive speech, write them on the left side of a piece of paper. On the right side, write their life-affirming and creative counterparts, so when you next notice yourself in the negative mindset, you can shift your experience to a more enjoyable reality by remembering your positive affirmations.

One very destructive thing I've done in life was rushing. I felt afraid that if I didn't get lots of things accomplished, I'd miss out. I constantly strained to be at the next place I was supposed to be, rather than fully appreciating being where I was at any moment. I felt I never had enough time to do what I needed and wanted to do. This problem became impossible to ignore when I got a speeding ticket for driving too fast! I'd had warnings to slow down prior to getting that ticket, when a person asked me to drive more slowly on a country road ... but I must have needed a more memorable message. The police officer told me that for every five miles an hour faster people drive, there is an exponential increase in the amount of damage that occurs. His explanation about destructive effects of speed helped me see how I'd been stressing my body with all my rushing around. I felt fortunate to have received such a clear message so that even in an emotionally stressful time of my marital separation and divorce, I came to understand that I still didn't need to rush things.

When I got home and thought about why I felt a need to rush, I wrote down destructive things I was thinking that corresponded to my perceived need to hurry, alongside positive affirmations for taking life as it comes:

Reasons to Hurry:	Reasons to Take Life as it Comes:
I may be missing out	I'm at the right place
I need to do things faster	I do what I'm doing well
They're waiting for me	They can wait a bit
I need to keep moving	I feel where I am

I felt so moved by this exercise that I put these affirmations on my refrigerator where I can see them and say them aloud often! I've been surprised to find I'm getting as much done as ever, without the feeling of rushing and stress I used to feel so much of the time. I feel *much* better since I started reminding myself to take life as it comes rather than hurrying! When I change beliefs that cause me discouragement and worry, I shift my reality to a lifestyle of relaxed productivity.

You can discover where your belief boundaries are constraining you by identifying patterns that continue to appear in your life (in the form of something annoying, such as a police officer giving you a ticket). You can expand your belief boundary by listing supporting reasons behind the belief most closely associated with what's troubling you, and then listing the new possibility. The beliefs on the other side are ones that free you from feeling trapped.

I talk lovingly to parts of my body that feel sick or injured, noticing immediate improvement when I speak with love rather than annoyance, anger, or fear. My body loves to cooperate; all it needs is a clear sense of my intentions. When I know my priorities, my body understands, too. As a healer, everyone I help to heal also benefits from feeling how much I care for myself, since any stinginess or closed-in tendencies on my part limits the love I can channel to others.

Understand Emotional Patterns of Health

Physical illnesses begin as emotional or psychological problems, and you may find during a healing that in addition to feeling physical sensations, you are sensing emotional energy disturbances. When we have trouble with love and intimacy in our lives, these problems are reflected in our physical health.

Eloquent authors such as Barbara Ann Brennan, Leonard Laskow, and Carolyn Myss describe many different kinds of energy imbalances in their books on healing. If you notice you or someone else blocking good health with a harmful belief, you can assist the person to replace that belief with something healthier. While no belief is intrinsically wrong, some are less healthy than others, and can continuously damage the body if left unexamined and unchanged. People can continue to believe what they want to believe. Our bodies do their best to inform us that *something is wrong* and we are forgetting something important!

Caroline Myss found patterns of emotional and spiritual traumas corresponding to physical ailments. Heart disease patients often block out intimacy or love from their lives, low back pain patients suffer from financial stress, cancer patients have unresolved emotional issues, and blood disorder patients often have conflicts with the family they grew up in. Many medical practitioners understand their patients need *more* than surface-level treatments. In order to truly heal those who seek healing, we need to illuminate the deeper emotional and spiritual issues. As Carolyn Myss writes in *Anatomy of the Spirit*, our bodies tell us energetically that we are losing vitality when we suffer prolonged lethargy and depression. Our consciousness or spirit knows and remembers every judgment we make, every attitude we choose to hold, and every way we fill every second of every day. As we notice how our fears control us, we can see how we shut ourselves off from the energy of life.

You can get a fairly good idea of the kinds of energy imbalances people establish and maintain in the five patterns of illness Dr. Leonard Laskow found in his herpes patients: difficulty receiving love, difficulty receiving pleasure, difficulty expressing and releasing anger, difficulty forgiving, and difficulty trusting. You can shift reality and heal each of these problem areas by recognizing that the beliefs causing the illness can be flipped around, and transformed into affirmations.

People who have *trouble receiving love* often felt manipulated by conditional love when they were growing up, being told that they'd be loved if only they would just do what others wanted them to do. Feeling disapproval and the withholding of love, many people develop feelings of betrayal, shame, abandonment, humiliation and rejection. If you have trouble receiving love, you'll be sure to subtly signal others that you are not willing to be loved. After all, it's much easier to be rejected than to show yourself truly to someone else and end up being abandoned, abused, or betrayed again like you felt when you were growing up. To heal from this belief, say aloud:

"I am lovable just the way I am."

People who have *trouble receiving pleasure* usually believe one must pay a high price for pleasure. This belief can block some people from experiencing much pleasure at all, with the result that they feel a general lack of joy in living. To heal from this belief, say aloud:

"I live to enjoy the pleasures of feeling love."

We learn how to *express and release anger* in childhood, and often our first experiences of being angry were ignored or belittled by our parents. Another common problem with anger is control-hurt pattern that occurs with people who were harshly punished as children physically or emotionally, and who subsequently link the otherwise unrelated ideas of anger, hurt, and control. Suppressed anger becomes a 'negative' or 'contracted' emotion, which turns inward and leads the individual to feeling a sense of isolation and separation. To heal from this belief, say:

"Anger flows out of me freely, and I express it in ways that do not frighten, control, or hurt others."

People who hold onto blame as a way to protect themselves from being hurt more, or in order to punish others have *difficulty forgiving*. Self-pity is often a kind of silence that speaks louder than words, and is a way to punish oneself and others. To heal from this belief, say:

"I forgive myself and others; we are all doing the best we can, and being true to ourselves."

People who have *trouble trusting* become sick as a way of testing a partner's love. Becoming sick or injured is a substitute for actually trusting the other person, since a test becomes available for observing how the partner behaves. "If you *really* loved me, would you sacrifice your career ... your friendships?" To heal from this belief, say:

> *"I accept you just the way you are, and I know I am loved."*

I've found affirmations useful for countering deeply ingrained inner negativity. When I notice and examine the beliefs I've suffered from, I replace them with healthier beliefs. We can all replace our inner dialogues with healthier messages, and shift reality by transforming our lives when we change these innermost beliefs. Beliefs run so deep that shifting them will transform your life, and a commitment to healthy beliefs will make a tremendous difference in your life. Be patient, and appreciate and savor every small improvement.

Maintain Good Health

Spirit gets our attention by influencing how we feel emotionally and physically. When we get "a funny feeling" about something, it's a signal that something isn't quite right. Similarly, when we feel light, warm, buoyant and radiantly happy, that's a signal all is well. We can learn a lot about ourselves by observing when we feel our best and when we don't. Our physical health is inextricably interconnected with our emotional and spiritual wellbeing. If we neglect any area of ourselves, we end up feeling that neglect. Discovering what we need and making sure we get that is a simple and effective way to take good care of ourselves.

I live the fullest life by listening to myself and by doing what I need to do ... eating what I am hungry for when I am hungry ... resting when I am tired ... exercising when I need to move ... stretching when I feel tight and constrained. My body is my connection to feeling my inspiration. When I listen to what my body says, I can find my true path in life. In addition to caring for basic bodily needs, having close interpersonal relationships has been shown by health researchers to be one of the best things we can do to significantly increase our health and longevity. Love, intimacy, and relationships provide us with the most powerful way to stay healthy.

Every illness, discomfort, and pain has a distinct message for you. Similarly, every joy and exhilaration and ecstatic epiphany has an important message for you! If you are quiet and relaxed enough to listen, without suppressing or rejecting the symptoms you feel, you may even hear them speak to you about where they came from and what your body and spirit need from you. You can keep your body feeling vibrantly alive by spending some quiet time with yourself each day in listening meditation to nourish every cell in your body with love as you feel the neglected parts of you speak up and explain their messages to you. Remembering good health is the key to staying healthy, and you can remember good health when you feel relaxed and energized.

If you are not yet able to hear your body talk to you, then begin by "listening" to your body's pain. Each hangnail and blister has a message for you in this waking dream of life, which you can interpret using a dream symbol book or your own intuition. When I get something in my eye, I look more closely at what I thought I was already fully seeing. When I get a ringing in my ear, I listen more closely to what I am hearing. A tickle in my nose reminds me that I "know" a *lot* about the world through my intuition and senses.

The better I listen to my body, the better I feel. I have much fewer problems with colds, asthma and allergy, which have troubled me in the past, and I feel physically energized. When I feel a cold or allergies or asthma coming on, I raise my energy by meditating and healing myself as soon as possible. I can feel myself vibrating at a higher frequency when I meditate, and the very intention of focusing on my health and remembering how much love there is in this universe that can flow through me is powerful medicine. I do my best to notice as soon as possible when I am feeling sick, because once I get really sick it's hard to remember to heal myself! Sometimes when I feel really sick, I am so low on energy that I actually forget I can ask for help directly from the highest source.

Healing Experiences

I was stunned to see that healing *really works* when I began shifting reality to heal three people who were very sick. These experiences surprised me because they showed to my satisfaction that we can feel connected and send someone effective healing intentions across great physical distances, when I'd never before believed such a thing could be possible.

Healing Synchronicities

In September 1995, my friend's mother went into the hospital for observation because of an irregular heartbeat. Joan had an episode of heart failure, and the staff called in the new cardiac specialist. He diagnosed her with atrial fibrillation, and gave her an injection directly into her heart, which seemed to straighten everything out.

Joan was released after a few days, and then had a terrible night, which resulted in a second trip to the emergency room and a diagnosis of pneumonia! The pneumonia was battled in the same hospital room, and upon her release, it seemed she was on the road to recovery. A few days later, she was rushed once again to the emergency room, since she was in a frightening stupor that could indicate a stroke. The CAT scan was clear, but a spinal tap revealed a suspicious bug the doctor identified as some form of meningitis. He immediately arranged for her to move into intensive care. My friend was with her for three hours in the "ER" while her mother was not conscious of her presence, only pain, and my friend felt her mother was close to death.

After recovering from these two excursions to the hospital, Joan again got violently ill with a 103+ degree fever several hours after taking her prescription pills, and made another midnight trip to the emergency room in October 1995. This marked the third time she got violently ill with a 103+ degree fever. My friend suspected some of these relapses were caused by the medication, but her family felt frightened by the way the doctors and nurses discussed the probability of an immanent blood clot in her brain if she stopped taking them.

When I felt Joan's illness at this point in time remotely from my home, I could feel her symptoms of nausea and dizziness, so I lay down and prayed and meditated that these incapacitating feelings would go away. I felt how much I love this wonderful woman, and what a nurturing mother she is. I opened my heart to her, requesting that pure total love heal her, and that I may feel that healing in my body. After about half an hour of focused prayer, I could feel her symptoms disappearing, as my body began returning to feeling a state of healthy vigor. I took this as a clear indication the healing had been received and was taking effect, so I phoned my friend to let her know I'd been praying for her mother's recovery. As it turns out, at the exact time I was feeling those sensations of nausea and dizziness and praying for relief, Joan's friend was asking her entire church congregation to pray for Joan, unbeknownst to my friend, or Joan, or me.

The same day as Joan's friend and I were praying for Joan, her doctors suddenly noticed her medications *were* causing the side-effects of dizziness and nausea I had been feeling, and when the doctors reduced the levels of medication they'd prescribed, the debilitating side-effects went away! One of the drugs Joan had been taking for years, and was still on, can actually *cause* atrial fibrillation—which was the very reason she was first taken to the hospital for observation. My friend suspected her mother's subsequent symptoms were for the most part caused by overdoses and hospital viruses. I was deeply moved to note the simultaneity of my observations of her symptoms as I prayed for her, her friend's serendipitous request for a church congregation to pray for her, and the doctor's sudden insight that her medications were causing trouble.

Joan *did* recover, and her doctor said there seemed to be no permanent effects. Her family was grateful to enjoy a celebratory dinner together at long last. My friend later wrote to me,

> "I'm so thankful that she has recovered from such a serious problem that I feel as if I could

float. I really haven't been too conscious of my normal life this week as a result of everything that's happened. I'm now starting to realize that everyone else is still with me and that I might be able to ease back into some of my normal routines in the next few days. Nothing at all seems normal or ordinary to me today, though. Everything has a special alrightness to it now. I'm so grateful for you and your concern. I can't tell you how much your mental support (consciously & unconsciously given) meant to me, especially in the moments in which I felt that I could do very little in the way of concrete physical helping. *It's never true that 'there's nothing more anyone can do' because each second is an opportunity to pray and call for invisible help.* It seems weird to write such words, but I've spent the last few days really living in my mind and soul from moment to moment in complete and (unfortunately) rather desperate support of my mom."

Mystery Ailment Healed

In February 1996, my friend's brother, Chris, became suddenly and seriously ill with a condition that eleven doctors were unable to diagnose. He initially came down with a case of the flu, which became walking pneumonia. He then got a prescription for antibiotics from his doctor, but his condition worsened after a few days. He was admitted to the hospital, where he was given intravenous antibiotics, which also didn't work, and then things became quickly worse. He was unable to breathe on his own, because his lungs filled up with fluid.

I knew Chris best from times when we'd played chess together in high school. In 1996 he lived in Arizona and I lived in California, and we hadn't seen each other in years. I longed to help him, so shortly after he became hospitalized in the Intensive Care Unit, I asked my friend to bring me a photograph of him so I might better focus my prayers for his recovery.

I concentrated on sending healing prayers to Chris, without knowing whether this would help, or quite what to expect. I got a sense his breathing was severely limited, and he was fighting with every ounce of strength in his body. I shared these sensations, and told my friend what I felt. I had the unexpected sensation of something being done to his throat. My friend confirmed the next day that my feelings of something intrusive in her brother's throat were correct. A tube had been inserted in his neck, so doctors could better administer medications Chris needed to keep breathing. His lungs were filling with fluid (bilateral bronchial tubes), and Chris was hooked to a respirator, breathing O2 with a mask. In addition to breathing difficulties, he was running fevers between 104 and 106 degrees every night.

Chris later told me that before becoming mysteriously ill, he wasn't a church-going man. He found God in the trees and rocks, and went to church once in a while. He'd asked to be baptized because he'd promised his family his children would be raised Catholic. The deacon came to the hospital to baptize him, and he couldn't take communion because he had a ventilator in his throat. He slipped into a coma shortly after his baptism, and a month and a half later, his every major organ began to fail.

Every day I prayed for Chris, while tuning in and getting his body's sensations in return. One day I thought I must have done something terribly wrong, because I got a feeling of tremendous pain around his heart. I couldn't understand how he could be having heart trouble, and it occurred to me I didn't really know what I was doing with remote intuitive healing! I relayed my feelings of heart pain to my friend, who floored me by informing me that her brother did have fluid near his heart, causing great pain, so doctors were now removing the fluid. It was astonishing to me that I'd picked these feelings up so accurately, so I continued daily prayers with some reassurance that I really was connected to him.

Chris later explained to me that his heart started showing mysterious arrhythmias at that time. His wife was an ICU nurse, and she noticed something was wrong when she looked at the monitor, and noticed his heart beating unusually. She immediately discussed this with the ICU nurse, and persistently requested a cardiologist, since her husband had heart problems before. The cardiologist came and requested an ultrasound, which indicated the presence of a liter of extra fluid in the sac around his heart (the pericardium). Without emergency surgery in the pericardial window to relieve pressure around his heart, he would have had only twelve hours to live.

One day while I was praying for Chris, I got a clear feeling he felt like giving up ... so I left a message imploring my friend to call and write her brother immediately, and let him know how much she loves him. I felt a bit foolish to leave this phone message, but had renewed faith the feelings I got from her brother were correct.

My friend called me back, to confirm Chris had written his wife a note stating he was losing the will to live ... just as I'd felt. I'd overheard a dialogue between him and spirit in which his spirit wanted to know what he was really living for. I felt his initial response of needing to be a dutiful father and husband and a responsible employee, and I heard that was *not* satisfactory to spirit. Spirit insisted Chris consciously embody much more of his higher self—and if he did not do so, his life would be over.

After my friend's brother's heart condition was stabilized, his kidney and liver started shutting down. The doctors thought this was a massive infection of the body, although they couldn't get a culture to grow (perhaps due to the antibiotics). The doctor removed his gall bladder, which turned out to be healthy after all. At about the same time as when he went in for surgery of the gall bladder, a lupus specialist came in to examine him and determine whether steroids would be appropriate. Since steroids negate the effects of antibiotics, there was some risk associated with their administration. The doctors conferred, and agreed to go ahead with steroids, starting them 24 hours before gall bladder surgery. Chris was still in a coma, and the doctor came out, saying to his wife, "I want you to understand that your husband is probably not going to survive surgery because he is so sick already, the clotting is poor, and he will probably bleed out." Fortunately, surgery went well, and at the time of surgery they cut a tracheotomy for a different ventilator. The sutures broke in the tracheotomy, and Chris began aspirating blood into his lungs. Then, 48 hours after the steroids, and 24 hours after gall bladder surgery, at about 4:00 AM, Chris woke up.

Chris later told me that just before he woke up, he had a vision he was standing in front of Satan. He explained this did not feel like a dream, but something much more vivid. He wanted to run or close his eyes, but couldn't. There were no eyes to close, no legs to run. The first thing going through his mind was, "Oh, Damn ... it's true!" He was upset to see that there is a Hell and a devil. Chris saw a huge, muscular, beastly creature with scaly skin, clawed hands and feet, opaque eyes, large curly horns thick in diameter, and wings that went from above his head to ankle level, flapping. The devil paced back and forth across a neutral background ... not saying anything ... not doing anything. This seemed to last forever. Then Chris awoke from his coma, terrified!

He pressed his buzzer and the nurse came in, asking Chris, "Are you OK?" He couldn't talk because of the ventilator, so he motioned for a pencil and paper to write, "How come I can't talk?" She explained what was happening. Chris asked about his chest pain, and she described his gall bladder and heart surgeries. She asked if he knew his name, and names of people in family photos by his bed. As Chris wrote their names, she reassured him, "You're doing just fine!"

On the morning of his vision and awakening from coma, Sister Claire, an Irish Catholic nun, came into the hospital room with his wife to pray for him, as she did every day. Chris noticed the strangest thing happening as he looked at Sister Claire; she started to GLOW. This little seventy-year-old nun from Ireland actually started to *glow*! At that moment, he felt tremendous peace and calm, and knew he would be OK. He looked at his wife... but she didn't seem to see anything unusual at all, so he didn't mention his devil vision or the glowing nun.

Chris occasionally found himself thinking back to the vision of the devil on occasion, as his health improved in record time. In another two and half weeks, he left the hospital and went home! The doctors had no idea WHY he stabilized so quickly, but they could clearly see he was continuing to get better and better.

When the deacon visited Chris at home, Chris asked the deacon, "So ... why did you become a priest?" The deacon explained his appendix burst when he was fourteen, living a long way from any hospital, and a religious family friend came to pray for him. It felt like warm oil being poured over his body—the most peaceful feeling he'd ever felt—and he was cured. The ailment went away, and nobody knew what happened. The deacon said, "I felt like I'd been touched by the healing hand of God." Chris cried when he heard this story, and described how he'd seen the nun glowing, and had a vision in the hospital. He asked, "Why would God choose to save me, of all people? I've broken many commandments." The deacon explained he had been baptized before he went into a coma, which cleansed him of sins when he was forgiven. When asked what the vision of the devil meant, the deacon replied, "Sometimes God lets you see the other side!" Chris feels a new peace, certain there is a God and a devil, and accountability.

The Sacred Heart picture of Jesus shows a glowing heart. Chris had looked at a version of that picture, without yet having spoken to the nun, and said to his wife, "That's what it was!" When he asked Sister Claire to lunch to tell her what he'd seen, she said, "Thanks be to God. That's just beautiful! I took a vow when I become a nun," turning over her necklace pendant to show the inscription, "Oh, Sacred Heart of Jesus, I trust in thee." This was her private prayer when becoming a nun forty years earlier.

Chris said, "Very honestly, I tell as many people as I can my story so they hear about the love and healing power of God from the view of a former non-believer. What happened has changed my life forever, and I feel fortunate to have been through this experience, sickness and all."

Inoperable Tumor Healed

I heard from a friend that a woman's newborn baby suffered from a deadly brain tumor in an inoperable location. When I felt the baby's health problems overlaid on my body, I sensed this problem was serious. Doctors had scanned the baby's brain, and the tumor showed up as a dark spot too close to the medulla oblongata to operate.

It seemed the only thing to do was pray, so that's what we did. As I attuned my energy with the baby, I felt the tumor, and a sensation of numbness. This feeling concerned me at the time, since I usually get an energized and vibrant feeling of feedback from the person's body during healings, not sensations of lethargy and numbness as I pray for love energy to flow and heal. I continued praying anyway, with faith that even though these feelings seemed unusual, prayer works, and I should not give up.

I was thrilled to learn the baby's tumor later miraculously relocated from the inoperable location to resituate in an operable place. The baby was put under general anesthesia to surgically remove the tumor, and it dawned on me the feelings of numbness I'd felt may have been anesthesia's effects.

Vanishing Bruises

I had a truly remarkable experience with a healing reality shift in June 1998, when I saw bruises on my left hand knee heal before my eyes! I didn't know how I got the bruises, and sensed they represented darkness I'd accepted in my life.

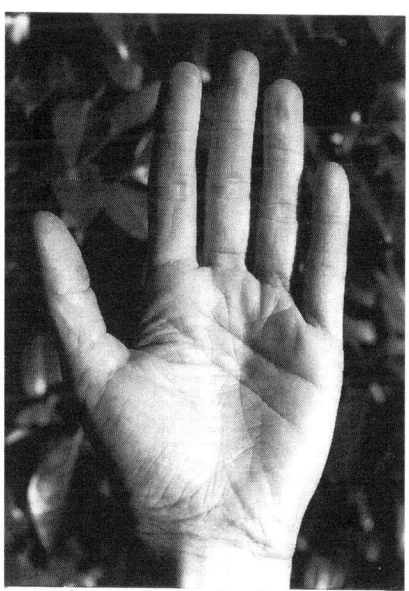

The author's healed hand

As I interpreted the meaning of the dark spots on my left knee and hand (what I need to receive and what I am actually receiving), I was shaken to discover these bruises represented dark feelings and thoughts I'd routinely made a "normal" part of my life. I realized how much I desired to stop bringing negativity into my life, and made a commitment to be as conscious as possible about what I receive from the universe, only taking love and support into myself with no negativity.

The moment I made this promise, I could actually *see* the bruise on my left hand *start to go away*! I had goose bumps watching this. Within minutes, the bruises were barely noticeable, and in a few hours, both bruises were completely and totally *gone* without a trace. I'd never seen bruises vanish so quickly; I had many other bruises on my right side still remaining, and it usually takes weeks for my bruises to clear, not hours.

When I called my friend Laura, whose hair curled when mine did, she told me bruises on her left side had vanished at that same time, too! I was amazed to hear she had also recently wished to take no more negativity into her life any more, and also had bruises vanish!

Choosing to Live

On August 25, 1998, I was getting ready to leave on a short trip with a healer friend of mine one morning, when I was interrupted by a constant series of delays. I had the distinct feeling I was waiting for something, without knowing exactly what that might be. I was happy to finally be loading the car around noon, when I saw my neighbor walk up to me with a serious look of sorrow on his face, and the heavy steps of a man facing something terrible. I immediately asked, "What's wrong?" and he explained that his mother had just slipped into a deep coma. He described his mother's health problems leading up to the coma; she had been drinking alcohol for many years, and when she recently fell down she got pneumonia. She first went into a light coma, and then slipped into a deeper coma a couple of days ago.

I asked my neighbor for pictures of his mother, since I'd never met her, and so my friend and I could focus better on her for healing prayers. My neighbor came back with two pictures of his mother that helped me sense who she is and how she was feeling. I felt her body was in good condition, though I sensed that she seemed tingly all over, as if in a heightened, energized state of awareness. My healer friend said he saw white; that she was feeling her life is too hard, and she was considering dying as an alternative to being a burden on her family. My friend and I sensed that coming back or dying was entirely her choice; she could decide either way. I told my neighbor that now is the time to massage his mother, touch her, kiss her, and speak to her from the heart. I felt a large part of the reason she slipped into a coma was because she wasn't feeling connected with those she loves. I sensed she could hear and feel her family around her even while she was in the coma, and if she truly feels reason to live, she might decide to come back. I felt she needed to speak and listen from her heart, in order for her life to feel worth living. I sensed if she chose to live, she would need to honestly communicate her feelings with her family.

I told my neighbor I felt his mother's presence with us as we spoke in my driveway, and that she wanted to hug, kiss, and reassure him. My healer friend felt this, too, and hugged my neighbor. My neighbor told us he was going to see his mother at the hospital, and I gave him a hug before he left, asking if I could keep the photos with me while I was out of town.

I checked in on my neighbor's mother remotely each day, feeling how her body was definitely viable, and noticing how she was regaining strength. When I returned, I discovered she'd made a *remarkable* recovery. She'd come out of her coma and off the respirator a couple of days after my neighbor spoke with me, and her health was steadily improving! My neighbor was impressed with his mother's recovery, because her doctors had said there was an 80-90% chance that she wouldn't wake up, and at each step in her recovery, the doctors told him they were uncertain she would clear the next hurdle.

Smashed Fingertip Healed

On October 12, 1998, I opened my car door to get out on the driver's side, when I reached over to retrieve my purse with my left hand up on the doorframe. I was horrified to feel the car door slam shut in the locked position, with my left index finger trapped inside. It took me several seconds to unlock and open the door.

I immediately put my finger in my mouth to soothe and cool it, feeling incredible pain. My finger felt mangled, bruised, and swollen, although not broken or sprained. After a few moments, I removed my finger from my mouth to see a quarter-inch deep dark purple indentation, and the beginnings of a nasty-looking bruise. I thought to myself, "*Great.* Now I'll need to put ice on this for 20 minutes and it will still feel mangled and bruised all day, because I bruise so easily." Immediately after thinking this, I thought, "No, I don't need that! I'll use Reiki and heal myself right now."

I held my finger in my right hand and used Reiki energy to heal my finger. I felt extreme heat and energy intensifying in my finger, and then after a couple of minutes I could feel my finger seeming normal again. I uncovered my finger, and saw no swelling or bruises of any kind. In fact, my finger felt nearly exactly the same as all the rest of my fingers after another 20 minutes!

Spontaneous healing is a *wonderful* example of how much enjoyment we can experience with reality shifts. It is often important to take time to receive messages from the illness or injury, in order to know the deepest levels requiring healing love. As healers, we are energy conduits and communicators who clarify the dialogue between spirit and person—but we cannot force a healing to work for someone who doesn't believe in the power of prayer to heal, doesn't wish to be healed, or who is unwilling to cooperate with spirit.

Healing Things

> *"Every loved thing is the center of a paradise."*
> – Novalis

People aren't the only ones that can be healed. All physical things can be healed, even what we think of as inanimate objects. Inanimate objects are *very* responsive to us and to our love. Many people have special feelings about their things; cars, boats, and airplanes are often loved as if they were alive. In some ways, they seem alive, since they require energy to run and frequent maintenance to run well. My friend, Lisa, felt her little old Datsun car cared about her, because it never broke down at night, even though she often drove at night.

People can be happier with their relationships with things when they are more conscious of them. My friend once saw a TV ad for Sears' Repair Services that stated, "all your kitchen and laundry appliances are waiting to betray you." She turned the volume down, but suspects it did its dirty work. Once that negative idea took hold, her microwave broke, and had to go to the shop. It's best to bless our appliances—they do such a good job for us everyday!

When I was a little girl growing up in the 1960's, our television set had lots of tubes that needed changing. I watched my father's methodically slow process of replacing tubes, and found that when I felt loving toward him and the TV set, the repair job went much more quickly and easily. Similarly, our Chevrolet sedan coughed and sputtered on start up, and when I shut my eyes, relaxed, and felt how much I loved the car. It started beautifully the next time my dad turned the key in the ignition.

Copy Machine Healings

My friend used to work in a copy shop for a spiritual boss who hung religious tapestries inside the shop. He kept the atmosphere of the copy shop really nice, even during first-week-of-the-quarter rush, when people started feeling stressed and short-tempered from the heavy volume of jobs being run.

One of the most impressive things about my friend's boss was that he had the power to keep the copy machines running, even when they were *missing* critical parts. He prayed over the machines, and they worked—at least until the repairman came with the needed part.

Camera Healing

One day in August 1998, I was loading my Olympus SLR camera with a roll of film, when the mirror locked up. After a sinking feeling of great disappointment and frustration, the realization hit me that this camera could be healed, just as anything animate can be healed!

A soaring feeling of hope returned to me as I sensed whether there were errant thoughts that might interfere with the camera's functionality. I found there was some negative feeling that needed to be exorcised. I used sharp exhalations as I visualized cleansing the camera, and then continued to heal the camera with energy flowing through my hands. I felt the camera become radiant with energy, and sensed when it was healed.

Sure enough, when I picked up the camera again after this healing, the shutter snapped shut and didn't jam again until several weeks later when the batteries ran low. The amazing thing to me is that the batteries *had* been low many weeks earlier, but praying and healing the camera gave them many more days of useful life!

Healings are a focused way to combine inspiration and intention to shift reality. It's possible to enjoy the way consciousness shifts by considering this waking dream to be fully malleable, and by opening our hearts and minds to allow miracles to enter our lives. We allow miracles when we stop limiting what we believe to be possible, and allow ourselves to more fully experience love and joy in our life.

Shifting Reality for Healing Exercises

Healing Spoken Words

Consider the impact of your words as you choose to speak them. Think about how they impact your health and the health of others who hear you. Your words and voice have the power to carry *all* your emotions, whether you are sharing love and warmth, cold fear, or riotous rage is entirely up to you. If you desire to change the way you relate to your loved ones, ask them to help you identify the things you say that feel destructive to them, then thank them for helping you become more conscious of the effects of your words.

Healing Unspoken Words

Take a few moments to consider the unspoken beliefs you have that may be adversely impacting your health. These destructive words can cause damage if left inside you, so take some time to get them out by writing some of them down on the left hand side of a piece of paper. On the right hand side of the page, write down the opposite of the negative beliefs, creating your own most powerful personal affirmations. You don't need to share these with anyone else, but it is very healing to put them somewhere you can see them every day.

Healing Beliefs

Do any of the emotional patterns of illness mentioned in this chapter apply to you? Take a few minutes to write down healing words to help you transform your energy imbalances. Put these healing words in a place you can see every day, and remember how loved you truly are.

Healing Messages

Think about your most recent injury or ailment. Consider what you were thinking or feeling at the time, and what message it might have for you. If you are open to listening to your body, you may find you will receive much more information about what *really* matters to you and who you really are. The more you learn about your self, the healthier and more fully connected to others you can be.

Healing Intentions

Choose a healing intention statement for yourself, and write it down.

Healing Someone

If there was one person you could heal right now, who would it be? How would you most wish to heal yourself?

Chapter 10

Everyday Life With Reality Shifts

*"Let yourself be silently drawn by the stronger pull
of that which you really love."*
– Rumi

I've been asked, "How do you live every day, knowing that reality shifts? Once you know about shifting reality, where do you go from there?" I've learned from witnessing reality shift that both our waking and sleeping time is dreamtime. In other words, there is a symbolic nature of people and events. We are much more than our physical bodies. Everything is connected. When I see reality shift, I no longer assume that what I see is all there is. As soon as my conscious awareness opens to accept the possibility that I am conscious somewhere else besides here in this body I call myself, I find myself living lucidly ... that is, realizing that consciousness is unlimited. Witnessing reality shift is a way of awakening to a sense of being "much more than this," a way of realizing that boundaries I've felt constrained within are not absolute and don't actually confine my spirit or conscious awareness.

My experiences of witnessing reality shift give me a clear sense that we are continually dreaming our lives into existence, and that every present moment connects to an infinite number of possibilities. I feel great appreciation for where I am each moment because I see how much goes into creating this moment. I sense the significance of each moment in every day, no matter how apparently trivial. I can feel how each moment is dreamlike, and how I can allow all possibilities to manifest by opening boundaries in my mind.

My wakeful state of mind enjoys a state of ecstatic rapture and energization during times of meditation or prayer, and when I feel so energetically aligned, my feeling of connection with everything is enhanced, so I experience heightened awareness. Such heightened awareness attunes me to the sensations of how others feel, and provides me with intuitive insights to where someone or something is, so I can walk directly there. I believe each and every one of us is equally connected and capable of communicating with all that is, and we can open ourselves to experiencing this sense of connectedness.

Feet in Two Worlds

Living with the waking dream experience of reality shifting around me feels a lot like walking with my feet in two (or more) worlds. Since I've acknowledged reality shifts, my life has continued to be much the same in most respects. I still sleep at night, and go about my regular daily activities. I still need the simple basic necessities I always did, and I still occasionally feel burning desires to see an exhilarating movie, go for long walks in natural surroundings, read good books, or eat delicious meals. In other words, to all outward appearances, my life seems the same as usual. I still do all the mundane things I need to do for survival, so much of the time I am living a life of habitual response. The biggest change in me is mostly one of attitude and mindset, as my sense of what's real has changed. My mind seeks a stable place to consider solid or real, and that sense of reality is no longer based simply on what I see in front of me or what seems to be solid. My sense of self is not limited to being confined to my body, since I so often experience feelings, sensations, and realities that don't happen where my body is.

By welcoming a waking dream state of consciousness, I allow for the unexpected to occur. Even ordinary things like cooking dinner have a different feeling for me. Sometimes I've opened my refrigerator to get something, shut the door, opened it again a few minutes later, and found a jar had vanished and reappeared in that short space of time. I savor these sensuous experiences of feeling awake in a dream, because I am aware of my wishes, desires and feelings shaping reality all around me. I often find my passing thoughts answered by the universe, as I engage in a continuous dialogue with all that is. I feel this communication best when I also feel how loved I am and how everything around me is here for my benefit and appreciation, surrendering myself as fully as possible to knowing I am love.

In the process of writing this book, I found one of my reference books inexplicably changed. When I first read this book after bringing it home from the bookstore, I was disappointed to find the writer was noticeably uneasy with associating himself with the material in his book. I found myself so offended by the tone of this book that I placed it high out of sight on a bookshelf, until one day when a discussion with two friends prompted me to bring the book down to show it to them. As my friend read aloud from this book, I was shocked to notice the tone of the book was now written with the courage of one who is willing to stand his ground when confronted with skepticism. I was astonished to see the book's style change so dramatically, and I picked the book up to see for myself how thoroughly the tone of this book had changed. The cover and title were the same, but the entire book was now written in a courageous voice. I took this reality shift to be a message to consider the impact of my tone and attitude on everything I communicate.

The biggest difference, now that I know reality shifts, is that I am *much* less likely to worry about things or get upset. I have a greater sense of awe and respect for the underlying essence of reality, and my sense of awe is inextricably intertwined with a feeling of deep love and appreciation for all creation. Every physical experience and interaction in my life feels like a great gift, because I know that each and every thing around me might not always be here. I feel our world exists for us to appreciate as fully as possible, and I care much more deeply knowing reality arises from consciousness.

We're All Creating This Dream

I love talking to people about reality shifts because when I tell people that reality shifts are an ordinary part of everyday life, rather than something peculiar, weird, or strange, people often agree, and share their own reality shift experiences. I've only met a few people who insist they've not yet noticed reality shift. Reality shifts are happening all around us all the time, yet they largely go unnoticed. In a more wakeful state of mind, we can observe some of larger discontinuities from one stream of consciousness to another, and these sudden leaps can help us grasp how reality is truly created from the energy of our thoughts and feelings.

I feel love is the strongest force in the universe, and that it has the power to bring us what we most need. Prayer may be the truest, highest form of our consciousness when we feel it resonating through every fiber of our body and soul as a full-body experience, since these are times when we are most in harmony with our conscious and unconscious desires. When you feel your entire being crying out in desperate appeal for something, you are wise to honor this feeling as a matter of great importance. At such times, we sometimes feel we are "falling apart" or "hitting bottom," but from these emotional depths we can most fully comprehend what breaks our heart is also what touches us to our very core. What we fall for is what we are living for, what we most truly love. We can all learn to trust our intuition and the deepest longings of our souls, for these bring us what we most need to learn from and experience in life.

I love to think about how we are all orchestrating reality together, collectively and cooperatively. It feels best to me to help others become their best, because we are all interconnected, and constructive interference feels *so good!* There is no need to fight or squelch dreams of others, since it feels so much better to live dreams-come-true as each one of us pursues our own unique reason for living. I pay attention to what I care for and what I don't care for, and marvel at the difference. I find joy in appreciating as much of life as I can. If I really pay attention, I know love is everywhere, and in everything. This whole universe is alive with love.

When I face doubts about myself and my path in life, I feel great comfort knowing that this life is all a waking dream. I am able to view my life from a more detached perspective, knowing I am much more than the "me" I seem to be. I can then care for myself as one would care for one's true love, rather than getting caught up in petty concerns of the moment or thinking this life is all there is. It feels healthier to see my daily concerns as messages for me, full of symbolic meaning.

This Universe is Alive

My appreciation for the interaction between reality and consciousness has grown gradually with time. The first reality shifts I experienced were such shocks to me that I had no idea how to integrate my experience of seeing, for example, a dead cat come back to life again. As I became more accustomed to feeling reality shift, I became more aware of how *alive* this universe is. These reality shifts now feel like consciousness quakes to me as they show me how it is possible for everything to change in a moment of time.

When my daughters and I were visiting some friends, my daughter borrowed my favorite pen so she could write some words on a paper toy we made. She ran upstairs with her friend, and I called after her that I'd like my pen back. She replied "I need your pen!" so I waited for her to return it. A few minutes later, my daughter's friend came downstairs to tell me something, and as I talked with her, I saw a silvery flash, and my pen appeared on the carpet between our feet! I asked if she'd brought my pen back for me, and she said, "No." I'd seen my pen materialize out of thin air, but I asked anyway, on the off chance she'd dropped it there. I didn't see it drop—I saw it *sparkle itself back into existence!*

I now keep my mind as open as possible, welcoming changes rather than attempting to confine reality or consciousness to any restrictive parameters. I read books and find things with much more faith in "random access" methods. I am pleased to find what I need is usually easily accessible, and I don't need to expend as much mental, physical, and emotional effort as I used to think necessary. I love to browse libraries and used bookstores to find reference materials, and when I read books, I often flip pages open randomly, reading in depth whatever section I turn to.

I also work that same fluid way, starting wherever I am and doing a good job at what I'm doing at that moment. I feel more relaxed and confident that I'm focusing my attention exactly where it needs to be, knowing that when I'm relaxed and energized, reality shifts around me.

Reality shifts have balanced my attention from being focused primarily on details, to being more equally focused on consciousness. The consciousness I notice feels like the universe's underlying intent to convey a dimension of creative awareness and insight to life. I feel this when I carry on discussions with the universe as I walk, feeling how much I *love* the Earth, then glancing up to read a bumper sticker, "Arborists are TREEMENDOUS!" I no longer feel so tied down to the limitations and constraints I'd internalized through habitually viewing the world through sets of dualistic frameworks, such as cause and effect, or me and not-me.

Our ordinary, everyday alphabet is a perfect example of how we can take something so much for granted that we forget this starting foundation was something arbitrarily chosen to be the building blocks for constructing our language. With these limited tools in hand, we can create words to give others an idea of what we mean to communicate. Words convey as much meaning as we manage to put into them, but we are limited by boundaries of perception and conceptualization. The arbitrary nature of how we establish boundaries is made clear to me by reality shifts, as I discover boundaries between what I thought I couldn't possibly tolerate and what I thought I love, between crazy and sane, between analytical reason and accepting faith. All these boundaries mark artificial divisions between what seems to be one thing in contrast and opposition to another, and reality shifts show how arbitrary all this divisiveness truly is. By demonstrating that even what seems most *real*, the very essence of how a thing exists in time and space can be in fact *changed*, reality shifts show us that everything in this universe is not what it seems. We are not constructed of this/not-this so much as we simply *are*. This universe is ALIVE and we are a part of it—not some distinct, separate, cast-off part of it, but an intrinsically connected, living, breathing, dynamically conscious aware part of it.

Opening the Boundaries

Thanks to experiences with reality shifts, we no longer need feel a sense of being trapped by circumstance. We can have a different feeling now, when situations seem to hem us in, because we can remind ourselves that *somehow* there is a way to move through any seemingly hopelessly stuck situation. Reality shifts renew faith in the power of love to transcend all boundaries. By changing our states of mind, we can see our way through anything—knowing that what we think and how we feel can literally move heaven and earth.

Our conscious minds can feel overly constricting and even somewhat mechanical when we measure this universe by theories that we attempt to force-fit onto reality. Such mechanistic ways of thinking can block our ability to witness the flowering of the unconscious mind growing out of the machinery of logical rules.

When I accept this universe as it is, I find it to be a mysterious, loving, expansive presence that provides me with whatever set of experiences I need, based on how and where I focus my attention. I feel a sense of being simultaneously separate from everything and yet integrally connected to all that is. I feel the beauty in every moment that had once seemed elusive to me, because I know I can trust whatever the universe brings me to enrich my life with feelings of love and joy. I feel more capable of fluidly adapting to each new experience, realizing I have probably had much to do with unconsciously creating each situation for myself, and that we are all creating this world around us every moment.

Reality shifts show me how easily anything can be changed. By keeping our conscious self-reflexive mind fixed on one point of attention and ignoring instances where experience goes outside those lines, we can choose to limit our growth. By keeping our conscious mind open to new experiences, our awareness can grow more quickly as we explore and learn to appreciate and accept life as it is, without expecting it to follow our rules.

Our conscious and unconscious minds work together in partnership to create reality, and where they come together is what we experience as real. Reality shifts remind us to honor the wild, unconscious parts of ourselves without getting stuck in the mechanistic conscious view of life that often can feel so cold. Reality shifts invite us to awaken within this dream, and fulfill our greatest potential; they encourage us to live a waking dream in which we become more fully aware of multitudes of possible worlds welcoming us right here in this present moment now.

This Mysterious Universe

Throughout history, peoples of the Earth have told stories to explain the creation and true nature of the universe. The universe can indeed be viewed as being like the shell of a tortoise, or like an island in the ocean, or like parallel universes, or like a hologram—but it seems much more likely that the truest, deepest nature of the universe will remain mysterious until such time as we are consciously capable of directly experiencing all that is.

At its very essence, our universe is a paradox of unified dualities, not something that wishes to be consciously constrained by any conceptualization of its behavior for purposes of predictive observation. All attempts we make to "know" the nature of how our consciousness relates to the universe will constantly be limited by the very symbology and thought constructs we are using to organize the universe in ways we can comprehend.

We need to encompass the range of all possibility in order to see the universe as it really is; yet we are continually hindered by our inability to step outside of the universe sufficiently to comprehend it. When we set our minds free to openly experience this universe, we allow ourselves access to the greatest surprises and delights. Whatever boundaries we use to define ourselves also affect our ability to perceive self and other. Perhaps the best perspective for comprehending all that is comes from the point of view of nothingness, because there are no boundaries to nothingness.

When I feel as close to nothingness as possible, as my smallest most essential bit of "me-ness," I am able to view the rest of all creation with rapture, awe, and the deepest sense of appreciation. I feel such love and am *so* joyous to be alive ... to be living the life I always wanted for myself. I sense how this universe and I are interconnected, and how we change and grow together. The limitations we may have thought were confining us no longer seem like impediments at all.

Affirmations

I enjoy experiencing different realities
I create my own reality
I create opportunities with conscious intention
We think our world into existence every day
When we change our minds, the world changes too
Surprises can open our minds to new worlds of possibility
This world is an illusion projected by our minds
We create more love and joy by greeting the world with love and joy
Every experience brings us messages
Love transforms nightmares into the happiest of dreams
We are all created from love
Reality shifts for those who feel total love
We can all shift reality when we feel love
Reality shifts for those who whole-heartedly wish it to
Open-minded optimism prepares us for receiving miracles
Love knows no boundaries
Reality shifts whenever we need it to
An open heart is the gateway to divine intervention
Heaven starts with open hearts
Our fortune in life is what we allow ourselves to receive
We live in a generous universe that gives us everything we need
Our wishes and thoughts flow through every cell of our bodies
We attract to us what we most love when we feel loving
We are in constant dialogue with the universe
I am a loving person, ready to receive more love in my life
I am the living embodiment of what I most love
I am totally, truly loved every minute of every day
I believe in myself
Nothing is too good to be true
Reality shifts for those who allow it to
What I spend my time, energy, and attention on is what my life is
Love is the strongest thing there is
Love binds the whole universe together
I shift reality when I choose to feel love instead of fear
Reality shifts through me right now
All physical and emotional obstacles are illusions

Reality shifts when I allow my consciousness to shift
I trust what I know & reality shifts towards what I most love
When I built my intentions with love's inspiration, I shift reality
I love it when reality shifts to bring me more joy in life
I shift reality every moment to arrive at the future I most desire
I create the situations I need to learn from
When I suspect I am dreaming, I probably am
I am my own best friend
Love is everywhere and in everything
This universe is alive with the energy of love
Reality shifts are an ordinary part of every day life
Our world exists for us to appreciate as deeply as possible
We are energy ... our thoughts and feelings create our experience
I am dreaming right now
I create my experiences in life
I choose how I feel every moment
I choose to feel love instead of fear
I let go of my wishes, like releasing butterflies to the breeze
It's never too late to make a change
Just for today I will choose not to be angry
Just for today I will choose not be worried
Just for today I will be kind to my neighbor and every living thing
Just for today I will do my work honestly
Just for today I will choose to be grateful for my many blessings
When I open my mind and heart, new opportunities open up for me
When I experience reality shift, I remember I'm awake in this dream
When I find the joy in my life, more joy comes to me
There really aren't any mistakes in life, just learning experiences
My life is a work of art that is continually being revised
As a work of art, what matters most in my life is the process
I have everything I need to succeed
I choose my future in every moment
Reality shifts are gifts
An infinite range of possibility is present in every moment
Reality is constantly shifting based on what I think and how I feel
Right now, at this very moment, I am shifting reality
I shift reality to become what I most love
Through love, anything is possible in every moment
We are all interconnected in love
I remember that I am loved
Love has no limits

Bibliography

Abbott, Edwin Abbott, *Flatland: A Romance of Many Dimensions*, Dover Publications, New York, NY, 1992

Bach, Richard, *Illusions: The Adventures of a Reluctant Messiah*, Dell Publishing Company, Inc., New York, NY, 1977

Ban Breathnach, Sarah, *Something More: Excavating Your Authentic Self*, Warner Books, New York, NY, 1998

Berger, Arthur S. and Berger, Joyce, *The Encyclopedia of Parapsychology and Psychical Research*, Paragon House, New York, NY, 1991

Bethards, Betty, *The Dream Book: Symbols for Self-Understanding*, Element Books, Rockport, MA, 1995

Black, Vern, *Love Me? Love Yourself: A Guaranteed Guide to Ecstatic Relationships*, Vern Black and Associates, San Francisco, CA, 1983

Brennan, Barbara Ann, *Hands of Light: A Guide to Healing Through the Human Energy Field*, Bantam Books, New York, NY, 1988

Brennan, Barbara Ann, *Light Emerging: The Journey of Personal Healing*, Bantam Books, New York, NY, 1993

Cameron, Julia, *The Artist's Way*, The Putnam Publishing Group, New York, NY, 1992

Cameron, Julia, *Blessings: Prayers and Declarations for a Heartful Life,* Jeremy P. Tarcher/Putnam, New York, NY, 1998

Dossey, Larry, *Be Careful What You Pray For ... You Just Might Get It*, HarperCollins Publishers, New York, NY, 1997

Dossey, Larry, "Healing Happens: The Miracle of Distant Healing," *Utne Reader,* September-October 1995, issue #71, pp. 52-59.

Feuerstein, Georg, *Lucid Waking: Mindfulness and the Spiritual Potential of Humanity*, Inner Traditions International, Rochester, VT, 1997

George, Leonard, *Alternative Realities: The Paranormal, the Mystic and the Transcendent in Human Experience,* Facts on File, New York, NY 1995

Godwin, Malcolm, *The Lucid Dreamer: A Waking Guide for the Traveler Between Worlds*, Simon & Schuster, New York, NY, 1994

Goswami, Amit with Reed, Richard E. and Goswami, Maggie, *The Self-Aware Universe: How Consciousness Creates the Material World*, J.P. Tarcher/Putnam Books, New York, NY, 1993

Green, Michael, *Unicornis: On the History and Truth of the Unicorn*, Running Press Book Publishers, Philadelphia, PA, 1983

Grimwood, Ken, *Replay*, Ace, New York, NY, August 1992

Jamal, Michele, *Shape Shifters: Shaman Women in Contemporary Society*, Arkana, Viking Penguin, New York, NY, 1987

Jampolsky, Gerald G. & Cirincione, Diane, *Love is the Answer*, Bantam Books, New York, NY, May 1990

Johnson, Robert A., *Ecstasy: Understanding the Psychology of Joy*, HarperCollins Publishers, New York, NY, 1987

Harman, Willis, *Global Mind Change: The Promise of the 21st Century*, Berrett-Kochler Publishers, Inc., San Francisco, CA, 1998

Hoffman, Donald, *Visual Intelligence: How We Create What We See*, W.W. Norton and Company, New York, NY, 1998

Kingma, Daphne Rose, *The Future of Love: The Power of the Soul in Intimate Relationships*, Doubleday, New York, NY, 1998

LaBerge, Stephen, *Lucid Dreaming*, Ballantine Books, New York, NY, July 1986

Laskow, Leonard, *Healing With Love: A Breakthrough Mind/Body Medical Program for Healing Yourself and Others*, HarperCollins Publishers, New York, NY, 1992

Levey, Joel and Levey, Michelle, *Living In Balance: A Dynamic Approach for Creating Harmony and Wholeness in a Chaotic World*, Conari Press, Berkeley, CA, 1998

Linn, Denise, *The Secret Language of Signs*, Ballantine Books, New York, NY, 1996

Lozoff, Bo, *We're All Doing Time: A Guide for Getting Free*, Human Kindness Foundation, Durham, NC, 1995

McNamara, William, *Mystical Passion*, Element, Rockport, MA, 1991

Miller, Carolyn, *Creating Miracles: Understanding the Experience of Divine Intervention*, H.J. Kramer, Inc., Tiburon, CA, 1995

Miller, Hamish, *The Sun and the Serpent*, Pendragon, Cornwall, England, 1989

Miller, Hamish, *It's Not Too Late*, Penwith Press, Cornwall, England, 1998

Mishlove, Jeffrey, *The Roots of Consciousness: The Classic Encyclopedia of Consciousness Studies Revised and Expanded*, Council Oak Books, Tulsa, OK, 1993

Myss, Caroline, *Anatomy of the Spirit: The Seven Stages of Power and Healing*, Three Rivers Press, New York, NY, 1996

Myss, Caroline, *Why People Don't Heal and How They Can*, Three Rivers Press, New York, NY, 1997

Needleman, Jacob, *Time and the Soul: Where Has All the Meaningful Time Gone? ... And How to Get It Back*, Currency/Doubleday, New York, NY, 1998

Newton, Michael, *Journey of Souls*, Llewellyn Publications, St. Paul, MN, 1994

Novak, Michael, *The Experience of Nothingness*, Harper Torchbooks, New York, NY, 1970

Palmer, Harry, *Living Deliberately: The Discovery and Development of Avatar*, Star's Edge International, Altamonte Springs, FL, 1994

Ponder, Catherine, *The Healing Secrets of the Ages*, Devorss and Company, Marina del Rey, CA, 1985

Pribram, Karl, *Languages of the Brain*, Wadsworth Publishing, Monterey, CA, 1977

Radin, Dean, *The Conscious Universe: The Scientific Truth of Psychic Phenomena*, Harper Edge, New York, NY 1997

Reed, Anderson, *Shouting at the Wolf*, Citadel Press, New York, NY, 1990

Resnick, Stella, *The Pleasure Zone*, Conari Press, Berkeley, CA, 1997

Roberts, Tom, *The Three Billy Goats Gruff*, Western Publishing Company, 1989

Schneider, Meir, *The Handbook of Self-Healing: Your Personal Program for Better Health and Increased Vitality*, Penguin Books, New York, NY, 1994

Snider, Jerry, "Poisoned Prayer: An Interview with Larry Dossey," *Magical Blend*, March 1998, issue #59, pp. 32-37, 80.

Spangler, David, *Everyday Miracles: The Inner Art of Manifestation*, Bantam Books, New York, NY, January 1996

Stein, Diane, *The Essential Reiki*, The Crossing Press, Freedom, CA, 1995

Strauch, Ralph, *The Reality Illusion: How You Make the World You Experience*, Station Hill Press, Barrytown, NY, 1989

Swimme, Brian, *The Universe is a Green Dragon*, Bear & Co., Santa Fe, NM, 1984

Talbot, Michael, *The Holographic Universe*, HarperCollins Publishers, New York, NY, 1991

Targ, Russell and Katra, Jane, *Miracles of Mind*, New World Library, Novato, CA, 1998

Tcherkezoff, Serge, *First Contacts in Polynesia — The Samoan Case (1722 – 1848)*, ANU E Press, 2008, p. 132

Thurston, Mark, *Discovering Your Soul's Purpose*, A.R.E. Press, Virginia Beach, VA, 1996

Toben, Bob, *Space-Time and Beyond*, Dutton Paperback, New York, NY, 1975

Tulku, Tarthang, *Gesture of Balance: A Guide to Awareness, Self-Healing, and Meditation*, Dharma Publishing, Berkeley, CA, 1977

Tulku, Tarthang, *Openness Mind*, Dharma Publishing, Berkeley, CA, 1978

Tulku, Tarthang, *Skillful Means: Patterns for Success*, Dharma Publishing, Berkeley, CA, 1978

Tulku, Tarthang, *Love of Knowledge*, Dharma Press, Berkeley, CA, 1987

Tulku, Tarthang, *Knowledge of Time and Space*, Dharma Publishing, Berkeley, CA, 1990

Tulku, Tarthang, *Time, Space and Knowledge*, Dharma Press, Berkeley, CA, 1990

Walsch, Neale Donald, *Conversations With God: An Uncommon Dialogue Book 2*, Hampton Roads Publishing Company, Charlottesville, VA, 1995

Walsch, Neale Donald, *Conversations With God: An Uncommon Dialogue Book 3*, Hampton Roads Publishing Company, Charlottesville, VA, 1998

Walster, Elaine & Walster, G. William, *A New Look at Love: A Revealing Report on the Most Elusive of All Emotions*, Addison-Wesley Publishing Company, 1978

Watson, Donald, *A Dictionary of Mind and Spirit*, Andre Deutsch Limited, London, England, 1991

Weiss, Peter, "Atom Tinkerer's Paradise: Innovations to Atom-Imaging Microscopes Create Labs on Tips," *Science News*, October 24, 1998, volume #154, pp. 268-270.

Wilber, Ken, *A Brief History of Everything*, Shambhala Publications, Inc., Boston, MA, 1996

Wilber, Ken, *The Holographic Paradigm and Other Paradoxes: Exploring the Leading Edge of Science,* New Science Library, Shambala Publications, Boulder, CO, 1982

Wolf, Fred Alan, *Taking the Quantum Leap: The New Physics for Non-Scientists,* Perennial Library, Harper & Row Publishers, New York, NY, 1981

Wolf, Fred Alan, *Parallel Universes,* Touchstone, New York, NY, 1988

Wolf, Fred Alan, *The Eagle's Quest,* Touchstone, Summit Books, Simon & Schuster, New York, NY, 1991

Wolf, Fred Alan, *The Dreaming Universe: A Mind-Expanding Journey to the Realm Where Psyche and Physics Meet,* Touchstone, New York, NY, 1994

Wolf, Fred Alan, *The Spiritual Universe: How Quantum Physics Proves the Existence of the Soul,* Simon & Schuster, New York, NY, 1996

Zweig, Connie and Wolf, Steve, *Romancing the Shadow: Illuminating the Dark Side of the Soul,* Ballantine Books, New York, NY, 1997

About the Author

Cynthia Sue Larson is an author and life coach whose favorite question in any situation is, "How good can it get?" as she helps people understand how our thoughts and feelings literally change the world. Cynthia received a BA degree in physics from UC Berkeley and an MBA degree from San Francisco State University, and has helped people set and achieve extraordinary goals in optimal alignment with their core strengths. Her popular *RealityShifters* ezine can be read and subscribed to at:

www.realityshifters.com

Printed in Great Britain
by Amazon